WILLIAM WATKINS LTD

London's First Major Towage Company

© Black Dwarf Publications and John E. Reynolds 2019
Designed by Mike Day

British Library Cataloguing-in-Publication Data.
A catalogue record for this book is available from the British Library
ISBN: 9781903599266

BLACK DWARF PUBLICATIONS
Unit 144B, Lydney Trading Estate, Harbour Road, Lydney, Gloucestershire GL15 5EJ
www.lightmoor.co.uk
Black Dwarf Publications is an imprint of Black Dwarf Lightmoor Publications Ltd

Printed in Poland
www.lfbookservices.co.uk

WILLIAM WATKINS LTD

London's First Major Towage Company

John E. Reynolds

Black Dwarf Publications

Contents

About the Author

John Edward Reynolds was born in April 1943 into a tugging family. He was employed in 1958 by Ship Towage (London) Ltd, as cook of the Racia. He married in 1962 and has three sons, a daughter and nine grandchildren. All his sons also being tugmen. In 1987 he was made a regular Master by the Alexandra Towing Company (London) Ltd. He retired in 2008.

Acknowledgements

I would like to thank the many crew members and office staff who over the years have given me many accounts of incidents and tows that they, or their fathers and other family members, have carried out. Also, the many documents and photographs that have been given to me over the years.

Particular thanks goes to Len & Percy Smith, Jack Simmonds, Bill Russell, Peter Scott, Peter Bryant and Steve Leach. My daughter-in-law Lisa Reynolds for typing the manuscript and daughter Victoria Holloway for editing and arranging the text ready for the book.

Preface

William Watkins Limited was founded in the summer of 1883 by John Rogers Watkins and his son William. John Rogers Watkins was born 1790 and was the son of Captain Giles Watkins, a coastal master, who was married to Judith Rogers. His wife's maiden name, Rogers, was passed down through the generations as a second christian name. John Rogers Watkins was a freeman of the River Thames and worked as a waterman. He purchased their first tug, the *Monarch*, from the River Tyne in 1833, at that time she was recorded as the finest on the river. At that date Limehouse was the seaward limit to tow a ship, later it became Blackwall and in the 1840s it had become Gravesend. Watkins were also owners of sailing ships, but this book only covers the tug owning side of the business.

As the tugs became bigger, more reliable, and the boilers not so extravagant on coal consumption, tugs would go seeking down channel looking for sailing ships and then negotiate a price with the master to tow it to its discharge port. Watkins were also one of the first companies to undertake coastal, and later ocean, towage, becoming a major force in that area in the early days. The first recorded long tows by Watkins were by the *Britannia* in 1855 when she towed the *Columbia* of 735 tons from Deptford to Calais for £90, and the *Victoria* which received £105 for towing the *Julia* of 1,070 tons, also from Deptford to Calais. By 1875 the *Anglia* carried out tows both from St. Helena and

to St. Petersburg, and also from Port Said, remarkable distances considering the coal consumption of the *Anglia*. She once burnt thirty tons running from Gravesend to Beachy Head a distance of 113 miles.

Salvage was also a big part of the tugs work, Watkins Tugs earned some big awards, but some were poor awards considering the work undertaken. The Thames Estuary was not the easiest of areas for a sailing ship to navigate. With its narrow channels and numerous sandbanks. Watkins had an agreement with the salvage association working to salve ships on a tidal basis. This agreement was not popular with many tug owners but Watkins got an income that they would not otherwise have had. The big paddlers were often chartered by ship owners to attend on their ships at naval reviews in the Solent. The after hold being converted into a ladies' saloon. By the turn of the century the screw tug was fast replacing paddle tugs on the Thames.

On the outbreak of the First World War the Government requisitioned all the tugs in the port. Mr John Stewart Watkins went to Whitehall to protest and to point out to the Government that without a certain number of tugs to handle the ships, London would grind to a halt. The Government relented and Mr Watkins was made an advisor to the authorities on tugs, part-time at first, but full-time from July 1917. For his work Mr J. S. Watkins received both the MBE and OBE. The requisitioned tugs

Fossa.

ranged far and wide during the conflict, from the *Hibernia* at the Gallipoli landings to the *Racia* in the White Sea. The tugs on the Downs Boarding Flotillas saved numerous ships that had been mined or grounded on the Goodwin Sands, the value of their cargoes running into millions of pounds. Captain George Wood of the *Hibernia* and Captain William Anning of the *Chub (Vincia)* both received the OBE for their wartime service.

During the depression of the 1930s the tugs were put on three rates of pay: *Fabia* and small tugs on the lowest rate; The 'Teddy Bears', *Java, Scotia* etc. on a middle rate; *Kenia, Gondia, Muria,* and *Hibernia* etc. on the full rate.

On the outbreak of the Second World War, Watkins tugs were soon in the thick of the action, some being requisitioned and back on the Downs Boarding Flotilla as they had been only twenty-five years earlier. The Watkins tugs distinguished themselves from all of the London companies at Dunkirk in keeping the troops supplied with water, food, and ammunition carried in sailing barges which they towed over, beached them, and then came back with troops. All Watkins tugs that took part in the Dunkirk evacuation received in March 1941 a brass plaque which on most tugs was mounted on the foreside of the bridge. Engraved within a lifebelt motive were the words 'Dunkirk May-June 1940', with the tugs name and house flag within the centre.

The tugs were also at the D-Day landings, positioning the ships that were sunk to make a rudimentary harbour until the Mulberry harbour units could be towed over from England and built. Watkins tugs were involved in all aspects of its construction. Mr J. R. Watkins was advisor to the Government on the tugs, first with the Ministry of Shipping and then the Ministry of War Transport; he received an OBE in 1942. In 1944 he was put in charge of all red ensign tugs taking part in the invasion of Europe. The war inflicted a heavy price on the tugs; *Napia, Muria* and *Persia* were victims of the mine with the loss of their crews. Managed tug the *Empire Wold* was lost off Iceland in adverse weather with all hands.

After the war Watkins went back into ocean towing with the acquisition of the *Rumania, Zealandia* and *Empire John* on charter. Tows were undertaken to all parts of the globe: America; Australia; China; Africa; and Mediterranean and European ports, until 1956 when the *Rumania* was lost assisting *Loide Honduros* on the Long Sand.

In January 1948 there was a strike over hours from the 23rd to the 28th. A 54-hour week was agreed with $1\frac{1}{3}$ overtime rate and double time on Sundays. When the author started work ten years later in 1958 it was a 50-hour week, $1\frac{1}{3}$ overtime and double time on Sundays.

On the 1st February 1950, William Watkins Limited, joined forces with the Elliott Steam Tug Co. (1949) Limited and both then acquired the assets of Gamecock Tugs Limited and commenced traded as Ship Towage (London) Limited. Mr J. R. Watkins became joint Managing Director. All tugs kept their own funnel colours and house flags until September 1965 when the Ship Towage funnel colours and house flag were introduced. On the 1st March 1965 Ship Towage (London) Limited acquired the four largest tugs of Gaselee & Son Limited, together with all their ship towing contracts on the rivers Thames, Medway and Swale.

On the 20th August 1963 John Rogers Watkins died aged 69, his ashes were scattered at the Nore on the 27th August 1963 from the deck of the *Hibernia*.

On the 27th January 1969 London Tugs Limited was formed with W. H. J. Alexander Limited (Sun Tugs) being acquired. The funnel colours were then again changed but the house flag remained the same. This brought all ship towing tugs on the

This is the artists original from which the printers block was made for William Watkins Ltd cheques. It is believed to date from 1917 when the firm became a limited company. The frame was made by Charles Rochefort and it was hung in Williams Watkins Ltd chairman's office until the company moved to Gravesend in 1971. It was given to the author when the company moved offices from the 'White House' on The Terrace to the W. H. J. Alexander (Sun Tugs) offices alongside Royal Terrace Pier when London Tugs was formed.

Thames under one banner, with the exception of the Port of London Authorities ship towing dock tugs.

On the 4th November 1973 Mr William Watkins died aged 47, he had become joint Managing Director in 1963 on the death of his father. With his death, it brought to an end 140 years of the Watkins family involvement in towage on the River Thames. On the 1st January 1975, just thirteen months later, London Tugs was acquired by the Alexandra Towing Company of Liverpool and so ending the ties with the old Thames Ship Towage Companies.

In conclusion, Watkins Tugs have been present at many notable events that have taken place along the historic waterway of the river Thames. The *Monarch* immortalized in oils by Turner when in 1838 she towed Nelson's ship of the line *Temeraire* from Deptford to be broken up at Rotherhithe. Watkins tugs attended at the launch of Brunel's *Great Eastern* in 1858 from Russell's Yard at Millwall on the Isle of Dogs.

In 1860 Watkins tugs attended at the launch of the Ironclad *HMS Warrior*, now preserved at Portsmouth, and at the launches of all of the major warships built by the Thames Ironworks at Poplar through to 1911 when *HMS Thunderer*, the last battleship built on the Thames, was launched. In 1878 the *Anglia* towed Cleopatra's Needle from Cadiz to London and then the *Era* took over towing it under all of London's bridges to the spot on the Embankment where the obelisk stands to this day.

The *Muria* towed the tea clipper, *Cutty Sark* on her last sea voyage from Falmouth to the Thames in 1938 when she joined

Worcester at Greenhithe as a training ship. In December 1954 *Gondia*, *Kenia* and *Java* towed the *Cutty Sark* from East India Dock to the purpose built dry-dock at Greenwich where she is preserved. This was carried out free of charge. These are just a few of the memorable tows carried out by William Watkins tugs from the 1830s.

While Mr J. R. Watkins was joint Managing Director of Ship Towage (London) Limited Mr A. J. Page of the Elliot Steam Tug Company (1949) Limited was the other. During the period from 1950 – 1969 when Ship Towage (London) Limited was in being, eight tugs were built and a further four were acquired when taking over Gaselee & Son Limited, ship towage contracts in 1965.

Of the tugs built, four were built and registered under William Watkins Limited ownership and were included in the fleet listing being *Dhulia* 1959, *Ionia* 1960, *Hibernia* 1963 and *Burma* 1966. The four acquired from Gaselee in 1965 were *Fossa* 1961, *Culex* 1958, *Rana* 1951, *Vespa* 1934. The four not included in the fleet list are, *Vanquisher* 1955 under Elliott colours, *Moorcock* 1959 sister tug to *Dhulia* 1959 under Gamecock colours, *Avenger* 1962 sister tug to *Hibernia* under Elliot colours and *Watercock* 1967 sister to *Burma* 1964 in Gamecock ownership in the new ship towage funnel colours.

Of the Ship Towage (London) Limited fleet in 1950 that were not part of William Watkins fleet were the *Challenge* 1931 and *Contest* 1933. Elliot Steam Tug (1949) Limited, *Ocean Cock* 1932, *Atlantic Cock* 1932, *Crested Cock* 1935 and *Watercock* 1923, Gamecock Tugs Limited.

Watkins' Family Tree

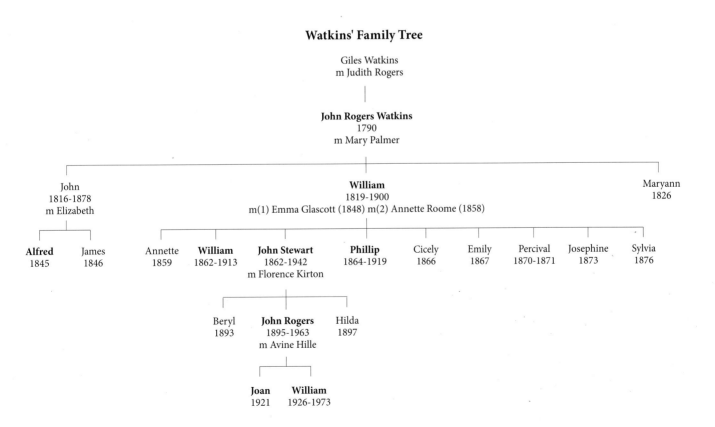

Giles Watkins
m Judith Rogers

John Rogers Watkins
1790
m Mary Palmer

| John 1816-1878 m Elizabeth | **William** 1819-1900 m(1) Emma Glascott (1848) m(2) Annette Roome (1858) | Maryann 1826 |

Alfred 1845 — James 1846

Annette 1859 — **William** 1862-1913 — **John Stewart** 1862-1942 m Florence Kirton — **Phillip** 1864-1919 — Cicely 1866 — Emily 1867 — Percival 1870-1871 — Josephine 1873 — Sylvia 1876

Beryl 1893 — **John Rogers** 1895-1963 m Avine Hille — Hilda 1897

Joan 1921 — **William** 1926-1973

Tugs Livery

	William Watkins	**Ship Towage (London) Ltd**
House Flag	Red dovetail with large white 'W'	Red dovetail with Elliot Steam Tug Co. house flag in centre.
Funnel	Black with broad red band	Black. Broad red band with Elliot Steam Tug Co. house flag. Narrow blue band beneath the red.
Hull and Bulwarks	Black with white line at bottom of bulwarks at deck level	Black with white line at top of bulwarks beneath top rail
Whale Mouth	Green	Red
Casing	Teak. Wooden doors varnished	Teak. Wooden doors varnished
Deck	Red	Red
Masts	Wood varnished or Steel painted teak	Wood varnished or Steel painted teak
Halfrounds (if fitted)	White	n/a
Handrails and Boat Davits	White	White
Towrails, Deck fittings, Bollards, Windlass etc.	Black	Black

1. Company Vessels: Chronological Listing of Tugs from 1833

MONARCH 1833 – 1876

Official No. 15862
Gross Tons 26.28
Draft 5ft fwd. 5ft 3ins aft
Dimensions 64ft 10ins x 13ft 11ins x 7ft
Built 1831 by J. & J. Wait, North Shields

Powered by a single-cylinder 20 NHP Grasshopper engine with a piston 26ins in diameter and with a stroke of 32ins. Clench built of wood, speed seven knots (under steam and sail seven and a half knots). Bunker capacity 7 tons. Consumption per 24 hours, 7 tons. Steam supplied by a flue boiler with a jet condenser. In 1833 acquired by John Rogers Watkins and credited as being the finest tug on the river.

In 1834 *Monarch* was considered the only tug on the river capable of towing *Iberia* the first steamship built for P&O Line from the builder's yard at Limehouse to the fitting out yard at Blackwall. The owners were so pleased with her performance that they promised Watkins all P&O work from then on, which they honoured when P&O returned to the Thames.

In 1838 the artist Turner was picnicking on the riverbank when *Monarch* was towing Nelson's *Temeraire* from Deptford to Rotherhithe to be broken up. The artist sketched tug and tow as they passed and from it produced the famous canvas 'The Fighting Temeraire' which immortalized forever the little *Monarch*. Being single engined, it was difficult to turn 'short-round' and Mr J. R. Watkins is credited with inventing the chain box, which, as the name implies, was a box filled with chain hauled across the deck on rails. This would immerse one paddle deep and lift the other clear of the water allowing the tug to turn in its own length. The chain box hauled back amidships put the tug back on even keel.

1848 re-boilered with a tubular boiler which greatly improved her efficiency and reduced her coal consumption.

1857 fitted with new patent paddle wheels and her engine, hull and boiler were repaired at a cost of £1,000.

1861 again fitted with a new tubular boiler.

When the *Monarch* arrived on the Thames, Limehouse was the limit to where tugs would tow ships, this later became Blackwall and then, in the 1840s, Gravesend. All mates had to prove they could handle the *Monarch* before they were promoted to Master of other tugs in the fleet She was worked hard in the upper reaches but in September 1876 she was surveyed and condemned.

After forty-three years she was sold to Stewart the Engineer for £40. Mr Watkins buying a silver tea and coffee set to commemorate their first and very successful tug.

Monarch towing Temeraire to Rotherhithe for Scrap   © *National Gallery, London*

FIDLER 1840 – 1847

Gross tons 78
Net Tons 20
Dimensions 69ft 5ins x 16ft 3ins x 8ft 5ins

Built in 1840 at Limehouse as a more powerful successor to the *Monarch*. Powered by a single-cylinder engine. Very little is recorded of the *Fiddler's* career but Captain Alfred E. Soaves was her Master in 1846. In 1847 she was sold to J. Bond, Millwall and then in 1848 to W. Sutcliffe, Millwall.

LORD WARDEN 1845 – 1853

Gross ton 107
Net tons 43
Dimensions 100ft x 17ft beam across paddle boxes 35ft 9ins
Powered by two Grasshopper disconnecting engines by Stewart, each with a cylinder of 30ins diameter and a stroke of 3ft 6ins
Nominal Horse Power 60
Bunker capacity 18 tons
Consumption per 24 hours 16 tons
Draft 6ft
Speed 10 knots

Built in 1845 at Millwall. William Watkins' third tug was built when even more powerful tugs than *Monarch* and *Fiddler* were required. Only used as a river tug.

Her machinery appeared to be too powerful for the wooden hull and she was broken up in 1853 and her engines were placed in a much larger **Punch** being built by Money, Wigrams and Sons, at Blackwall.

PUNCH (i) 1846 –1850/1

Built 1846 for John Rogers Watkins and his son William. A river tug built of wood with a single engine. Sold early 1850s to Constantinople shortly before the beginning of the Crimean War. She was one of the first tugs in that port and was kept very busy with the transport ships supplying the Army with men and stores.

PAUL PRY 1847 – 1866

Official No. 12757
Call signs LDFM
Gross tons 83
Net Tons 39.5
Dimensions 80ft x 15ft 5ins x 8ft 7ins
Draft 4ft 6ins fwd. 6ft aft

Wooden clench built paddle tug built at Millwall 1847. Powered by a 35-nominal horse power single-cylinder Grasshopper engine built 1842 by Waite, North Shields. Speed 8 knots.

Bunker capacity 14 tons, consumption 24 hours 9 tons.

1st January 1859 new boiler, patent wheels and repairs to hull and engine.

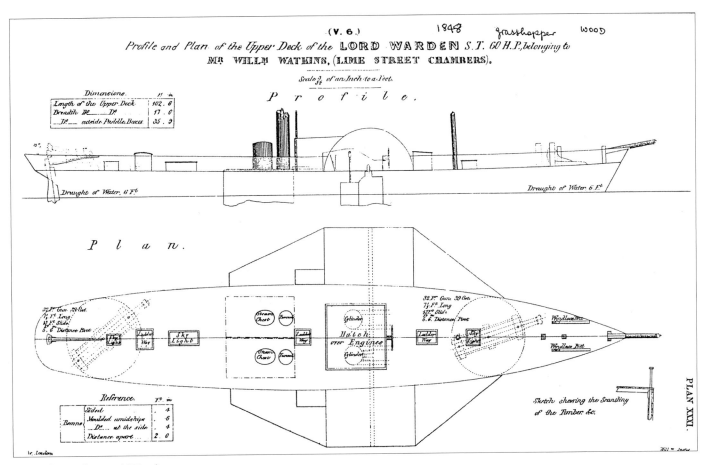

Plan of Vessel - *Lord Warden*

1863 boiler taken out and repaired.

1865 boiler again taken out for repair, new bottom fitted to hull and engine overhauled at a cost of £408.

Built with a clipper stem and a figurehead that could be unshipped when likely to be in the way when towing.

Used in the early days mainly on the river, a large proportion of her work being associated with the thriving shipbuilding and dry dock industry at that time.

1st December 1866 sold to Hockly Gill & Company, trading as The Commercial Towing Company, for £500 for service on the river.

One of the mainstays of her work in the latter half of her life was seeking in the Thames estuary for schooners and 'onker' barques.

JOHN BULL 1849 – 1878
Official No. 22036
Gross tons 114.58
Net tons 34.93
Call sign NJTB
Dimension 96ft x 18ft 2ins x 9ft 7ins

Wooden carvel built paddle tug built at Millwall 1849. Powered by a single-cylinder 60 nominal horse power engine with a cylinder diameter of 29ins and stroke of 3ft 6ins.

Jet condenser.

From 1853 – 1859 she worked on the River Mersey when Mr John Watkins Jnr attempted to establish himself as a tug owner there. On her return to the Thames in 1859 she was fitted with new boiler.

1866 had another large refit and rebuilt and fitted with new side-lever engine.

23rd November 1878 sold to A. Lentner, London for £1,150.

1879 sold to Wreck Recovery and Salvage Company for salvage work from Dover. This company went into liquidation in the early 1880s and *John Bull* returned to the Thames owned by A. Barker. Soon re-sold to A. Lentner who re-sold her to G. J. Spicer, Gravesend. Again, sold to J. Jackson & Company the London contractors and used in keeping craft away from the workings of Tower Bridge during its construction.

1904 converted to a hulk.

UNCLE SAM 1849 – 1900

Official No. 22037
Call Sign NJTC
Gross tons 159.07
Net registered tons 77.25
Dimensions 107ft x 20ft 3ins x 10ft 9ins

Built 1849 by R. & H. Green at Poplar (other sources state C. J. Mare & Co. West Ham). The first tug built by R. & H. Green who normally built sailing ships and was built of top quality timber left over from a sailing ship. Carvel built hull with a fine clipper bow and a short bowsprit with a figurehead and twin funnels abreast.

Powered by two side-lever disconnecting engines producing 80-nominal horsepower, each having a single cylinder with a diameter of 34ins and stroke of 4ft. Steam supplied from two multi-tubular boilers with four furnaces with a pressure of 181 psi. Jet condensing.

Owned originally by John Rogers Watkins and his son John, who had been master of the barque *Royal Exchange* and was setting up as a tug owner in Liverpool. A large number of American vessels were using Liverpool and in 1849 America was not very popular with England, so she was given the name *Uncle Sam* to encourage work with these sailing ships.

After ten years she returned to the Thames and was thoroughly overhauled in Wigram's Dock, new engines and boilers being fitted and paddle beams shifted, returning to work for Watkins

on the Thames on 30th June 1860.

A very popular tug at the various yards for launches in the river and Samuda's Yard always insisted on her being in attendance at the launch of vessels from their yard. She was also popular with the various dock companies who chartered her for towage in the enclosed docks.

1867 her boilers were unshipped and completely overhauled, cylinders bored out, new condensers, new pistons and hull overhauled.

1879 boilers removed and repaired.

1881 fitted with new paddle boxes and bridge.

1884 major repairs to hull including a new stern.

1886 fitted with new steel boilers and again major repairs to the hull.

1900 sold to be scrapped.

Another claim to fame: she was the first merchant vessel through Tower Bridge after its official opening in 1894, following through astern of the Trinity House vessel *Irene* who had officially opened it.

Uncle Sam

Uncle Sam

JOHN LEE 1850 – 1855
SAUCY JACK 1855 – 1862
JOHN LEE 1862 – 1866

Official No. 12755
Call Sign LDFJ
Gross tons 104.3
Net tons 34.8
Dimensions 90ft 2ins length 17ft beam 9ft depth of hold 6ft draft

Paddle tug clench built in 1844 by A. Woodhouse, South Shields for a consortium of London owners headed by Mr Mark Melville of Shadwell.

Powered by a 60-nominal horsepower Grasshopper engine built by Marshall. Bunker capacity 11 tons, consumption per 24 hours 12 tons

The first tug on the Thames over 100 gross tons, she was not a success and was sold April 1845 to the Southampton Dock Company when Southampton was expanding into a major port.

1850 acquired by William Watkins Limited.

1856 major repairs were carried out to the hull and engine and a new boiler fitted at a cost of £1,400. Renamed *Saucy Jack*.

1862 again re-boilered with a boiler from the steamer *American* and repairs to engine and hull, name changed back to *John Lee*.

A successful tug in Watkins ownership until October 1866 when she was sold for scrap to Messrs Beech and Castle for £175.

BRITANNIA 1852 – 1855

Official No. 24594
Gross tons 73
Net tons 48
Draft 6ft 8ins
Dimensions 100ft 5ins x 16ft 7ins x 10ft 8ins
Built 1852 by Money, Wigram at Northam near Southampton.

Powered by a 110-nominal horsepower side-lever engine by Stewart, Blackwall. Bunker capacity 20 tons, consumption per 24 hours 14 tons. Speed 9 knots.

A well built wooden paddle tug with pleasing lines, fitted with a figurehead and bowsprit. Watkins most profitable tug during the period she was in their ownership.

In 1855 the *Britannia* towed the sailing ship *Columbia* 735 tons, from Deptford to Calais Roads, for a fee of £90. At that time this was considered a very long tow, much further than had been attempted before.

1855 sold to owners in Constantinople, this port being very busy during the Crimean War.

VICTORIA 1853 – 1906

Official No. 12754
Call sign LDFH
Gross tons 151.85
Net registered tons 34.96
Dimensions 117ft 2ins x 19ft 3ins x 10ft 8ins

Built 1853 by Money, Wigram & Sons, Blackwall of oak and teak with metal fastenings, iron trussed, solid bottom. Effective horsepower 450.

Powered by two engines each with a single cylinder with a diameter of 34ins and a stroke of 4ft. Steam supplied by two cylindrical boilers with a working pressure of 35 lbs. Jet condensing. Fitted with a steam windlass. Speed 11 knots.

The largest and most up to date tug on the river when built she was very successful and built for long distance towage. With the outbreak of the Crimean War, and with most of the transports that shipped out all equipment, food and ammunition to the largest army to be sent overseas based in London, tugs were in short supply, towing the ships to the various loading points on the river.

Victoria didn't undertake any long-distance towage until after the war ended. Fitted with clipper stem and twin funnels, placed side by side. She was a fine looking tug and had a carved Victorian crown in the boss of her paddle box.

The boilers of these early tugs were not very reliable and she had new boilers in 1859 plus new paddle wheels and engines repaired. In 1864 she was re-boilered again and fitted with feathering paddle wheels, which cut down the power loss, at a cost of £2,500. In 1876 again re-boilered, repairs to engines and hull, at a cost of £4,500. In 1880 boilers were removed and repaired and new beams and paddle boxes fitted and sponsons shortened. In 1885 new steel boilers were fitted and the quality had improved that these lasted her for the next twenty years.

Her first long tow was a 1,000-ton ship from Deptford to Calais, which was considered quite a feat at the time. In 1870 she

Victoria

attended at the trials of the cigar ship *Ross Wymans*, which proved a failure of the design. The *Victoria* and *Anglia* towed her from West India Dock to Le Havre, her shape making the tow very difficult. Yarrows the shipbuilders insisted on her attendance at the launches of large torpedo boats at their Poplar yard.

Her steam windlass was very popular when seeking, being able to heave up quickly against the backbreaking work by hand.

At the turn of the century she was laid up most of the time and was sold for scrap to James Livingstone & Son on 5th January 1906 for £200.

Punch 1854 – 1895

Official No. 12756
Call Sign LDFK
Gross tons 115.14
Net registered tons 30.84
Lengthened in 1858 to 101ft 7ins breadth 18ft 1ins depth 9ft 9ins
Draft 6ft 6ins
Nominal Horse Power 60

Paddle tug built of iron 1854 by Money, Wigram and Sons, Blackwall. Powered by two single-cylinder side-lever Grasshopper disconnecting engines that had been taken out of the *Lord Warden*. Each engine having a cylinder diameter of 30ins and a stroke of 3ft 6ins. Two multi-tubular boilers with a working pressure of 25 psi.

Lengthened and re-boilered in 1858.

New boilers and engines and paddle wheels thoroughly overhauled in March 1868, at a cost of £1,800.

1879 boilers taken out and repaired at a cost of £920.

1866 Hull repaired £1,200.

Sold to Chas Dyble, North Shields 6th December 1895 for £1,600, re-sold two or three times before being sunk in a collision off the River Tyne, October 1911. She was salved, but condemned to be broken up.

When built she had two carved figures of Punchinello, one on each paddle box, but one was unshipped down channel and ended up in a public house in Newhaven.

Highly regarded when new, she carried out a number of long tows and was engaged in various salvages in the estuary; one being the *Famenoth*, which was refloated from the Pan Sand by the *Punch* and *Titan* under charter to the Salvage Association.

Watkins did a lot of work with the Salvage Association re-floating ships on a charter basis. In later years she was classed only as a river tug and did a lot of work towing old wooden walls to Castles ship breaking yard, Watkins having the contract for this work. Also chartered by the various dock companies at different times, for towage in the enclosed docks. These charters being quite profitable to the owners.

Don 1855 – 1866
Official No. 4279
Call Sign JRTG
Gross tons 45.1
Net tons 20.6
Dimensions 72ft 2ins x 14ft 9ins x 8ft 4ins

Paddle tug, clench built in 1841 at East Jarrow, River Tyne. Powered by a single-cylinder engine of 30ins diameter.

Acquired by William Watkins from the River Tyne in August 1855 from Mr William Hughes Jnr at a cost of £410.

Extensively repaired and fitted with a new boiler and paddle wheels and her hull repaired at the exorbitant price of £1,400; resuming work after this rebuild on 8th November 1856.

Don was not of any great power and was only used on the river. Her hull must have still been leaky as she sank while anchored off the South West India dock but was salved and put back to work.

In 1866 she was condemned and sold for scrap for £55 Hull £10 Boiler £30 Engine £15.

Defiance 1856 – 1871
Gross tons 81
Net tons 36
Official No. 16954
Call sign MDQG
Dimensions 81ft 5ins x 17ft 7ins x 9ft 3ins
50 nominal horsepower

Paddle tug built of iron in 1856 by Marshall and Co., South Shields.

Re-boilered 1860 and again in 1869.

Major repairs carried out to her boiler and her engine fitted with new pistons and slides in 1864.

Used by Watkins as a training ship for future 'Big Tug' Masters.

Sold May 1871 to East and West India Dock Company for £1,300. Used by Watkins mainly as a river tug.

Used as a dock tug mostly in the West India Dock, after being acquired by the East & West India Dock Company in 1871. Her masts being unshipped at this time.

Scrapped 1883.

Toby 1856 – 1862
Official No. 16959
Call sign MDQM
Dimensions 80ft3ins x 17ft x 8ft 7ins
Gross tons 73
Net tons 9

Built Greenwich 1855 and acquired by William Watkins in 1856 Other sources state built Millwall in 1856 for William Watkins.

A composite paddler, clinker built on iron frames. Completed without any frills during the Crimean War when the number of vessels built was of prime importance. A mizzenmast not being fitted, just the main, so being unable to carry any sail to help eke out the coal consumption, most contemporary tugs carried some sail. A successful river tug, giving good service until being sold in 1862 to owners in Jersey.

1879 sold to France.

1882 acquired by Mr James Watkins a shipbroker and nephew of Mr W. Watkins who sold her the following year to owners at Hull.

1904 scrapped.

Napoleon 1857 – 1881
Official No. 19885
Call sign MTSN
Gross tons 156.69
Net tons 29.45
Dimensions BP 120ft 8ins x 20ft 4ins x 11ft 3ins

Wooden (teak) paddle tug built in 1857 by Money, Wigram & Sons at Northam, near Southampton. Powered by two engines, each with a single cylinder of 34¾ins diameter, later changed to 33ins, with a stroke of 43ins. 100 nominal horsepower.

Jet condensing boilers with a working pressure of 20 lbs.

Built to undertake economic long-distance towage of which she was very successful. *Napoleon* completed a number of tows to Spain with dredging equipment and also towed the large sailing ship *Clara* from Sunderland to Liverpool. She was also one of the many tugs that attended the launch of Brunel's *Great Eastern*, which at 22,0000 gross tons was by far the largest ship built, when she was finally launched and taken across the river to Deptford to be fitted out on 1858.

1862 her boilers were taken out and repaired. New furnaces fitted and the engines thoroughly overhauled.

1870 fitted with new boilers, engines, practically renewed, extensive repairs to hull and new decks fitted at a cost of £4,000.

1876 new boilers again fitted and a thorough overhaul of engines at a cost of £3,000.
1880 new spring beams and sponsons, new slides and boilers

overhauled. On 14th October 1881 when under the command of Captain William Houghton, she foundered with the loss of all nine crew, going to the assistance of the James Norse sailing ship *Allanshaw* in distress off North Foreland in hurricane force winds. She was running in company with the *Victor* in very heavy seas. The *Victor* lost sight of her in a squall and when it cleared the *Napoleon* had disappeared. The *Victor* assisted by the *Hibernia* who had been sheltering behind North Foreland successfully rescued the *Allanshaw*, but no trace was found of the *Napoleon*.

Antagonist 1857 – 1867

Gross tons 90.02
Net tons 36.34
Official No. 12874
Call sign LDQG
Dimensions 91ft 6ins x 17ft x 8ft 8ins lengthened in 1864

Antagonist

Built 1857 by Chas Lingley, Deptford. Clench build of iron. 50-nominal horsepower engines by Stewarts & Sons, Blackwall.

A successful tug she did a lot of work in the Lower Reaches.

1863 chartered by the Isle of Wight Steam Packet Company to run a passenger service between Littlehampton, Sussex to Ventnor, Isle of Wight in competition with the *Annette* who had been chartered to run between Ryde, Isle of Wight and Stokes Bay, Gosport.

During September 1864 her Master sighted an abandoned vessel when on passage from Ventnor and after landing the passengers at Littlehampton sailed to find the wreck, which she towed into Portsmouth. After this incident her charter must have been terminated as she returned to the Thames and was lengthened by James Ash & Co. at Cubitt Town, fitted with a new boiler, new condensers, engines and paddle wheels completely overhauled at a cost of £3,000.

1867 sold to Messrs A. Brett & Co. to work at Amsterdam for £2,300.

Her Master from 23rd October 1864 to 25th October 1865 was David Valentine Glue.

Victor 1859 – 1894

Official No. 20546
Call sign NBPR
Gross tons 219.24
Net registered tons 59
Dimensions 136ft 3ins x 20ft 2ins x 11ft 8ins
Draft 8ft fwd. 9ft aft

Built 1857 by Charles Lingley, Deptford, of iron, clench built paddle tug. Powered by two single-cylinder engines with a bore of 34½ins bored to 35ins in 1877, length of stroke 4ft 6ins. Effective horsepower 100. Bunker capacity 60 tons. Two tubular boilers and six furnaces.

1859 acquired by William Watkins Limited. She was a very large tug when built with a clipper stem and two funnels abreast. A fine sea boat, powerful and fast. One of her first jobs was assisting the *Great Eastern* down river, after she had been completed. She had been acquired for long distance towage and safely delivered many dredgers over distances thought to be out of range of any tug at that time. In 1860 she towed the dredger *Navigator* from Gravesend to Cadiz, and the dredger *Industrious* from the Thames to Ferrel, and two more to Spain in 1861. She was also employed during this period towing wooden wall warships from Nelson's time, to Castle's scrap yard on the Thames. These had all been made obsolete with the development of steam and ironclad.

In 1862 her boilers were removed and overhauled and in April 1866 she was given new boilers and her engines were thoroughly overhauled and fitted with a surface condenser in place of her jet condenser, which greatly improved her efficiency at a total cost of £3,000.

The *Victor* was also the first Watkins tug to be involved in cable work, spending three months during 1861 repairing the cable between Beachy Head and Dieppe. She was chartered many times in the following years for cable work, making a name for herself in the process.

She was a lucky tug for salvage, but her most memorable salvage was the James Norse sailing Ship *Allanshaw*, in distress off North Foreland in hurricane force winds on 14th October 1881. Running in company with the *Napoleon*, both tugs ran into the squall, but when it cleared the *Napoleon* had disappeared, lost with all hands. The *Victor* was later assisted by the *Hibernia* who had been sheltering behind North Foreland. Watkins claimed £1,000 but the court was so impressed by the performance, that they awarded £2,000 to the *Victor* and £1,000 to the *Hibernia* and also praised the Master of the *Victor*, Captain John McCarthey, for his gallantry in the rescue.

Given new cylinders in 1883, new pistons in 1890, but age was creeping up on her and after spending a lot of time laid up at Blackwall, she was sold to Messrs Castle and Sons for £200 on 8th January 1894 and scrapped.

Times 1861 – 1886

Official No. 19887
Call sign MTSQ
Net tons 10.55
Gross tons 78.6
Dimensions 81ft 3ins x 19ft 8ins x 9ft

Clench built of wood in 1857 by Andrew Woodhouse, South Shields. Powered by two side-lever disconnecting engines, each with one cylinder with a diameter of 25ins.

50-nominal horsepower.

Steam supplied by two tubular boilers with four furnaces.

1861 acquired by William Watkins during a shipping slump at a very low price. Not up to Watkins standard, and given a thorough refit on arrival in London.

June 1864 fitted with new tubular boilers, engines thoroughly overhauled and fitted with new pistons.

Repairs carried out to engines March 1869 at a cost of £539.

Repairs carried out to engines September 1869 at a cost of £288.

Two new paddle shafts and one beam fitted May 1871.

Sunk in collision with the steam ship *Emily*, in May 1874 off Greenwich, other reports state off Gravesend.

Salved, her hull was extensively rebuilt and engines thoroughly overhauled, giving her a new lease of life.

In 1886 repairs were proving too costly and she was sold on the 12th March to J. Stewart the builders at Blackwall who were short of work and wanted a small job to keep his skilled workforce together.

Her hull was later sold to H Westbrook.

Annette 1861 – 1869

Official No. 47404
Gross tons 118
Net tons 44
Dimensions 103ft x 18ft x 10ft 3ins

Iron paddle tug built by James Ash & Company, London. Twin engines, each with a single cylinder of 29ins diameter manufactured by Stewart's and when built considered the finest machinery available.

Fitted with feathering paddles and super heaters on the boilers.

Named after Mr William Watkins wife Annette.

Soon after completion she was chartered to run a ferry service between Ryde, Isle of Wight and Stokes Bay, Gosport.

The *Antagonist* was chartered at the same time, by rival Isle of Wight Steam Packet Company, to run in competition between Ventnor, Isle of Wight and Littlehampton. These early tugs were often used in the passenger trade. The *Annette* was bareboat chartered during August and September 1865 for a whaling voyage to Iceland at £170 per month.

The following year she assisted in laying a cable to Belfast, and was fortunate to get a tow from London to Belfast from the steamer *Monarch* for £300 which made the cable charter much more profitable.

January 1869, she was sold to Mr Percy Acatos of Mark Lane for £3,300 for owners on the River Danube.

Britannia 1862 – 1875

Official No. 13748
Call sign LJGN
Gross tons 96
Net registered ton 42
Dimensions 91ft 4ins BP x 18ft 4ins x 10ft 3ins

Iron built paddle tug built 1856 by Marshall & Co., South Shields Powered by two side-lever disconnecting engines of 60 nominal horsepower.

Steam supplied by two multi-tubular boilers with four furnaces.

1860 fitted with new boilers supplied by J. Stewart and new paddle wheels.

She was owned on the River Tyne by J. Broder & Co. and was purchased in June 1862 by William Watkins. When purchased she was highly regarded as an ideal size for river work but was used outside the river when first purchased, such as when the *SS Regina* was ashore at Dungeness in 1863 working on a tidal basis with the Salvage Association. *Victoria, Uncle Sam* and *Britannia* were chartered, the *Britannia* getting £20 a tide and when refloated the *Regina* was towed to Limehouse for repair.

1866 *Britannia* and *Annette* were chartered to attend the long drawn out trials of the experimental cigar ship *Ross Winans* in the lower reaches and estuary. These being a complete failure the *Ross Winans* was laid up.

1868 *Britannia* and *Napoleon* shared £530 for the salvage of the steam ship *Forfarshire*.

With bigger tugs joining the fleet, *Britannia* was confined to the river. 22nd June 1875 she was surveyed and her hull and engines were worn out. The boilers were removed andrefurbished for future use, the engines were broken up onboard and the hull sold for scrap, July 1875.

Express 1864 – 1880

Official No. 17036
Call sign NDWQ
Gross tons 93
Net tons 37
Dimensions B P 88ft 9ins x 18ft 6ins x 10ft 1ins
Draft 6ft 6ins

Iron paddle tug built 1856 by Marshall & Co., South Shields for a Gravesend consortium of Edward Gregory, William Gunn and John Wood.

Powered by two side-lever disconnecting engines each with a single cylinder with a diameter of 28ins.

60 nominal horsepower.

Jet condenser.

1860 new boilers and feathering paddle wheels, engines overhauled by J Stewart.

April 1864 acquired by William Watkins.

1867 Boilers taken out and repaired, engines overhauled and extensive repairs carried out to hull.

1876 again thoroughly overhauled. Boilers replaced by the boilers taken out of the *Britannia* in 1875 when she was scrapped. These had been refurbished and stated to be as 'good as new'.

Sold 18th June 1880 for £1,500 to Mrs Caroline Jackson of Milford Haven.

Sold November 1887 to John Coram of Neyland and converted to a trawler.

Worked on the Welsh coast until broken up in 1898.

Anglia 1866 – 1894

Official No. 54745
Call sign HTKN
Gross tons 273.64
Net tons 77
Dimensions 114ft 4ins x 22ft 2ins x 12ft 4ins
Draft 9ft fwd. 8ft 6ins aft.

Iron built in 1866 by Thames Iron Works, Blackwall. Powered by two single-cylinder engines, with cylinder diameters of 38ins and having a stroke of 5ft developing 700 ihp, 140 nominal horsepower Bunker capacity 90 tons.

Anglia was to have been fitted with four boilers and funnels placed abreast in pairs, but Watkins considered this would be

Anglia   ©*Arthur O'Pollard Jnr, Gravesend, Kent*

very extravagant on coal and settled for three funnels and boilers, two abreast abaft the paddle boxes and one placed forward, giving her the nick name of 'three fingered Jack'. Her design was so good and ahead of its time, that it won first prize for tugs in an exhibition at the Institute of Naval Architects in 1877 eleven years after completion.

The *Anglia* completed the longest tow ever undertaken in 1875 when she towed the Union liner *Syria* from St. Helena to Southampton for a fee of £4,800; towage over this distance had been thought to be impossible. Other notable tows that Anglia undertook was the dredger *Friend of All Nations* from Cardiff to St. Petersburg (Leningrad) fee £1,350. The *Princess Amalia* from Port Said to Glasgow, fee £2650.

A tow she will always be remembered for was in 1878 she was sent down to Ferrol in Northern Spain to tow back to London the cylindrical pontoon, which housed the obelisk 'Cleopatra's Needle'. It had broken adrift from the steamship *Olga* that was towing it to England from Egypt. Found drifting by Spanish fishermen it was towed into Ferrol. The children of Gravesend were given a half-day holiday from school, to be able to see the *Anglia* pass with her unusual tow. The *Anglia* received £500 for this small but very awkward tow.

To keep these early tugs in tip top condition was very expensive. In 1871 her boilers and engines were overhauled at a cost of £800. In 1878 her boilers were removed and overhauled, fitted with new shafts, paddle wheels and pistons at a cost of £3,000

Her boilers were again removed in August of the same year at a further cost of £1,200. In 1880 she was dry-docked and had new boilers, pumps and shafts fitted and a general overhaul at a cost of £4,200.

On 19th January 1894 she was classed as obsolete and sold for scrap to Constants for £300 but her hull was still in a very good condition and she was purchased by Messrs Palmers ship builders on the Tyne and was converted to a barge for transporting iron from the River Tees to the River Tyne. During World War One she was towed between the north-east coast and France, usually by a French warship, loaded with coal to keep the allies munitions works supplied.

Albion 1868 – 1869
Official No. 4283
Call sign JRTM
Gross tons 168
Dimensions 107ft 6ins x 20ft x 9ft 5ins

Built 1851 of iron by Thomas Toward, Newcastle-upon-Tyne as *Friend of all Nations* for Thomas Petley, one of the first tug owners on the river Thames

1860s sold to William Collins, London.

1868 sold to William Watkins and re-named *Albion*.

The *Albion* had very large paddle wheels with the shaft being above deck level, ramps were fitted over it to enable the crew to get from forward to aft.

Used by Watkins seeking down channel, as far as Lands End, but though she was quite large and a good sea boat, she was underpowered for this work and not up to their standards.

1869 sold to owners in Trieste for £5,000.

Era 1869 – 1882
Official No. 60986
Gross tons 30.31
Net tons 6.32
Dimensions 65ft B P x 12ft 7ins x 6ft 5ins Draft 7ft

1869 built of iron by John Stewart & Co.. Blackwall.

Watkins first screw tug and built to evaluate the potential of the screw propeller.

Powered by a two-cylinder compounded engine with cylinders of 13ins and 18ins with a length of stroke of 16ins, producing 104 ihp, 24 nominal horsepower.

Steam supplied by a multi-tubular boiler, two furnaces with a working pressure of 60 psi

The early screw tugs were not very successful, most being quite small and shallow drafted for ship towage and they did not have sufficient weight to grip the water when towing a heavy ship.

Era was fitted with a variable pitch propeller when built but this was changed after a few weeks and was a reasonable success despite her small size. Also fitted with a drop funnel, the only Watkins tug so fitted until 1965 when four tugs of Gaselee & Son were acquired. Watkins had very little work above the bridges but *Era* was very popular on university boat race day, to take the Watkins family and friends to view the rowing.

1874 *Era* was re-boilered and extensively refitted.

One occasion when her drop funnel was needed was in 1878, when she relieved the *Anglia* of the tow of Cleopatra's Needle and towed it to its berth on the Embankment in Kings Reach.

1880 she was chartered by the East India Dock Co. at £5 a day for towage within the dock.

5th May 1882, with more modern screw tugs in the fleet, she was sold to Mr J. Beckett of Greenwich for £800 for craft towage.

Later sold to R. & W. Paul, Sailing Barge & Tug owners of Ipswich and in the latter half of the 1890s she came back to London owned by the Era Steam Tug Co. managed by Mr A. Watkins and Mr J. Watkins. Re-boilered and completely refitted she was principally used towing schooners and colliers on the lower river.

Cambria

Cambria 1870 – 1914

Official No. 63623
Call sign WQFH
Gross tons 208.82
Net tons 54.82
Dimensions Length BP 138ft 8ins, breadth 20ft, depth of hold 11ft 5ins, draft 8ft 3ins.

Iron paddle tug built 1870 by Thames Ironworks and Shipbuilding Company Limited.

Powered by two twin-cylinder side-lever engines by John Stewart & Sons Ltd, 700 ihp cylinder diameter 34ins, length of stroke 54ins.

Bunker capacity 50 Tons.

Speed 11 knots.

Steam supplied by two multi-tubular boilers with a working pressure of 35 psi. Re-boilered 1891 cost to build £10,000.

Built as a more economical successor to the *Anglia*, apart from steering badly the *Cambria* was a very successful tug and an excellent sea boat. Fitted with large cabins where the crew slung hammocks.

These large cabins were very useful when chartered as a passenger tender to various large steam yachts or liner companies such as P&O and Castle Line; she was also popular attending at the Spithead naval reviews. Her after hold converted into a ladies saloon when on passenger work.

When new the *Cambria* salved the *Willem III* and was awarded £2,500 the largest salvage award William Watkins had received at that time. Also in 1870 with the outbreak of the Franco-Prussian War, *Cambria* was chartered for eighty-four days cruising off the Irish coast warning French ships of the conflict. For £31.10s a day, Watkins had an agreement with the Salvage Association working for them on a tidal basis for an agreed amount. In 1898 they chartered her for twenty-eight tides re-floating the *Ballisteros* ashore near Cape Barfleur on the Cherbourg Peninsular. On 12th December 1899 the Glasgow registered Barque *Mandalay* grounded on the Goodwin Sands off of Sandown and was re-floated by the *Cambria* after thirty-six hours and this ship had jettisoned 200 tons of cargo.

Cambria

Launch of *HMS Thunderer* 1911

On 8th November 1904 *Cambria* and five other Watkins tugs attended the launch of the cruiser *Black Prince* from the Thames Iron Works, Blackwall.

1911 *Cambria* and *Vincia* were among nine Watkins tugs at the launch of *HMS Thunderer* from the Thames Ironworks Co. Blackwall; the last battleship built on the Thames. She was towed to her fitting out berth at Dagenham on the north shore of Halfway Reach. The berth is named Thunderer Jetty and is still in use to this day as an oil tanker berth.

After a long career *Cambria* was sold February 1914 to Bolchow Vaughan for scrap.

Albion (ii) 1870 – 1872

Official No. 63606
Gross tons 109.74
Net tons 26.59
Dimensions Length BP 101ft, Beam 17ft 9ins, depth of hold 9ft 3ins, draft 7ft 6ins

Built 1870 by London Engineering & Shipbuilding Co. Limited, Cubitt Town, Isle of Dogs.

Powered by a 40-nominal horsepower twin-cylinder vertical direct-acting engine by Stewart. Cylinders 15⅝ins 26 ⅝ins with a stroke of 16ins.

Speed 12 knots.

Watkins second screw tug, a handy tug but still suffering from being designed with the hull too shallow for holding a heavy tow, as were most of the early screw tugs. When the Franko-Russian war broke out in 1870 the *Albion* was chartered to cruise between Falmouth and Ireland to warn French ships, then down to the Azores on the same charter. *Albion* spent seventy-four days at £36.15s a day, a total of £2,719.10s. A French officer was carried onboard for this charter.

In 1871 her small size did not stop her doing a tow from Cadiz to the River Tyne with the sailing ship *Karkal* 483 tons for a fee of £600, her shallow draft made her unsuitable for Watkins work and the *Albion* was sold to interests in Antwerp in January 1872.

Robert Bruce 1872 – 1892

Official No. 52660
Call Sign KWVH
Gross tons 192.27
Net Tons 49.4
Dimensions 121ft 3ins x 20ft 1ins x 10ft 9ins

Paddle tug built of iron 1865 by Westwood & Co. Poplar for the Caledonian Steam Towing Co., Poplar.

Powered by two single side-lever engines with a cylinders of 34ins with a stroke of 5ft. 120 nominal horsepower.

15th July 1872 acquired by William Watkins Limited for £8,000

when the Caledonian Steam Towing Co. went into liquidation.

1876 badly damaged in a collision with General Steam Navigation Company's *Nautilus* off Cuckolds point, Limehouse.

1877 the boilers were removed for repair

1879 the engines were removed to strengthen the hull

1881 the boilers were again removed for repair and new paddle shafts fitted.

Robert Bruce* at launch of *HMS Sans Pareil

9th May 1887 *Robert Bruce* assisted at the launch of *HMS Sans Pareil* from Thames Iron Works, Blackwall.
1892 sold to Castle & Sons for £180 for scrap
The hull was acquired by the City of London Corporation as the headquarters of the Port Sanitary Authority (now known as Port Health Authority) and moored off Gravesend and re-named *Hygeia*. Her paddle boxes and sponsons were removed and a large deckhouse erected, for accommodation for the doctors. She was finally scrapped in 1910 and replaced by the newly built *Hygeia*.

Atlas 1873 – 1887

Official No 14368
Call sign LMTS
Gross tons 100.22
Net registered tons 17.27
Dimensions 98ft 1ins x 17ft 7ins x 9ft 8ins
70 nominal horsepower
Wooden carvel built

Built 1854 by Charles Hill & Son, Bristol for Bradford & Co. Bristol. Fitted with two single-cylinder side-lever engines with cylinders of 32ins and a stroke of 4ft.

Two boilers fed by four furnaces with a working pressure of 15 psi

1873 acquired by William Watkins Limited.

1879 her paddle wheels were repaired and was re-boilered with

two tubular boilers from the steamer *Rainbow*
25th May 1879 boilers tested at 25 psi

1882 fitted with new spring beams, sponsons and paddle boxes, new shafts and her paddle wheels refitted and bottom sheathed in Ruggs Dock.

21st October 1887 she was dry-docked and surveyed and found to be unfit for repair and scrapped.

Atlas

Hibernia 1874 – 1884
Official No. 70651
Gross tons 237.54
Net tons 37.93
Length B P 139ft 2ins Breadth 21ft 1ins depth of hold 12ft 4ins
130 nominal horsepower

Iron paddle tug built 1874 by Westwood Baillie & Co., Cubitt Town, Isle of Dogs.

Powered by two single-cylinder side-lever disconnecting engines. Diameter of cylinder 34ins with a stroke of 5ft.

Steam supplied by two multi-tubular boilers with four furnaces. Working pressure of 35 psi

A near sister to the highly successful *Cambria*, the *Hibernia* and her sister *Scotia* soon made a good reputation for themselves.

In 1875 she had a lucky escape when bound to Madeira, to tow the steamer *Ariadne* to Antwerp for a fee of £1,500. Her bunkers were full and also a large deck cargo of coal to supplement the bunkers for a long trip. When in the Bay of Biscay in foul weather she was swept by the very large sea, which stove in her engine room casing and flooded it. By superb seamanship her Master,

Captain Edwin Reader who was her Master from new on 2nd October 1874 until she was sold on 18th January 1884, turned her on the crest of a wave, and limped back to Falmouth. The *Anglia* went down to Madeira to undertake the tow instead.

In 1876 she towed the obsolete ship of the line *Frederick William* from Portsmouth to the Thames where she was converted for the training of Merchant Navy cadets. Re-named *Worcester* she was the first of a line of training ships to be moored at Greenhithe with the name of *Worcester*. *Hibernia* also took part in the salvage of the *Allanshaw* in company with the *Victor*. The *Napoleon* being overwhelmed and lost with all hands prior to the arrival of the *Hibernia* who had been sheltering behind North Foreland. The *Victor* received £2,000 and the *Hibernia* £1,000 and the highest praise from the courts concerning the conduct of the three tugs.

In 1883 *Hibernia* was extensively refitted, including new boilers, at a cost of £2,760. Sold 18th January 1884 to French owners Societe Havraise de Remorquage at Le Havre for £7,000 and re-named *Tourville*. Acquired by G. Petrie of Middleborough in 1889 and given her original name of *Hibernia*. In 1911 William Watkins formed a partnership with Mr G. Petrie on the River Tees, so the *Hibernia* returned to her original owner in a roundabout way. In 1913 she was sold for scrap, but her hull was in such good condition that her engines were taken out and she was converted into a sailing ship. Owned during the First World War by the Brito France Shipping Co. and employed transporting coal to France in company with the hull of the *Anglia*, which had been reduced to a barge and used in the same trade.

After the Armistice there was an acute shortage of coastal vessels, so the old *Hibernia* was taken in hand and fitted with a screw propeller and motor engine. In this guise she was reputed to be the ugliest vessel on the coast, also this very early motor engine had constant mechanical problems. She was finally run down and sunk in the Barrow Deep by the Ellerman line *City of Birmingham* in February 1927.

Scotia 1874 – 1891
Official No. 70610
Call sign NJTV
Gross tons 235.91
Net tons 40.21
Dimensions 139ft 2ins BP x 21ft 1ins x 12ft 4ins
Draft 9ft 1ins fwd. 9ft aft
Nominal horsepower 130
Bunker capacity 52 tons

Iron paddle tug built 1874 by Westwood & Baillie, Cubitt Town, Isle of Dogs. Powered by two side-lever disconnecting engines, each with a single cylinder with a diameter of 34ins and with a stroke of 5ft.

Steam supplied by two condensing multi-tubular boilers with a working pressure of 35 lbs.

Scotia and her sister *Hibernia* were built as improvements on the *Cambria* and *Anglia*, for long distance towing and seeking.

Advancements in boiler efficiency improved the coal consumption of these early paddle tugs, which was always a headache when engaged in long distance towing.

Her first long tow was with the *Anglia* towing the dis-masted sailing ship *Duchess of Edinburgh* from Coruna to London for a record fee. She also had numerous hovels in the estuary and along the south coast, and in 1883 ran down to Lisbon and salved the sailing ship *Earl of Dumfries*. By the 1890s she had become outclassed by the new large screw tugs and was sold on 3rd March 1891 for £3,250 to Societe Havraise de Remorquage, Le Havre and re-named *Sucouf*. In 1900 she was acquired by G. Petrie of Middleborough and given her old name back. Petrie had also purchased her sister *Hibernia*, so when Watkins went into partnership with Petrie in 1911 forming Watkins, Petrie & Co. both the *Scotia* and *Hibernia* were back in the partial ownership of Watkins again.

This partnership was ended in 1913 and the *Scotia* sold for scrap in March 1913 for £1,500.

Titan 1874 – 1888
Official No. 45829
Gross tons 95.57
Net registered tons 41.27
Dimensions, length 85ft 5ins breadth 18ft 6ins depth of hold 9ft 7ins
Nominal horsepower 50

Iron paddle tug built 1865 by Gourlay Bros. & Co., Dundee, Yard No. 23, as the *Atlas* for Dundee, Perth & London Shipping Company, Dundee.

Two side-lever disconnecting engines, each with a single cylinder with a diameter of 28ins and a stroke of 3ft 9ins. One tubular boiler with three furnaces and a working pressure of 19 psi

Acquired by Watkins in 1874 and re-named the *Titan* as an *Atlas* was already part of the fleet. Thoroughly overhauled on arrival in the Thames to bring her up to Watkins standard.

Titan was unusual in having small paddles, which ran very

Titan as built with two funnels in Lawson Batey colours

fast. Fitted with a new boiler, July 1877, new pistons 1879, new cylinders November 1882, and new paddle boxes 1887.

Although mainly a river tug the *Titan* occasionally went out of the river and in 1884 towed the grain elevator *International* with the *Hibernia,* from the West India dock to Antwerp. The *International* was 80ft high and none of the other tug owners in London would attempt the tow as it was considered to be risky.

Sold on 10th October 1888 to John Batey of Newcastle for £1,350. Other reports state it was sold to Hartlepool for £1,700.

June 1920 owners Lawson Batey Tugs Limited.

September 1936 sold for £205 to Clayton and Davie Ltd, Dunstan, and scrapped.

Paddle Tug 'Titan' at Newcastle c. 1930

Titan **with single funnel in Lawson Batey colours**

Renown 1874 – 1903
Official No. 47351
Call sign VNGQ
Gross tons 165.05
Net tons 29.32
Dimensions 118ft x 19ft 2ins x 9ft 9ins
Draft 7ft 11ins
Nominal horsepower 100

Paddle tug built of iron in 1863 by Charles Lingley at Deptford for a Gravesend syndicate headed by Mr M. Martin.

Two side-lever engines, built by John Stewart of Blackwall. Single cylinder with a diameter of 33ins with a stroke of 4ft. Two multi-tubular boilers with four furnaces.

Sold soon after to Mr. Thomas Seed of Fleetwood. Later sold to W. & T. Joliffe, Liverpool.

Acquired by William Watkins Limited in 1874 for £3,000.

Extensive repairs to engines in 1876, a re-conditioned boiler from the Napoleon fitted by her engine builder J. Stewart, with a cost of £2,250. Re-boilered again in 1882, her reconditioned boiler being unsatisfactory, also major repairs to her engines and a new paddle box fitted at a cost of £2,500.

Sold 1903 to Dutch ship breakers at Rotterdam for £500.

Renown

Used by Watkins at first seeking, but mainly in the towing of sailing ships out of river and meeting ships, some already under tow inward bound and assist them through the narrow channels of the outer estuary to the docks in London.

Also used on salvage work around the coast in conjunction with the Salvage Association. Watkins had an agreement with the Salvage Association to supply tugs to transport gear and pumps to stranded and sunken ships to assist in their recovery on a daily hire basis.

Pilot 1875 – 1883

Official No. 27228
Call sign PQKP
Gross tons 70.89
Net tons 17.83
30 nominal horsepower
Dimensions Length 85ft 4ins, Breadth 16ft 2ins, Depth of hold 8ft 5ins

Wooden clench built paddle tug built 27th November 1858 by Andrew Woodhouse, South Shields.

Powered by two side-lever disconnecting single-cylinder engines with a cylinder diameter of 24½ins with a stroke of 3ft 9ins.

Steam supplied by two cylindrical boilers with a working pressure of 22 lbs. Jet condenser

Owned by Mr Richard Davis, Gravesend, mid 1860s.

Renown

Sold to Mr Arthur Read, Rotherhithe, early 1870s.

Acquired by William Watkins 21st May 1875 for £220.

In a very poor condition Watkins spent £2,000 on repairs immediately.

On the scroll work round her bow was a pilot with a telescope at his eye. Her hull was too lightly built for a tug and she leaked badly with high repair bills.

Sold for scrap August 1883. Hull sold for £15.00

India 1876 – 1894
Official No. 76969
Call Sign QRNH
Gross tons 218.12
Net tons 41.92
Nominal horsepower 90
Dimensions, Length BP 138ft 9ins, Beam 20ft 6ins, Depth of Hold 11ft 5ins

Iron paddle tug built 1876 by Westwood Baillie, Cubitt Town, Isle of Dogs, London.

Powered by two single-cylinder side-lever disconnecting engines with a cylinder diameter of 30ins and a stroke of 4ft 6ins.

Steam supplied by two multi-tubular boilers with a working pressure of 40 psi. Fitted with a surface condenser instead of the jet type which improved her economy.

Cost of build £9,245.5s 8d.

India

Built as a more economical version of the *Hibernia/Scotia* with smaller engines to enable her to be able seek further down channel than other tugs. One of the finest sea boats Watkins ever built, but was underpowered on heavy tows. The power being undercut too much, for the sake of economy.

On two tug tows she was very useful, her big boilers giving a steady constant supply of steam. In November 1878 she assisted the *Anglia* from Falmouth to Bremerhaven with the North German Lloyd liner *Neckar* for a £1,000 fee and £30 for use of tugs towropes. The *India* had numerous salvages and in 1880 she rescued the derelict sailing ship *Sorideren* off the Scilly Isles and towed her to Falmouth. Also in the same year she refloated the *Mabel* with the *Victor* ashore on the Goodwin Sands a fee of £1,000 awarded. In 1881 she salved the *SS Duke of Westminster* aground on the Isle of Wight.

The *India* had a passenger licence and was always in great demand attending yacht races in the river and estuary. In 1887 she was chartered to carry passengers from Fresh Wharf by London Bridge for a tour of inspection round the Victoria and Albert

docks and then down to Tilbury dock and return to London.

In 1891 the *India* was run down and sunk by a steam collier, not showing any lights off of Shoeburyness. She was soon salved and refitted, also in 1891 she was fitted with a bar and run excursion trips during the summer season from Margate. She carried these out successfully and was popular with the public. She did this for the following two years reverting to a tug in the winter months until on 19th January 1894 she was sold to J Constant for £1,000.

Resold to J. Spicer of Peckham who worked her for a short period on the Thames before selling her later in the same year to the Tees Tug and Lighting Company, Middleborough.

On 19th July 1895 she was chartered by the south coast excursion steam company Cosens & Co., Limited, Weymouth to supplement their fleet and provide trips from Weymouth to Cherbourg. Her charter was cut short when her owners wanted her back in Sunderland as the Royal Navy's channel fleet was paying a visit; she sailed from Weymouth on 7th September 1895.

India **on charter to Cosens 1895**

In the following year she was back on the South Coast chartered by a Mr J. Taylor of Portsmouth during July and August 1896 providing trips round the Isle of Wight, to Bournemouth and Southampton and trips across the channel to Cherbourg.

In 1899 she was sold to French owners at Dunkirk and re-named *Marine* and converted to a hulk January 1904.

Her Master's under W. Watkins were

Richard Thomas Reader	*1st September 1876 – 16th April 1886*
George Harris	*27th April 1866 – 4th February 1887*
Richard Thomas Reader	*5th February 1887 – 14th December 1888*
George Crouch	*16th December 1888 – 21st January 1889*
Richard Thomas Reader	*22nd January 1889 – 20th December 1889*
Richard Thomas Reader	*14th February 1890 – May 1892*
A. Frost	*13th May 1893 – 24th November 1893*
George Easdown	*1st December 1893 – 19th January 1894*

India **1896 on south coast after being sold**

Bristol 1877 – 1898

Official No. 69403
Gross tons 58.69
Net registered tons 39.91
Nominal horsepower 45
Dimensions Length 76ft 7ins, Breadth 16ft, Depth of Hold 8ft

Iron screw tug built 1876 by Leaker and Son, Bristol.

Powered by a two-cylinder compound engine with a cylinder diameter of 18ins with a stroke of 18ins. Steam supplied by a multi-tubular boiler with a pressure of 50 lbs.

Worked at Bristol before being acquired by William Watkins in 1877. On her way to London the *Bristol* broke down off Start Point and was towed into Plymouth. The *India* ran down to tow her from there to London.

A useful tug assisting the ships and schooners using the London and St. Katherine Docks, and was chartered for use in the London dock, by the Dock Company for a time.

In July 1883 her boiler was taken out and her hull given a new steel bottom and her deck layout improved.

The *Bristol* was conspicuous by her bell-topped funnel.

25th February 1898 she was in a collision with the *SS Winsloe* at the Nore and sunk. Trinity House later blew up the wreck to stop it causing shoaling.

Fox 1877 – 1878

Official No. 79602
Dimensions 76ft x 14ft 5ins x 8ft 4ins

Built by J Stewart, Thames Iron Works, Orchard Yard, Blackwall.

Powered by a two-cylinder compound engine built by the shipbuilder.

The *Fox* did not stay in Watkins ownership for long, joining the fleet on 12th October 1877 until her sale on 1st February 1878. During this time, she was under the command of Captain Sidney Hood.

1st February 1878 sold to Currie Line for use at Port Natal, South Africa. She sailed from London in July, taking 41 days to Cape Town where she arrived 5th September. From there she ran to Port Natal where she worked.

19th March 1912, sold to African Boating Company.

5th June 1912 sold to C. A. Johnson.

31st January 913 sold to Irvin & Johnson Limited.

1927 deleted from register.

Fox

Canada 1880 – 1936

Official No. 82785
Gross tons 72.33
Net tons 2.6
Dimensions 80ft 5ins x 16ft 9ins x 9ft 8ins draft 11ft 3ins
Bunker capacity 18 tons
Speed 11 knots

Iron screw tug built 1880 by Thames Iron Works, Blackwall. Powered by a high-powered two-cylinder engine with all pistons the same diameter of 19ins with a stroke of 18ins. In March 1884 re-engined with a compound engine with cylinders of 19ins and 33ins and a stroke of 18ins. In 1888 again re-engined with a triple-expansion engine built by J Stewart & Son, Blackwall with cylinders of 13ins 19ins and 33ins with a stroke of 18ins.

350 ihp steam supplied at 60 psi.

Re-boilered when fitted 3-cylinder engine with a multi-tubular boiler 10ft x 10ft with a pressure of 160 psi. She was re-boilered again in 1911 with a secondhand boiler at a cost of £600. In 1917, she was extensively refitted by Charlton & Co. at Grimsby, at a cost of £4000. Her original wooden bulwarks being replaced by iron at this time. An extremely successful tug designed for the smaller tows on the river, but also used on coastal tows.

Before the days of freezers, ice was brought to the Thames in sailing vessels from Scandinavia, and during very hot summers the ships were becalmed and the hospitals who relied on this source of ice, would be running short, so tugs would be sent seeking them in the North Sea and tow them to London, the *Canada* often being used on this work.

In July 1899 she was chartered to find an ice ship in the northern approaches and tow to Surrey dock, three days at £9.00 a day £27.0s.0d. During the Frst World War the *Canada* was one of the few tugs spared being requisitioned by the Government, subsequently being kept very busy on the Thames.

After the war Tilbury dock was extended and the *Canada* was used towing the hoppers away from the dock.

On completion of this contract the *Canada* was laid up at Ramsgate until being sold to G. Cohen & Son during May 1936 for £110 and scrapped.

***Australia* as built**   ©*A. Duncan, Gravesend, Kent*

Canada

Australia 1882 – 1908

Official No 85095
Gross tons 128.04
Net tons 18.21
Iron screw tug built 1882 by L Smit & Zoon, Kinderijk, Holland
Dimensions Length 90ft 4ins, Breadth 20ft 6ins, depth of hold 11ft 3ins, Draft 10ft 6ins

Powered by a two-cylinder direct acting 400 ihp compound engine with cylinders of 22ins and 40ins with a length stroke of 22ins. Steam supplied by two cylindrical multi-tubular boilers with a working pressure of 65 psi. Bunker capacity 40 tons.

The hull was built in Holland and then towed to Greenwich with her sister *Zealandia* by the *India* to be fitted with their engines and boilers by Appleby Bros., when built *Australia* had twin funnels placed fore and aft, with the steering wheel on deck level, the fore side of the forward funnel. Used in the coastal and seeking trades until 1896 when *Australia* and *Zealandia* were both modernized and fitted with one funnel and a bridge which greatly improved their appearance. They were then used as river tugs only, as bigger and more powerful tugs were being used on the coast.

Sold 30th July 1908 to Pas & Co., Rotterdam for scrap.

***Australia* after being modernised 1896**

Zealandia (i) 1882 -1912

Official No. 85094
Gross tons 128.04
Net tons 18.21
Dimensions 90ft 4ins x 20ft 6ins x 11ft 3ins draft 10ft 6ins
Speed 11 knots

Iron screw tug built by L. Smit & Zoon, Kinderdijk, Holland. Powered by a 400 ihp two-cylinder compound engine with cylinders of 22ins and 40ins with a length of stroke of 22ins. Steam supplied by two multi-tubular boilers with a pressure of 65 psi. Bunker capacity 40 tons.

The hull was towed from Holland along with the hull of her sister *Australia* by the *India*, to Greenwich, for the fitting of her high-pressure engines by Appleby Bros., London. These were not a success and were compounded by Stewarts soon after. When built she had two bell-topped funnels placed fore and aft, with the steering wheel on the deck level. When new she was used down channel seeking and on coastal tows, but was not all that suitable for coastal work. In 1896 *Zealandia* and *Australia* were both modernized while being re-boilered, the two funnels were replaced with one and a bridge being fitted at the same time. This gave them a much more modern and pleasing line. *Zealandia* was used mainly for river work from then on.

Sold May 1912 to the Shipping Federation and used on the river for the breaking of strikes. As soon as they acquired her, she was sent to Queenborough to bring 200 strike breakers to London. When not required for this she was laid up in Gravesend Canal Basin.

During World War One the Navy requisitioned her for a time.

1917 sold to Messrs. Duncan of Redcar for use on the River Tees.

1922 Scrapped.

Tasmania 1883 – 1897

Official No. 87107
Gross tons 81
Length 80ft

Iron screw tug built by E. Wates, Hull. Powered by a compound steam engine with two cylinders, with diameters of 17ins and 34ins, with a stroke of 20ins.

Steam supplied by a multi-tubular boiler with a pressure of 80 psi.

Cost to build £3,168.

Built as an improvement of the *Canada*, the *Tasmania* was very small for the type of towing she tackled. Coastal towing and salvage in the outer estuary being successfully carried out. The salvage of the sailing vessel *Firth of Solway* in 1894 with the *Mercia*, earned her a big award. Another was the refloating of the German ship *Pampa*; from off the Long sand with the paddle tug *Conqueror*.

In 1887 she was chartered at Great Yarmouth, towing sailing fishing smacks in and out of port. These smacks were trying to compete against the steam powered fishing boats that were being operated in larger numbers. In 1891 she was sunk in collision with the steam ship *Bengal*, salved and refitted. In 1894 she was re-boilered and modernized. Her wooden bulwarks being replaced with iron ones at this time.

Sold 10th May 1897 to William B. Hill, Liverpool (Liverpool Screw Towing Co) and re-named *Heathercock*.

1910 sold to Leith Salvage & Towage Company. (J. Nicholson of Leith). 1929 scrapped at Inverkeithing.

Malta 1883 – 1885

Official No. 87083
Gross tons 59.47
Net tons 12.13
Length 72ft 9ins
Breadth 15ft
Depth of Hold 8ft 6ins

Iron screw tug built 1883 by E. Wates at Hull. Powered by a 35-nominal horsepower two-cylinder compound engine with cylinders of 15ins and 28ins with a stroke of 20ins.

Steam being supplied by a cylindrical multi-tubular boiler with a pressure of 80 psi.

Built as a river tug she did not last long in Watkins ownership being sold to Cowes Steam Tug Co. Limited, Cowes, Isle of Wight on 5th March 1885.

1935 scrapped.

Columbia 1884 – 1912

Official No. 89649
Call sign JSBN
Gross tons 213.72
Net tons 42.34
Dimensions 121ft x 22ft x 12ft 5ins
Draft 12ft
Bunker capacity 110 tons
Speed 11 knots

Steel screw tug, built 1884 by De Maas Co. Ltd, Delftshaven, Holland.

Powered by a two-cylinder compound engine with cylinders of 23ins and 47ins with a stroke of 24ins.

Re-engined 1894 with a three-cylinder triple-expansion engine with cylinders of 15ft, 23ft and 44ft with a length of stroke of 24ins, 800 ihp.

Re-boilered in 1894 and again in 1897 with a multi-tubular cylindrical boiler 13ft x 10ft with a working pressure of 160 psi.

A sister to the *Hibernia* of 1884 but built of steel, which was in its infancy, as a trial instead of the more usual iron, which the *Hibernia* was constructed of.

A number of long tows were completed by the *Columbia*. In 1885, along with the *Hibernia*, they towed the dredgers *Egypt No. 1* and *Egypt No. 2* from the West India Dock to Alexandria for a fee of £1,200 each. In 1901 she assisted the *Oceana* from Madeira with the *Dunnoter Castle* that *Oceana* was towing from Dakar to Southampton.

Columbia again assisted the *Oceana* to tow the *Italia* from Fayal to Genoa in 1905. Both tugs then running to Port Said to tow the steamer *Balmoral* with rudder damage to London. Another difficult tow with the *Hibernia* was a naval floating dry dock for submarines from Barrow in Furness to Portsmouth.

The steel used in building *Columbia* was not as durable as the iron of the period, her hull being worn out, she was sold to French breakers in 1912.

Columbia

Hibernia 1884 – 1961

Official No. 89622
Call sign JPWG (Later) MGSR
Gross tons 213.17
Net tons 42.37
Dimensions: 121ft x 22ft x 15ft 5ins
After shortening 107ft 1ins x 22ft 1ins x 12ft 1ins
Draft 8ft 10ins forward 12ft 8ins aft
Speed 11 knots

Built 1884 by De Maas Co. Ltd, Delftshaven, Holland, of iron.

Powered by two-cylinder compound engine with cylinders of
23ins and 47ins with a length of stroke of 24ins. 825 ihp 120
nominal horsepower

Hibernia **as built**

Steam supplied by a multi-tubular boiler with a working pressure
of 110 psi. Fired from forward side of boiler. Her bunker being
foreside of bridge instead of usual position at after end of the
boiler casing as was normal in tugs fired from after side of boiler.
Bollard pull 5$\frac{1}{8}$ tons.

Bunker Capacity 120 tons, after shortening 80 tons.

Iron screw tug built in Holland with her sister *Columbia*, which
was built of steel as an experiment. The *Hibernia* being one of the
most successful and long-lived tugs in the Watkins fleet, giving
seventy-seven years' service before being scrapped.
Built for seeking and ocean towing Watkins being the world

Hibernia **towing HMS Grampion to Charlton for scrap 1899**

Hibernia ready for launching after being shortened at Ramsgate 1923

Hibernia as *HMS Carcass* entering Ramsgate harbour

Hibernia 1960

leader in distance towing at this period. She was nicknamed 'the three one hundred and twenties' being 120ft long, 120 nominal horsepower and her bunkers held 120 tons of coal.

Numerous ocean tows were undertaken. In 1886 amongst the other tows were three dredgers, which were difficult ungainly tows from Amsterdam to Oporto, Hook of Holland to Passajes, Spain and Antwerp to Lisbon. In 1903 the paddle vessel *Basrah* from Portsmouth to Basrah in the Gulf in forty-two days. A Dutch tug towing an identical tow taking fifty-three days. At the beginning of World War One the *Hibernia* was requisitioned by the Royal Navy and renamed *HMS Carcass* and placed in the Downs Boarding Patrol.

The *Hibernia* was relieved in the Downs, her large radius without bunkering being wasted there. Again renamed (the *Java* receiving the name *Carcass*) to *HMS Hibernia III* to avoid confusion with the battleship *Hibernia*. She was then sent out to the Dardanelles and came under hostile fire on numerous occasions taking part in the second landing and later evacuation of troops at Sulva Bay and Anzac Cove on the Gallipoli Peninsula. From Gallipoli the next tow was an Admiralty X lighter to Mesopotamia (Iraq) in the Persian Gulf. Her Master Captain George Wood was awarded the OBE being very highly regarded by the Navy. The *Hibernia III* then returned to England for an extensive refit from June – December 1916, by the Grand Central Engineering Co., Grimsby, at a cost of £6,700. On completion was employed as a rescue tug around the UK coast, until the end of the war. In 1923 it was decided there was insufficient long-distance towage, so *Hibernia* was sent to Ramsgate where her bow was shortened by 15ft 6ins enabling her to be used as a river tug. During the Second World War the *Hibernia* was one of the few ship towing tugs to remain on the river.

The *Hibernia* was finally scrapped at T. Ward's yard at Grays, Essex on 13th April 1961. The last iron tug in the fleet still with her original engine, serving the company for seventy-seven years. A fine record for a hard-working tug.

Mona 1884 – 1885
Official No. 89653
Call Sign JSRN (later) MJBP
Gross tons 119.15
Net registered tons 11.47
Dimensions: length 97ft 9ins Beam 19ft 1ins Depth of Hold 11ft 4ins
Designed by James Pollock, Sons & Co Ltd Shipbuilders at Faversham, Kent Ship No. 16
Built 1884 by L Smit & Zoon Kinderdyk, Holland
Engine by Charles Burrell, Thetford, Norfolk

Powered by a two-cylinder compound engine with cylinders of 40ins and 20ins with a stroke of 24ins. 80 nominal horsepower 600 ihp.

Multi-tubular boiler11ft 6ins in diameter with a working pressure 100 psi. Bunker capacity 40 tons.

Her Master was George Harris from 24th January 1885 to 10th

July 1885. The *Mona* was probably the only failure Watkins had built, becoming a salvage job on her first sea tow. She was towing the SS *Niobe* from Havre to Glasgow and when off Cherbourg had a complete engine failure and was towed to port. The *Anglia* was sent to complete the tow of the *Niobe*, and the *Mona* was towed back to London where repairs to her engine which included two new pistons were carried out. Her engine builders, Charles Burrell were successful traction engine builders and not known as marine engineers, so why Watkins had the *Mona's* engine built by them is a mystery. She was still having problems and after a few months was laid up and sold.

One report states she was sold 10th July 1885 to Cowes Steam Tug Company, Isle of Wight for £2,300 and sold 1890 to Queenstown. Another report stated she was sold 10th July 1885 to J. Miller, Queenstown, Ireland for £5,000.

1902 sold to Liverpool Screw Towing Co. and renamed *Fighting Cock*. On 12th September 1929 she sank after a collision with the sand dredger *G. B. Crow*. 1946 sold to Toyne Carter & Co., Fowey. 1947 sold to Fowey Tug Co. and renamed *Thethosa*. 1949 sold to W. J. Reynolds, Torpoint, Cornwall. 1963 sold for scrap to Demmelweek and Redding, Sutton Pool, Plymouth.

Mona as 'Fighting Cock'

Malta 1886 – 1888
Official No. 70712
Gross tons 112.93
Net tons 17.34
Dimensions: Length 103ft 2ins, Breadth 18ft 2ins, Depth of hold 9ft 4ins

Iron paddle tug built 1875 by J. Eltringham, South Shields as the *Benachie* for J. F. Gibb's, Ben Company.

Powered by a 90-nominal horsepower single-cylinder side-lever engine with a piston size of 27½ins with a stroke of 50ins by J. P. Rennoldson, South Shields.

Steam supplied by a multi-tubular boiler with a working pressure of 30 lbs. psi

Malta in France. Fenwick Tyne & Wear colours

© A. Duncan, Gravesend, Kent

Acquired by William Watkins Limited May 1886 on the collapse of the Ben Company from G. & W. Davidson of Aberdeen and renamed *Malta*. Several Aberdeen ship owners had interests in the Ben Company.

She did not last long in Watkins ownership. After breaking one of her paddle wheel shafts in September 1888, she was inspected by Mr M. Allen of Newcastle and acquired by him on 28th September 1888 in the damaged condition for £1,350.

1914 sold to J. Dry Steam Tug Limited. 1944 sold to France Fenwick, Tyne & Wear Company Limited. 1951 sold for scrap to J. A. White & Co. North Queensferry.

Burmah 1886 – 1889

Official No. 73663
Gross tons 179.54
Net tons 26.45
Dimensions: Length 121ft 7ins. Breadth 21ft 2ins.
Depth of Hold 11ft

Iron paddle tug built 1876 by Hall Russell & Co., Aberdeen for J. F. Gibb as the *Ben Lomond*.

Powered by two single-cylinder side-lever engines with a diameter of 33ins with a stroke of 54ins, nominal horsepower 100. Twin tunnels fore and aft.

Acquired by W. Watkins in 1886 for £7500 when the Ben Line collapsed. Renamed *Burmah*, she was sent to Scotland for a refit to bring her up to Watkins standard, starting work in February 1887. On the occasion of the Royal Naval Review at Spithead to mark the jubilee of Queen Victoria in 1887, the *Burmah* was chartered by P&O to attend on their liners *Rome* and *Victoria* and at the review of 1889 she attended on the Orient Liner *Ormuz*.

She did not last long in Watkins ownership, being sold 28th September 1889 to Bilbao, Spain for £2,900 and renamed *Bilbao*. Lost off Vigo, March 1903

Burmah

Iona 1886 – 1920

Official No. 73659
Call sign KLPH
Gross tons 179.54
Net tons 26.55
Dimensions: Length 121ft 7ins, Breadth 21ft 2ins, Depth of Hold 11ft, Draft 7ft fwd. 9ft 3ins aft.
Speed 11 knots

Iron paddle tug built 1876 by Hall Russell & Co., Aberdeen for J. F. Gibb, London as *Ben Nevis*. Launched by Mrs Richard Holland wife of her first Master.

Re-engined 1884 by T. A. Young of Blackwall and fitted with two twin-cylinder side-lever engines with a cylinder diameter of 34ins and a stroke of 5ft.

Steam supplied by two multi-tubular boilers, each with two furnaces, with a working pressure of 30 psi, nominal horsepower 120, bunker capacity 60 tons.

Acquired by Watkins in 1886 after the collapse of Gibb's Ben Company, along with the *Ben Lomond* (*Burmah*) and *Benachie* (*Malta*). All three were sent to Scotland to be refitted to bring them up to Watkins standard. A fine tug with twin funnels placed fore and aft, renamed Iona. Watkins used her seeking, coastal towing and she had numerous hovels in the Thames Estuary and English Channel.

Iona

Iona was also popular attending Spithead Naval reviews on 28th June 1897, she was charted for four days at £25 per day to run from Gravesend to attend a P&O steamer at the review and return to Gravesend. In 1899 she was reboilered with new steel boilers by Stewarts with a working pressure of 40 psi. In August 1904 the *Iona* and *Scotia* were chartered attending a channel swim at Dover for a fee of £37.10s and £20.

As more economical screw tugs replaced the paddlers, the Iona was used as a river tug only, the paddle tug still being very popular for stopping and steering dead ships on the river. 1920 sold to Mr. W. Alder of Middlesbrough for £1000 *Iona* was the last paddle tug on the Thames. 1928 scrapped at Sunderland.

Mercia 1889 - 1895

Official No. 96650
Gross tons 94.49
Net tons 9.63
Dimensions: 85ft 8ins x 18ft 1ins x 10ft 7ins Draft 11ft 5ins

Iron screw tug built 1889 by Westwood & Baillie, Millwall.

Powered by a three-cylinder inverted direct-acting compound with cylinders of 12½ins, 18½ins, 32ins with a stroke of 20ins by Stewarts of Poplar, of 400 ihp, 70 nominal horsepower. Reboilered in 1894 with a two-furnace boiler by Eltringham, 10ft 6ins x 9ft 6ins with an increased pressure of 160 psi which improved her towing ability.

Although small she was used successfully on outside work and lucky with salvage, in December 1891 the *Burma* and *Mercia* were Watkins representative in salvaging the *Alladne* and got two thirds of the award. On 24th November 1892 the 4 masted Barque *Glencairn* 1,564 tons grounded in fog at Thorpeness on the Suffolk coast. Ten tugs refloated her, three from Lowestoft, three from Great Yarmouth, one from Harwich, *Mercia* and *Iona* from Watkins and one other from the Thames. Salvage award was £2,175, the *Iona* and *Mercia* having the biggest share £650.

In December 1894 *Mercia* and *Tasmania* got a good award for services to the sailing ship *Firth of Solway*.

Sold 22nd April 1895 to Manchester Ship Canal Co for £4,000.

Mercia **in Manchester Ship Canal Co. colours**

Sold again in 1935 to C. Roberts, Commonwealth Steam Towing Co. Avonmouth.

April 1939 Fairplay towage and Shipping Co. Ltd acquired the Company and its tugs. The owners Lucy and Kurt Burchard had escaped from Germany with two tugs and a cargo ship and operated at Avonmouth until returning to Germany after the war.

Iona

On 14th January 1942 the *Mercia* was towing a barge from Newport, South Wales to Bristol and struck a mine on the Welsh Ground Sands Pos. 51° 31' 21" N 02° 46'44" W and was lost with all hands. The barge she was towing was undamaged.

Burma 1889 – 1904
Official No. 96664
Gross tons 94.49
Net tons 9.63
Dimensions: 85ft 8ins x 18ft 1ins x 10ft 7ins

Iron screw tug built by Westwood, Baillie & Co, Millwall, London Powered by a three-cylinder compound engine with cylinders 12½ins, 18½ins and 32ins with a length of stroke of 20ins, 70 nominal horsepower, 350 ihp. Steam supplied by a multi-tubular boiler with a pressure of 160 psi. Re-boilered 1894 by Stewarts.

A near sister to the *Mercia,* the *Burma* was a good towing tug for an early screw tug and was mostly used on the river, but had her share of salvage in the Estuary and Channel. In February 1901, she was one of the tugs that re-floated the *Rion* from the Goodwin Sands, and on Christmas day 1902 she salved the steamship *Gorbea* with the *Arcadia*. She was also hired for pleasure cruising; in September 1899 she sailed from Seaforth for four weeks cruising in the channel, charterer paying running costs for £30 per week. Sold 7th October 1904 to Messrs. Price, Wells and Reeves for £3,050 for service in Bombay being lost off the port in 1905.

Oceana 1889 – 1918
Official No. 95549
Gross tons 337
Net tons 2.18
Dimensions 140ft x 22ft 7ins x 13ft 1ins Draft 12ft 6ins
Speed 11 knots
Crew 13

Twin-screw ocean going tug built of steel by Gourley Bros. Dundee. Powered by two x two-cylinder compound engines each 500 ihp, total 1,000 ihp with cylinders of 19ins and 36ins with a length of stroke of 27ins. Steam supplied at 80 psi with a coal consumption of 10 tons per day.

Built as a modern replacement for the now ageing and increasingly obsolete *Anglia*.

The *Oceana* carried out innumerable long tows, too many to list in full. Her first tow was the *SS Cape of Good Hope* from Leith to London, then the *Argentino* from Lisbon to Sharpness, also in 1889 she towed the *Avery Hill* 3,140 tons from Pernambuco to Dunkirk for £2,150. In April 1894 she towed the *Dunbar Castle* from Las Palmas to East India Dock for £850. In February 1901 she went down to St. Helena to tow the *Lismore Castle* back to London for £2,800; and in December of the same year the *Dunottar Castle* from Dakar to Southampton for £1,600 assisted from Madeira by the *Columbia* £500, the ship had broken its crankshaft.

Oceana on buoy at Gibraltar   © Dr A.R. Lane, Oxon

In 1905 the oil hulk *Tancarville* was towed from the Tyne to Portland by *Columbia* who was relieved by the *Oceana* and towed to North Sumatra, a distance of 8,200 miles, the longest tow undertaken at that time, taking 45 days at an average speed of 7 knots for a fee of £3500.

In 1891 she was in collision in Gravesend Reach while towing a barque and was beached to stop her sinking. She was salved and repaired. 1903 one of her propellers fouled the clipper *Orontes* that unfortunately sunk.

1908 reboilered and her bridge extended at a cost of £200.

With the outbreak of the First World War, the *Oceana* was requisitioned by the Navy on 3rd August 1914 as an armed boarding vessel, being renamed *HMS Cerberus* and placed with the Downs Boarding Flotilla. She was not suitable at this, her twin screws often fouling ships hulls.

She was transferred to coastal towing, a role that used her potential to the full. Her name was changed back to *HMS Oceana* and was later transferred to Scapa Flow as a rescue tug, and attendant tug to the Grand Fleet.

On 18th October 1918 the *Oceana* was at anchor in Scapa Flow when the Navy tug *Stobo Castle* collided with her and she sank, fortunately without loss of life and was a total loss.

Guiana 1889 – 1918

Official No. 91809
Call Sign KGRL (later) QCWH
Gross tons 165.85
Net tons 4.9
Dimensions 110ft 5ins x 19ft 5ins x 10ft 9ins Draft 11ft

Iron screw tug built 1885 by Usk Shipbuilding Co., Newport, Mon. Designed by James Pollock & Sons Limited, Faversham Ship No. 28 for South West Steamships Co. Ltd, Plymouth as *Power*. 500 ihp, three-cylinder triple-expansion engine with cylinders of 15ins, 23ins and 40ins with a length of stroke of 25ins. With a boiler 12ft x 10ft 3ins with a working pressure of 150 psi.

March 1889 acquired by a Gravesend syndicate headed by the solicitor Mr Tolhurst.

7th June 1889 acquired by W. Watkins and renamed *Guiana* on 11th October 1889. Fitted with a two-bladed propeller as an experiment, but was not a success when going astern, this being changed to a three-bladed propeller from the *Oceana*, which was highly satisfactory. Reboilered 1896 with a working pressure of 160 psi, burning 6 tons of coal per day.

From 19th December 1897 until 19th May 1898 *Guiana* was chartered as a pilot cutter by the Dutch at the Hook of Holland while their steam cutter was being built. Charterers providing everything except Chief and 2nd Engineers at a fee of £180 per month £900 total.

Oceana on buoy at Gravesend

© A.Duncan, Gravesend, Kent

Guiana

Once in 1893 and again in 1894 the *Guiana* and *Hibernia* towed two new floating dry-docks from River Tyne to the Manchester Ship Canal, these being very unwieldy tows. In 1903 *Guiana* and *Arcadia* towed a dredger from River Clyde to Middlesbrough via the Caledonian Canal, the tugs and tow having to pass through the locks one at a time.

She was very successful with salvage in 1907 she got the *Cambrie* into Dover assisted by the *Gauntlet* and Dover tug *Lady Crundall*, which had extensive bow damage from a collision. In 1909 she got an award of £1,450 for rescuing the French sailing vessel *Quillota* which had lost her anchor off Dunkirk and towing her to Antwerp.

In 1906 she was towing the sailing ship *Portia* off of Flamborough Head, she blew the cylinder head off her NP and had to be towed into the River Humber for repair. In 1907 she had a similar accident when towing a ship off Great Yarmouth, she blew her LP cylinder head off. She sailed herself to the Britannia Pier at Great Yarmouth to telephone for assistance, the *Persia* being sent up to tow her home.

Requisitioned by the Navy on 7th November 1914 and stationed at Newhaven and later as a dockyard tug in the Firth of Forth.

On the 29th January 1918 she was struck amidships by the destroyer *HMS Bat* in fog off Whitby and sunk with the loss of her Master Captain V. Wood and three other crew members.

Nubia 1890 – 1935

Official No. 98149
Call sign MQGP
Gross tons 101.92
Net tons 18.41
Dimensions: 87ft 6ins x 18ft 6ins x 10ft 7ins draft 12ft 3ins
Bunker capacity 30 tons
Coal consumption 4 tons a day.
Speed 11 knots

Iron screw tug built 1890 by Westwood, Baillie & Co, Poplar. Powered by a 350 ihp, three-cylinder triple-expansion engine with cylinders of 12½ins, 19ins and 32ins with a stroke of 20ins. Steam supplied by a multi-tubular boiler with a working pressure of 160 psi.

A very useful class of tug capable of most jobs on the river also used coasting and seeking.

When the Thames froze over during the great frost of 1895, the *Nubia* was seeking and was signalled to return to the Thames, as the paddlers were unable to work in the ice. 1895 was a good year for salvage for the *Nubia*, the sailing ship *Alexander Yates* had refused the *Nubia's* offer to tow her to London, a gale blew up and she was dragging her anchor until the *Nubia* and Sandford's *Conqueror* were able to get her away from the beach at Dungeness. The *Nubia* later towing her to London for a very good award.

Nubia

On Boxing Day sailing ship *Atlanta* grounded on the Long Sand, the *Nubia* and *Cambria* plus other tugs refloated her after five days, the two Watkins tugs getting £566.13s.4d each from a total award of £2,200.

She was re-boilered in 1894, again 1902 and 1920. In September 1906 the *Nubia* was chartered seeking ice ships in the northern approach channels as the hospitals were running out of ice.

During World War One the *Nubia* was one of the few tugs left on the river to cover all the work, the others being requisitioned by the Navy. The *Nubia* still managed to get her share of salvage during the war; in 1916 she was one of six Watkins tugs that salved the *Parkgate*, and in 1917-8? *Nubia* was one of four Watkins tugs on the *Polglass Castle*.

1924 extensive hull repairs costing £2,000.

Laid up at Ramsgate during the depression of the 1930s until sold for scrap to G. Cohen and Son, Canning Town, for £140.

Cynthia 1892 – 1896
Official No. 99079
Call Sign MPSG
Gross tons 244.17
Net tons 107.2
Draft 6ft 10ins
Dimensions: 153ft 4ins x 21ft 4ins x 10ft 3ins x 35ft 4ins over paddle boxes

Iron paddle excursion steamer built 1892 by James T. Eltringham & Co, South Shields. Powered by two diagonal compound engines with cylinders of 23ins and 46ins with a stroke of 36ins by

Cynthia

Stewarts, Poplar. Steam supplied by a steel boiler with a working pressure of 90 psi speed 13 knots. Bunker capacity 48 tons. Cost to build £8,844.

With the success of the *India* in the excursion trade from Margate during the summer seasons of 1891, 1892 and 1893 it was decided to build a purpose-built paddle steamer to run from Margate across the channel to France. Her first Master for the 1892 season was Edwin Reader who had been Master of the *Renown*. For the 1893-1895 seasons her Master was John Jones who was Master of the *Cambria* and went back to the *Cambria* during the winter when the *Cynthia* was laid up in the South West India Dock. *Cynthia* was not a financial success, running a single ship service and being a pure pleasure steamer, she could not return to towing during the winter months as the *India* and other tugs in the excursion trade could. She was a week into the 1896 season when an offer was received from Mr C. E. Pollard from South Shields and she was withdrawn and sold.

Cynthia was chartered from the Tyne during August and September 1899 by Cosens & Co. Ltd, Weymouth to supplement their fleet of excursion steamers as the Royal Navy channel squadron was in Portland, and Cosens had the contract to attend on the fleet when in port. On her return to the Tyne at the end of 1899 season she was sold to H. C. Jones of London and run for two seasons from Rosherville Pier to Herne Bay and then on other routes as the Herne Bay route did not pay. Sold May 1905 to Hastings, St. Leonards & Eastbourne Steamship Co. Ltd, and run between Hastings and Eastbourne and mooring at Newhaven at night. *Cynthia* only had one mast at this time; her main mast had been removed.

Competition on the South Coast from the fleet of P. & A. Campbell was too great and she was sold September 1907 to Molville Steamship Co., Londonderry, running between Molville and Londonderry and as a tender to liners that called at Mŏlville to pick up passengers.

1917 requisitioned by Royal Navy as a minesweeper for a short period and returned to her owners 24th May 1917. 1923 sold to Anchor Line and used on the same tender service to its liners calling at Molville.

1931 sold to Stewart & Hewitt Ltd, Belfast for excursion work. In 1932 a large Eucharistic Congress took place in Dublin and the *Cynthia* acted as tender to the numerous liners acting as hotels anchored in Dublin Bay. On 26th January 1933 while laid up for the winter in Kinston Harbour at Dun Laoghaire the *Cynthia* sunk during a severe storm. She was raised and scrapped.

Scotia 1894 – 1935
Official No. 102862
Call Sign MQPW
Gross tons 136
Net tons 4.51
Dimensions 97ft 5ins x 19ft 5ins x 11ft 2ins
Speed 11 knots.
Bunker capacity 45 tons

Built in 1893 of steel by Anderson Laverick & Co. Ltd, Newcastle and engined by Stewarts of Blackwall with a 493 ihp triple-expansion engine with cylinders of 13ins, 21ins and 34ins with

Cynthia

Scotia

a stroke of 24ins. Steam supplied by a multi-tubular boiler, 11ft 3ins x 9ft 6ins, with a working pressure of 160 psi. Stewarts had the hull built to take the engine they had built for exhibition purposes, and when no longer needed she was laid up at Blackwall and put up for sale.

Acquired by William Watkins Ltd in 1894 who dry-docked her and altered her hull to their specifications. She was very economical to run and a very good sea boat. Her first Master, Captain Thomas W. Finch was in command until July 1897 and *Scotia* was used seeking and coastal towing. She was one of many tugs chartered to attend the needs of the ships of various shipping companies, attending the naval review to commemorate Queen Victoria's Diamond Jubilee at Spithead. *Scotia* attending Glen Lines *Glenartney*. She was re-boilered in 1907, which was unsatisfactory and resulted in a court case. During the First World War, *Scotia* was used towing barges from Holland for a time and when released by the Government she spent the rest of the war working the river and assisting many ships in the Thames Estuary that had been mined and damaged. *Scotia* had extensive hull and engine repairs and was again re-boilered with a boiler of increased pressure to 180 psi at a cost of £3,400.

After the war, while being repaired on the slipway at Ramsgate she fell over causing her some damage. With the world slump badly affecting shipping the *Scotia* was laid up at Ramsgate in 1934 and sold to G. Cohen & Son in May 1935 for £160 and scrapped at Canning Town.

Arcadia 1895 – 1952
Badia (ii) 1952 – 1962
Official No. 105766
Call sign MQTJ
Gross tons 179.85
Net tons nil
Dimensions 109ft 1ins x 21ft 5ins x 11ft 8ins, Draft 12ft

Steel screw tug built 1895 by Cook, Welton & Gemmel, Hull. Powered by 700 ihp, three-cylinder triple-expansion engine with cylinders of 14½ins 23ins and 37ins with a length stroke of 27ins.

Scotia

Arcadia **as built**

© *Dr A.R. Lane, Oxon*

Steam supplied from a multi-tubular boiler 12ft 9ins x 10ft 6ins with working pressure of 160 psi.

Bunker capacity 80 tons, speed 11 knots.

Bollard pull $5^1/_8$ins.

Arcadia was a fine sea boat and used extensively seeking and coastal towing, but on occasions going further afield. In 1896 with her sister *Manila*, towed the paddlers *Empire* and *Liberty* from Erith to Las Palmas with a price of £425 each and in 1899 towed the steamer *Riga* from Lisbon to Le Havre for a fee of £375.

With the outbreak of the First World War the *Arcadia* was requisitioned on 4th August 1914 by the Royal Navy and renamed *HMS Chichester*, Lt W. Hibberd RNVR was her Master with Watkins before the war and when requisitioned made a Lieutenant in the RNVR.

Allocated to the Downs Boarding Flotilla based first in Dover then Ramsgate and used examining ships passing through the Dover Straits for cargoes or personnel bound for Germany. Tugs were the ideal design for this job, all ships had to be cleared and a boarding officer was but aboard the ships in all weathers and tugs proved the most suitable craft for this work. Her Master, Captain W. Hibberd was drowned after falling from the top of the halfround during the examination of a ship. She remained under naval control until 29th May 1919 when she was returned to

Arcadia **as HMS Chichester**

Watkins and reverted back to the name *Arcadia*. When refitting after the war her halfrounds had six holes cut in them to make it easier to pass a heaving line from foreward where it was usually thrown onboard a ship to aft to pull the towrope direct to the towhook.

During World War Two the *Arcadia* was used on the River Thames and in coastal towing. Armed with twin marlins on the side of the wheelhouse and a strip Lewis behind the funnel and a rifle the same age as the tug, two D.E.M.S. gunners were also carried. Hired by Ministry of Shipping during December 1940 and was towing barges two at a time between London and Great Yarmouth, these barges were bound to Glasgow and were towed from Yarmouth by other tugs. Early in 1941 while towing

Arcadia after holes cut in halfrounds

Arcadia **with hole in funnel after being bombed**

two of these barges she was attacked by a German JU88 plane in the vicinity of the Rough Buoy, eight miles east of Harwich. The *Arcadia* was machine gunned and bombed and fortunately the bomb went straight through the funnel without exploding. Assisted into Harwich by the *Kenia*, the hole in the funnel causing a loss of draft to her fires so unable to maintain steam pressure.

During the blitz on 9th September 1940 the *Minnie De Larrinaga* was bombed in London and sunk. Salved she was taken to Silvertown, which had been badly hit with a heavy loss of life. The ship was loaded with the rubble from the bombed factories, this rubble contained human remains from the factories. The *Arcadia, Water Cock* and *Lady Brassey* towed the ship from Silvertown to Dover, the stench from the decaying remains was overpowering and she was sunk as a blockship in the western entrance of Dover Harbour on 5th February 1941. In late 1941 the *Arcadia* was towing a collier from Harwich to Sunderland and as they were not escorted they anchored at night, first night in Yarmouth Roads, second night off Cromer. When going through the Race, a channel off the Wash, the *Arcadia* grounded and damaged her rudder, she then lost her anchors in bad weather and drifted round the Wash for two days and was spoken to by a United Towing tug from Hull who towed the collier to port. The *Arcadia* was adrift for another two days before being found by a trawler who towed her to the Humber for repairs. She had a set of sails made while under repair, but I don't think she ever used them in anger.

Arcadia **unberthing** *Almeda Star* **from Tilbury landing stage**

When built the *Arcadia* had been fitted with sails, which was normal for tugs built in the 19th century, these were used when seeking down channel to save on coal until a sailing ship was sighted. Also on a couple of occasions when she had mechanical problems she sailed to a safe anchorage.

Arcadia returned to the Thames on river work in 1942 and assisted in the positioning of the Maunsell and Naval AA forts in the Thames Estuary. In 1944 she assisted shifting various sections of the Mulberry Harbour from their building berths to lay-by

Arcadia **renamed Badia 1952**

berths and handing them over to the sea tugs to tow away. She also assisted the numerous ships using the port with the build-up to the invasion. 1st February 1950, *Arcadia* became part of the Ship Towage (London) Ltd fleet with the joining of William Watkins Ltd, The Elliot Steam Tug (1949) Ltd, and Gamecock Tugs Ltd, all tugs keeping their own flag, funnel and hull colours.

In June 1952 her name was changed to *Badia* when the P&O Line asked for the name to be released for their new liner being built on Clydebank. *Badia* continued at work on the river for another ten years, being sold to Thos. W. Ward Ltd for £1,455 and delivered to Grays Buoy at 13.00 hours, 14th November 1962.

Manila

1895 – 1901
Official No. 105775
Gross tons 179.85
Dimensions 109ft 1ins x 21ft 5ins x 11ft 8ins
Draft 7ft fwd. 12ft aft

Single screw steel tug built 1895 by Cook, Welton & Gemmell, Hull. Powered by a 700 ihp, 99 nominal horsepower three-cylinder triple-expansion engine with cylinders of 14½ins, 23ins and 37ins with a length of stroke of 27ins. Speed 11 knots

Steam supplied by a steel multi-tubular boiler 13ft 1¼ins diameter with a working pressure of 160 psi. She was a successful tug, used seeking and coastal towing. In November 1896 she towed the

paddle steamer *Empire* from Erith to Las Palmas for £475 on the run home she towed the steamer *Inga* from Vigo to London for £260 inclusive of three-day detention at Vigo.

She also had her share of salvages; in 1900 she was one of a number of tugs which salved the German liner *Duisberg* off Margate with a damaged propeller and rudder. Later in the year she played a major part in refloating the *Sardonyx* ashore on the Mouse Sands, *Manila* getting a good share of the award from both ships.

During the Boar War, Cape Town was short of tugs, with the large volume of shipping transporting the Army and its stores. Watkins received a good offer for her from Messrs Chalmers Guthrie & Co. who sold her on 3rd June 1901 to Table Bay Harbour Board. Sold 7th December 1916 to Cape Town Stevedoring Co.

Sold 15th January 1917 to Ernest G. Nyman.

Sold 29th March 1917 to British Africa Shipping and Coaling Co.

Requisitioned by the Royal Navy and transferred to Port Said

Sold 5th August 1920 to Greek owners and renamed *Elzi 2*

Sold 1926 to Locas Matsas & Sons, Pireus and renamed *Aghids Nicolaos*

Scrapped 1957.

Manila

Simla

1898 – 1964
Official No. 108343
Call Sign MQZK
Gross tons 143.87
Net tons 2.67
Dimensions: 100ft 4ins x 20ft 1ins x 12ft.
Draft 12ft 6ins aft. 8ft fwd.
Bunker capacity 50 tons
Speed 11 knots

Single screw tug built 1898 by Lobnitz & Co., Renfrew Powered by a 500 ihp three-cylinder triple-expansion engine by the shipbuilder. Cylinders of 13ins, 22ins and 35ins with a stroke of 27ins. Steam supplied by a cylindrical multi-tubular boiler 12ft x 10ft with working pressure of 160 psi. Consumption of coal six tons per 24 hours. Bollard pull March 1953, 5¼ tons.

Soon after being delivered from the builders, the *Simla* was following the sailing ship *Blenfell* through the Gull Channel trying to negotiate a price to tow her to Thames Haven. Loaded with a cargo of naphtha, contemporary reports state that the steward entered the lazarette with a naked light, followed by an explosion, which blew her stern off. The *Simla*, under the command of Sidney Hood then went to the forward end of the ship and rescued the remaining crew over the bow, not knowing if the rest of the ship would explode at any moment. The *Simla's* crew received gallantry awards for their bravery.

Requisitioned by the navy from July 1914 until July 1915 and served

on the Medway before being sent to Havre and Rouen under the army and then to Scapa Flow, back under the navy, salving various ships on the Scottish coastline. One being the Norwegian *Sarpen* ashore in the Orkneys. The salvage claim was disputed because the *Simla* was under the Admiralty and could not claim salvage. A higher court found in favour of the *Simla* and was awarded £800.

Between the wars *Simla* used mainly on the river with the occasional coastal tow. Requisitioned again by the Royal Navy from September 1939 to October 1943 and stationed at Dover. During operation Dynamo the evacuation of the B.E.F. from Dunkirk, Dover was the main reception port for Naval vessels, ferries and larger merchant ships. The Admiralty Pier with eight berths was the main landing area, usually there were sixteen ships alongside, double banked most of the time, all needed tugs and *Simla*, George Low Master with *Gondia Roman* and *Lady Brassey* worked non-stop during the evacuation.

Apart from berthing and un-berthing the ships at the pier they needed help outside the harbour and they towed in *Themson* loaded with refugees after it had collided and sunk the *Efford*. On 27th May, towed in *Monas Isle* five miles out with bomb damage. 29th May destroyer *HMS Montrose* towed in stern first with the bow blown off. 30th May, *HMS Jaguar* bombed making water berthed Eastern Arm. 31st May *HMS Bideford* with her stern blown off towed in, berthed, submarine camber dock, then *HMS Impulse* with engine problems towed into port. *Simla* carried out over 140 towing jobs, they also had to take stores and ammunition off to the ships on buoys in the harbour and put them alongside the tanker *War Sepoy* for bunkers.

Simla towing PLA *Hercules* through Tower Bridge 1960. The signal of a Ball & Pennant being flown by *Simla* requests that the Tower Bridge Bascules be raised. This was before VHF was used. Ships inward bound flying the signal, would be seen by Cherry Garden Pier, who would inform the Bridge that a ship required the Bascules raised.

© *Star, Fleet Street*

She returned to the Thames in 1944 and was used towing sections of the Mulberry Harbour to Tilbury to be handed over to sea tugs to tow to France.

After the war *Simla* was stationed at North Woolwich Pier. Most of her work being the smaller ships that berthed in the various docks and river berths in the upper reaches. Also attending on the various P.L.A. heavy lift cranes. The *Simla* and *Java* would spend days towing the 60 tons lift *London Ajax* from ship to ship in the South West India Dock.

Simla © *World Ship Society*

On 1st February 1950 Ship Towage (London) Ltd came into being when William Watkins joined forces with the Elliot Steam Tug Co., both acquiring the interests of Gamecock Tugs Ltd. The tugs keeping their own funnel colours and house flags until 1965.

10th April 1964 arrived Sheerness for scrap by The Medway Drydock Co. *Simla* was put into No. 1 Dry-dock for dismantling.

Java (i) 1900 – 1901

Official No. 112731
Gross tons 154.5
Net tons 3.98
Bunker capacity 60 tons
Dimensions: 100ft 5ins x 20ft x 11ft 6ins Draft 12ft 6ins

Steel screw tug built 1900 by Mordey Carney & Co. Southampton Powered by a three-cylinder triple-expansion engine by the shipbuilder with cylinders of 13ins, 22ins and 35ins with a stroke of 27ins. Steam being supplied by a 12ft x 10ft multi-tubular boiler with a working pressure of 165 psi.

Java did not last long on the Thames being sold March 1901 to Unterweser Reederei G.M.B.H. Bremen and renamed *Unterweser 15*. 1909 sold to Svenska Statens, Jarnvagar, Sweden and renamed *Tralleborg S.J.*

1967 scrapped.

***Simla* docking Hellenic Lines Anglia into Greenland Dock entrance**

Java as *Unterweser 15*

Mashona 1902 – 1905

Official No. 115822
Gross Tons 153.12
Net tons 3.34
Dimensions 100ft 5ins x 20ft 1ins x 12ft 5ins Draft 12ft
Speed 11 knots

Steel screw tug built 1902 by the Irvine Shipbuilding & Engineering Co. Irvine. Powered by a 500 ihp three-cylinder triple-expansion engine with cylinders of 13ins, 22ins and 35ins with a stroke of 27ins. Steam supplied by a multi-tubular boiler with a working pressure of 160 psi. Bunker capacity 60 tons

The hull was completed in Scotland and towed to London by the *Columbia* to be engined by J. Stewart and Sons, Blackwall.

The *Mashona* did not spend much of her time in Watkins ownership on the Thames; most of it spent coastal towing. Soon after completion she towed the steamer *Neritea* 3,650 tons from Belfast to the Tyne with the *Oceana*.

In 1904 she assisted the *Arcadia* and *Simla* tow the ironclad battleship *Temeraire* from Plymouth to Jarrow to be converted into a training ship for Engineers.

Mashona was also a lucky ship for salvage, in 1902 refloating the *British Prince* from the beach at Dungeness with the *Persia*, *Columbia* and another Gravesend owned tug the *Cleveland*, the total award being £6,320 and in November salved the sailing ship *Calvan*. In 1904 *Mashona* had two noteworthy salvages, the *Phillippeville* and the James Norse sailing ship *Erne* damaged in collision was picked up by the *Mashona* and another tug, the *Mashona* suffering heavy weather damage in this incident.

1905 sold to Messrs. Price, Wills & Reeves for service at Bombay.

1915 requisitioned by the Royal Navy to assist in the Persian Gulf in stopping gun running and slavery.

Persia 1902 – 1908

Gross tons 149.79
Net tons 8.74
Dimensions 94ft x 19.65ft x 11ft draft 12ft
Speed 11 knots
Bunker capacity 50 tons

Steel screw tug built 1902 by Cochrane & Sons, Selby. Powered by a 500 ihp three-cylinder triple-expansion engine by J. Stewart & Son, Blackwall, with cylinders of 13ins, 21ins and 34ins with a stroke of 24ins. Steam supplied by a cylindrical multi-tubular boiler 11ft 3ins diameter with a working pressure of 160 psi.

This class of tug were very successful capable of any work on the river, or seeking and coastal towing.

When new she was the first tug to make fast to the *British Prince* ashore at Dungeness, receiving an award of £1300 out of a total award of £6,320. The *Persia* was unlucky being sunk twice. In September 1906 she was struck by one of the propellers of the P & O Line's *Marmora* at Tilbury Dock old lock entrance. She was quickly salved and refurbished and returned to work, but on 11th April 1908 while seeking north of the Sunk light vessel was in collision with the steamer *Hugenot* of Newcastle and sunk, the crew being rescued by the *Hugenot*. The *Persia* this time being a total loss.

Persia 1902

Liberia 1905 – 1911

Official No. 120612
Call sign HDPM (later) MCGY
Gross tons 128.06
Net tons 6.21
Dimensions 94ft x 19ft 6ins x 10.95ft draft 12ft
Bunker capacity 50 tons

Steel screw tug built 1905 by Cochrane & Sons, Selby. Powered by a 500 ihp three-cylinder triple-expansion engine with cylinders of 13ins, 21ins and 34ins with a stroke of 24ins. Steam supplied by a 11ft 3ins diameter cylindrical multi-tubular boiler with a working pressure of 160 psi.

Liberia

The *Liberia* was employed successfully in all aspects of the industry, seeking, salvage and river towage.

In 1911 Watkins went into partnership with G. Petrie of Middlesbrough under the name Watkins, Petrie & Co., Middlesbrough, the *Liberia* being transferred to the new company on the River Tees. This association only lasted until January 1913 when the Tees Tug Co. Ltd, acquired the interests of the company.

During the First World War, Watkins chartered her for work on the Thames as most of the Watkins' tugs had been requisitioned by the Navy.

30th July 1920 sold to Tees Towing Co. Ltd.

25th June 1930 sold to Newport Screw Towing Co. Ltd.

1937 broken up.

Java (ii) 1905 – 1965

Official No. 120611
Call sign MCGX
Gross tons 126.35
Net tons 6.21
Dimensions 94ft x 19ft 6ins x 10ft 95
Draft 12ft
Bunker capacity 50 tons

Built 1905 of steel by Cochrane & Sons, Selby. Powered by a 500 ihp three-cylinder triple-expansion engine by G. T. Grey & Co, South Shields with cylinders of 13ins, 21ins and 34ins with a stroke of 24ins. Steam supplied by a multi-tubular boiler 11ft 3ins diameter with a working pressure of 160 psi.

After being launched the hull was towed to the River Tyne for the fitting of her engine by the engine makers. Before the First World War she was successful seeking and coastal towing, with a number of salvage jobs to her name.

In 1911 W. Watkins Ltd formed a partnership Middlesborough tug owner G Petrie, the *Liberia* was transferred permanently to the River Tees and the *Java* for a short period of time also.

The *Java* stayed on the Thames for the first year of World War One until the Royal Navy requisitioned her on 27th July 1915 and sent her to Ramsgate as part of the Downs Boarding Flotilla and renamed *HMS Carcass*.

Her Master was Capt. James Walker and while under Navy control became a Lt. RNR. She relieved the *Hibernia* who had previously been named *HMS Carcass*, freeing her for long distance work with her large bunkers she was wasted on the Downs Patrol. The work of the Boarding Flotilla required all ships passing through the Dover Straits to be cleared and tugs were ideal vessels to go alongside ships in all sea states. The tugs were also in a perfect position to assist ships that got into difficulties on the Goodwin Sands.

Form A.

Certificate of Approval of the position (Alteration of the position) of the Centre of the Disc, and of the Lines to be used in connection therewith, in pursuance of the Merchant Shipping Act, 1894.

Lloyd's Register of British & Foreign Shipping.

ESTABLISHED 1834.

No. ~~8756~~ 7999

No. 71, Fenchurch Street,

LONDON, *11th November,* 1905.

This is to Certify that the Committee of this Society have approved, on behalf of the Board of Trade, the position (or alteration of the position) of the centre of the disc and of the lines to be used in connection therewith on the Steamship _"Java"_

Official No. _____, and hereby certify—

(*a.*) That the centre of such disc is placed at _one_ feet _two & a half_ inches below the _main_ deck line marked under the provisions of the Merchant Shipping Act, 1894.

(*b.*) That the position of the lines to be used in connection with the disc shall be as follows and as shown in the subjoined diagram :—

Maximum load-line in fresh water.—The upper edge of this line is _____ feet _two & a half_ inches above the upper edge of the horizontal line passing through the centre of the disc.

Maximum load-line in Indian summer.—The upper edge of this line is _____ feet _____ inches above the upper edge of the horizontal line passing through the centre of the disc.

Maximum load-line in summer.—The upper edge of this line is on the same level as the upper edge of the horizontal line passing through the centre of the disc.

Maximum load-line in winter.—The upper edge of this line is _____ feet _one_ inches below the upper edge of the horizontal line passing through the centre of the disc.

Maximum load-line in winter, North Atlantic.—The upper edge of this line is _____ feet _____ inches below the upper edge of the horizontal line passing through the centre of the disc.

Top of statutory deck line above the top of wood ~~or iron~~ deck at side _three quarters of an_ _____ inches.

This Certificate is to remain in force only so long as the vessel remains in her present class, provided that no change has taken place in the structural condition of those deck erections in respect of which deductions have been made for freeboard.

NOTE.—In accordance with the Regulations made by the Board of Trade, the disc and lines must be permanently marked by centre punch marks or cutting, and the particulars given in this Certificate are to be entered in the official log. This Certificate must also be framed and put up in some conspicuous part of the Ship.

If and so soon as the class of the ship is either changed or withdrawn, or if and so soon as any change is made in the structural condition of the deck erections above mentioned, this Certificate will be cancelled and must be delivered to the Committee of Lloyd's Register for that purpose, and the owner must then apply for a new Certificate.

Witness my hand,

Geo. T. Henderson
for **Chairman.**

A. Scott
Secretary.

The *Summer freeboard* applies to voyages from European and Mediterranean ports, from April to September inclusive. In other parts of the world this freeboard should be used during the corresponding or recognised summer months.

The *freeboard for Indian Summer* applies to voyages in the fine season in the Indian Seas between the limits of Suez and Singapore.

The *freeboard for Winter North Atlantic trades* applies to vessels sailing to, or from, the Mediterranean, or any British or European port, and which may sail to or from, or call at, ports in British North America, or Eastern ports in the United States, north of Cape Hatteras, from October to March inclusive.

Lloyds certificate for stating position of Plimsoll line on hull of *Java*

Among the notable salvages rendered by the *Carcass (Java)* were the *Sigrum I*, which had been abandoned on 3rd November 1915, the *Addington* on 18th March 1916 and the *City of Manilla* refloated from off the South Goodwins with the *Chub (Vincia)*, *Doria* and *Commonweal (Commonwealth)* 20th/21st June 1918. The *Java* was returned to her owners on 14th May 1919 and returned to the Thames.

When the Second World War was declared on 3rd September 1939 the *Java* was off the Isle of Wight towing two barges from London to Portsmouth, she then went to Devonport and in company of the *Tanga* both were sent to Brest and St. Nazaire during October 1939. On her return to the UK the *Java* was requisitioned by the Royal Navy and placed on the Dover Patrol once again examining ships passing through the Dover Straits, until Operation Dynamo, the evacuation of the British Expeditionary Force from Dunkirk was set in motion. The *Java* was in the first wave sailing from Ramsgate 15.00 hours, 28th May 1940 for Dunkirk in company with four drifters and five motor launches. At first light the next day, the *Java* launched her boat and with the four drifters was transporting troops from the beaches and filling ships offshore, she was ordered along the coast to La Panne and transferred troops to the cruiser *Calcutta*. *Java* then returned to Dunkirk and spent the afternoon filling ships lying onshore, she then proceeded to Ramsgate. Five miles from Dunkirk she rescued two British airmen from a plane in the sea and then troops from the sunken paddle steamer *Waverley*. *Java* arrived at Ramsgate at 9.30, 30th May and landed 120 troops. The following day she rescued 150 troops from the trawler *Jacinta* that had stranded

on the wreck of the *Merl* near the North Goodwin lightship and landed them at Ramsgate.

For their work ferrying troops from the beaches in the tugs boat, the deckhand Harry Griffith was awarded the D.S.M. and the mate Victor Smith was mentioned in dispatches. After Dunkirk, the *Java* was transferred to Milford Haven with the *Gondia*, on harbour duties and from there to Londonderry, Northern Ireland, later being joined by the *Cervia* and *Fabia*, attending the North Atlantic convoy escorts based there.

The *Java* remained at Londonderry until relieved on 1st August 1945, she then went to Colraine and towed an RAF pumping unit to Rye, Sussex, then on to London for a boiler clean, before going to Harwich attending on the troopships running between Cuxhaven and Harwich with the British Leave Army until January 1946 when she was relieved. *Java* was then coasting between Kings Lynn, Southampton and the continent.

On the 11th September 1946 she received orders to run to Southampton via Ramsgate to Flushing, but the crew refused saying she was unseaworthy. The crew was laid off and the tug run to Ramsgate on 17th September by her Master and shore staff as crew. On 1st October Lloyds passed her as seaworthy, the old crew were sacked and the new crew shipped. On 2nd October she towed on the *Fort Vermillion* ashore on the Goodwin Sands, she had grounded on 29th September fully laden with iron ore. The ship refloated on 5th October by 5 tugs after jettisoning 2,000 tons of ore over the side, the *Java* was waiting her turn to get hold of the ship when she refloated.

1st January 1926. *Java* **alongside a section of a large German drydock that was towed to Sheerness from Germany in September 1920**

Java and ***Doria*** **on Dover patrol during the Second World War at Ramsgate**

On 7th October towed on fore half of *Helena Majeska* with three other tugs but only managed to move it 150 ft. She had grounded on 12th September and had broken in two before the ship could be lightened sufficiently to refloat. Both halves were later salved. On 27th December the *Java* refloated the Harrison Lighterage tug *Markrock* ashore 2 miles up Hole Haven creek after towing on her for 2 hours and then towing her up to Tilbury Dock tidal basin.

Owing to the fuel crisis the *Java* was laid up on 3rd March 1947 and the crew laid off owing to the shortage of coal.

1st February 1950 Ship Towage (London) Ltd was formed by the merger of William Watkins Ltd with the Elliot Steam Tug (1949) Ltd and the acquisition of Gamecock Tugs Ltd.

10th December 1954 the *Java*, *Gondia* and *Kenia* towed the clipper *Cutty Sark* from East India Dock to her permanent dry berth at Greenwich, this towage was carried out free of charge.

The *Monte Urquola* 7,723 gross tons sailed from New Fresh Wharf in the Upper Pool at 16:15 on 27th January 1954 and touched the ground aft. The flood tide swung the bow of the ship round and the forward tug being unable to hold her, she laid athwart of London Bridge completely blocking the river. It was not until 19:00 that the combined efforts of *Tanga*, *Java*, *Kenia*, *Crested Cock*, *Sun V*, *Sunbird* and *Sunfish* pulled her clear.

The *Java* was based at North Woolwich for the remainder of her working life, attending on the smaller ships that berthed in the upper docks and reaches. A large part of her work was attending on the smaller P.L.A. heavy lifting cranes. The *London Ajax*, *London Atlas*, *Hercules* and *Leviathan*, towing them around to and from the enclosed dock systems to riverside wharfs.

The *Java* was finally sold for scrap to Southend Ship breakers in May 1965, the hull being resold to Metaalhanel En Sloopwerken H.P. Heuvelman N.V. Krimpen A/D Ijssel, Holland.

1966 the hull resold to Bruges Scheepssloperij, Belgium and scrapped March 1966 at Bruges.

Helena Majeska **being towed before she broke in half**

Java on slip at Ramsgate 1950's

Monte Urquiola **athwart of London Bridge 27th January 1954**

Java

Java in Gallions Reach

Watkins Tugs on buoy at Gravesend. Badia, Tanga, Java, Kenia, Hibernia

Doria 1909 – 1947

Official No. 125767
Call sign MCXT
Gross tons 146.96
Net tons nil
Dimensions 96.2ft x 20.6ft x 10.9ft draft 11ft aft 6ft fwd.

Built of steel in 1909 by Philip & Son, Dartmouth. Powered by a 500 ihp, 3-cylinder triple-expansion engine by the shipbuilder, with cylinders of 13ins, 21ins and 34ins with a stroke of 24ins.

Bunker capacity 50 tons, consumption fout tons per day, speed 11 knots. Steam supplied by a 12ins x 10ins multi-tubular boiler by Riley Bros. Stockton with a working pressure of 165 psi

The first of a class of three tugs known as the 'Teddy Bears' how this nickname came about has not been established. They were improved *Java's* of middle range power, capable of carrying out most of the work on the river or coast.

In 1909 the French barque *Colbert* was in difficulties off Berry Head, Devon having lost one anchor and dragging the other onto a lee shore. The *Doria* was undergoing builder's trials, but manned by a Watkins' crew, went to her assistance and towed her to Dartmouth. The builders claimed £100 salvage award, as the *Doria* had not been handed over to Watkins at that time.

On 15th July 1914 the *Doria* and *Simla* were requisitioned by the Navy and went to Chatham to assist two cruisers out of lay up and swing their compasses. The Navy next sent *Doria* to Scotland under the command of Capt. Jack Smith and later Capt. Keeble, later returning south as an armed boarding vessel with the Downs Boarding Flotilla under Capt. Albert Cross who was given the rank of Lieutenant in the RNVR. The flotilla examined ships for contraband and giving them routes through the minefields in the Dover Straits. The tugs of the flotilla were also in a good position to assist the many ships that were mined or got into difficulties. The *City of Manilla* grounded on the Goodwin Sands in June 1918 with a cargo worth £1 million; the *Doria* was one of four tugs to get her off into deep water. *Doria* was returned to her owners on 2nd January 1919 after five and a half years under Naval control.

Between the wars the *Doria* was used mainly on the river with the occasional coastal tow. In August 1939 the Royal Navy again requisitioned the *Doria* initially stationed at Southend and later at Ramsgate. During the evacuation of Dunkirk during May – June 1940 the *Doria* did not go into Dunkirk but was patrolling offshore and is credited with rescuing forty soldiers of the B.E.F. *Doria* remained at Ramsgate until October 1940 and in 1942 was transferred to Southampton until May 1945 under Risdon Beazly. She was returned to Watkins and worked the Thames until 1947 when she was sold with the *Vincia* to Rimorchiator Riuniti, Genoa and renamed *Euro*. The *Empire John* towed both tugs from Ramsgate 29th November 1947 to Genoa; a severe gale was encountered in the Gulf of Lyons causing the tugs some structural damage.

1954 renamed *Venezuela*.1956 renamed *Cile*.1957 scrapped.

Corsea salvaged by *Doria*, approximately 1940

Doria as *Euro*, November 1947

Doria

Bravor (Norwegian) mined 22nd April 1940. 1 mile south of Gull Buoy, 4.1 miles East of Ramsgate

Convoy being bombed off Deal. Taken from *Doria* 1940

***Doria* under white ensign, Downs patrol 1940**

Crew of *Doria* relaxing

Nuritos salved by *Doria* after hitting a mine off south east coast

Badia 1909 - 1947

Official No. 125778
Call Sign MGXY
Gross tons 146.96
Net tons nil
Dimensions 96ft 2ins x 20ft 6ins x 10ft 9ins Draft 11ft aft 6ft fwd.

Steel screw tug built 1909 by Philip & Son, Dartmouth. Powered by a 500 ihp 3-cylinder triple-expansion engine by the shipbuilder, with cylinders of 31ins, 21ins and 34ins with a length of stroke of 24ins.

Steam supplied by a 12ft x 10ft multi-tubular boiler with a working pressure of 165 psi, bunker capacity 50 tons, consumption four tons per 24 hours, speed 11 knots.

One of the three sisters built by Philips and known as the 'Teddy Bears'.

The *Badia* had her share of salvage; in 1910 she was one of four Watkins' tugs that refloated the French sailing ship *Marechal Suchet* that grounded on the Shingles while under tow.

Requisitioned by the Royal Navy 31st July 1914 and renamed HMS *Chester III* and placed with the Down Boarding Flotilla until 7th September 1917. Transferred to expeditionary force service and given back her name *Badia* and stationed at Calais until the end of the war.

20th January 1919 transferred back to the Royal Navy until 23rd May 1919 then returned to W. Watkins Ltd. Between the wars she was fitted with a Kort nozzle.

In 1926 her Master Capt. J Russell was who her Master since 16th April 1909, apart from when the tug was at Calais when he was Master of a Naval tug, was lost overboard and drowned. Also in 1926 the *Badia* was one of a quartet of Watkins' tugs salving the *Spanker* on fire off Greenhithe. In January 1928 she refloated the *Hindustan* ashore in Northfleet Hope, assisted by *Muria* and *Arcadia*.

During the Second World War she was one of the few Watkins tugs to remain on the Thames for the duration of hostilities. She assisted in the towage of the Maunsell and Naval forts built on the Thames at Northfleet to plug the gap in the anti-aircraft defences in the Estuary. *Badia* was also involved in the towage of the sections of Mulberry Harbour from where it was built to storage in the docks and then in 1944 towing them to Tilbury to hand over to the bigger tugs to tow them across to France.

2nd October 1947 sold to Fowey Tug Co. Ltd, Fowey and renamed *Penleath*

1961 sold to V.D. Marel & De Korte, Holland and scrapped at Bruinisse.

Badia

Badia and *Hibernia* with two other Watkins tugs docking a P&O liner in Tilbury Dock old entrance

Badia with Kort nozzle fitted

Vincia 1909 – 1947

Official No. 129004
Call sign MCYZ
Gross tons 150.08
Net tons Nil
Bunker capacity 50 tons.
Consumption 4 tons per day.
Speed 11 knots
Dimensions 96ft 2ins x 20ft 6ins x 10ft 9ins, draft 11ft aft 6ft fwd.

Steel screw tug built 1909 by Philip & Son, Dartmouth. Powered by a 3 cylinder 500 ihp. Triple-expansion engine by the shipbuilder, with cylinders of 13ins, 21ins and 34ins with a stroke of 24ins. Steam supplied by a 12ft x 10ft multi-tubular boiler by Riley Bros. Stockton, with a working pressure of 165 psi.

The *Vincia* was the last of three sisters built by Philips and known as the 'Teddy Bears'. A good all-round tug for the river and coastal, having good sea keeping qualities and being very economical on coal. Her first Master was Captain William J. Anning.

At the beginning of the First World War, the *Vincia* was requisitioned by the Royal Navy on 30th July 1914 renamed *HMS Chub* and became part of the Downs Boarding Flotilla examining and directing all vessels passing through the Dover Straits, Capt. Anning being made a Lieutenant in the RNR while the tug was under the white ensign.

The *Chub* and all the other tugs of the Boarding Flotilla were based at Ramsgate and were in a good position to assist ships that had suffered mine damage in the Dover Straits area and ships that grounded on the Goodwin Sands. Amongst those salved by the *Chub* was the *Galicia*, mined off the Elbow Buoy and beached at Deal assisted by three other tugs before she sank. The tanker *Perth* loaded with whale oil worth a quarter million pounds struck a mine near the Tongue Sands and was towed up the Thames assisted by the *Gamecock* and two patrol vessels and beached on the Mucking Flats.

On 7th February 1915 the Boarding Flotillas mother ship *Peel Castle* caught fire and with ammunition exploding the *Chub* rescued seventy sailors from the burning ship. Another big salvage was the *City of Manila* that grounded on the Goodwin Sands in June 1918 with a cargo worth one million pounds and in danger of breaking up, but was refloated by the *Chub*, *Carcass*, *Doria* and *Commonweal*. The *Chub* was returned to her owners on 15th December 1919 and her Master Captain W. Anning was awarded the OBE for his wartime services.

Between the wars the *Vincia* was mostly on the river with the occasional coastal tow and salvage. In 1922 the Orient liner *Orcades* grounded off Southend and *Vincia*, *Hibernia* and *Arcadia* refloated her, in February 1928 the *Kota Radja* was in collision with the *Esperance Bay* off Tilbury and the *Vincia* managed to berth her on Tilbury Cargo jetty.

With the outbreak of the Second World War the *Vincia* was again requisitioned by the Royal Navy and became part of the Downs Boarding Flotilla as she had been in the First World War.

In May 1940 the evacuation of the British Expeditionary Force from Dunkirk was gathering pace, the *Vincia* under the command of Captain A. V. Hoiles sailed from Ramsgate on 31st May towing three lifeboats for the beaches. Off the Sandettie Buoy

Vincia on Downs boarding patrol 1939

Vincia

German seaplane being towed to Deal July 1940 by *Vincia*

she rescued an RAF gunner who had parachuted into the sea, the wounded flyer was transferred to the destroyer *Venomous*. The *Vincia* anchored off Bray at 21:00 and started loading troops with the three lifeboats and the tug boats. With around 300 troops she was on her way back to the UK when she was stopped by the destroyer *Keith* and told to put the troops on the destroyer *Sabre* and stop at Bray. At 8:15 on 1st June she witnessed the *Keith* being bombed and the *Vincia* took off survivors and rescued men from the water. *Vincia* was under continuous air attack until clear of Dunkirk and returned to the Kent coast and landed 108 survivors, 1 officer and 83 ratings from the *Keith* and 24 men from the British and French HQ staff at Margate.

After the fall of France, the *Vincia* remained on station in the Downs area based at Ramsgate. A German hospital seaplane was forced down on 9th July 1940 and it landed in the sea, the *Vincia* captured the crew and towed the seaplane to Deal where it was beached, these planes were used to rescue German aircrew that had ditched in the sea.

By 1943 the *Vincia* had been released by the Navy and she returned to the Thames and was stationed at Woolwich, the workload had increased with the buildup of stores and equipment prior to the D-Day invasion. Many of the Mulberry Harbour units were built on the Thames and the *Vincia* towed many of them from the docks up river to Tilbury where they were passed over to the sea tugs for on towage to France.

On 3rd July 1944 the *Vincia* was on forward of the *Fort Gibraltar*

German airmen from seaplane captured by *Vincia* **9th July 1940**

bound for the Victoria Dock, there was an air raid warning so the ship had to wait for the Connaught Bridge to open. A V2 rocket dropped in the dock alongside the *Challenge*, which was the stern tug causing her damage.

After the war she remained on the river until 1947 when she was sold along with her sister tug *Dora* to Societa Rimorchia Tori Riuniti, Genoa and renamed *Eolo*. Both tugs sailed from Ramsgate undertow of the *Empire John* on 29th November 1947 bound for Genoa.

1954 renamed *Peru*. 1957 scrapped.

Vincia in Limehouse Reach

Alboa **salved from Goodwin Sands**

Racia 1915 – 1919

Official No. 139116
Gross tons 399
Net tons 26
1200 ihp, 65 nominal horsepower
Bunker capacity 380 tons
Dimensions 149ft 2ins x 28ft 3ins x 12ft 4ins

A single screw ocean going tug built of steel in 1894 by L Smit & Zoon, Kinderdijk, Holland for L. Smit & Co., Rotterdam, Holland, as the *Oceaan*.

Powered by a 1,200 ihp triple-expansion engine with cylinders of 18ins, 28ins and 46ins with a length of stroke of 30ins. Steam supplied by a multi-tubular boiler with a working pressure of 160 psi.

Acquired 1915 from the Dutch by Mr John Watkins on behalf of the Admiralty as Holland were a neutral country, the Admiralty was unable to purchase the *Oceaan*, Mr. John Watkins acting as a go between. Although officially owned by Watkins and renamed *Racia*, contemporary reports state Watkins on behalf of the Navy managed her.

Racia was acquired because of an acute shortage of large salvage tugs that were desperately needed to tow damaged ships to safety. *Racia* made about six trips to the White Sea, one to tow the Royal Mail liner *Arlanza*, which was serving as an A.M.C. to *Belfast* with mine damage. One very difficult tow was a ship loaded with pit

props that had been torpedoed and towed into Stornoway with great difficulty by destroyers. The ship drawing 41ft forward was towed stern first to Barry, South Wales by the *Racia* where her cargo was badly needed.

In 1919 there was an acute shortage of timber in the country and ships to carry it, so the Government had a timber raft built at Trondhjem, Norway as an experiment to see if it could be safely towed across the North Sea. The raft was 360ft long, 42ft beam with a draft of 10ft 6ins, displacing 4,200 tons and contained 1,292 standards of timber and fitted with a steel stern frame and a rudder. It was registered as a ship and named *Merakerbrug* for legal reasons in case of collision. It was planned that four light cruisers would tow it across but Mr Watkins convinced the authorities that the only chance of success was a proper tug and good weather. The *Racia* towed it across the North Sea to Ipswich at a best speed of two and a half knots, and although it arrived safely the experiment was not repeated.

1919 (other sources state June 1920) sold to Messrs Crichton Thomas, London.

Resold to Dutch owners at S-Gravenhage.

1925 sold to Port du Bouc in the South of France. 1930 to Italian owners.

No further details known.

Racia

Muria (i) 1920 - 1940

Official No. 13608
Call sign GTVM
Gross tons 192
Net tons nil
Dimensions 106ft 3ins x 23ft 1ins x 11ft 7ins Draft 11ft 7ins.
Speed 12 knots.

Built 1914 by Scott & Son, Bowling as the *Wrestler* for Steel and Bennie Limited, Glasgow. Powered by a two-cylinder compound engine by Aitchinis Blair with cylinders of 21ins, and 42ins with

a stroke of 27ins. Steam supplied by a multi-tubular boiler with a working pressure of 120 psi. Bunker capacity 110 tons. Coal consumption per 24 hours towing 10 tons.

She was sold to Turkey before completion but was still in the UK when Turkey entered the First World War, so the Navy requisitioned her in January 1916 and later purchased her and renamed her *HMS Hotspur* in 1918. Used by the Navy at Havre and later as a rescue tug.

June 1920 acquired by W. Watkins Ltd and renamed *Muria*. Watkins had intended to name her *Mercia* but not allowed by Board of Trade as Watkins old *Mercia* was still trading under that name. In 1931 her mizzenmast was lengthened and was fitted with wireless taken from the *Gondia*. Stanchions that were fitted from the boat deck to the top rail, which gave her a yacht like appearance, were also removed at this time.

One of the most powerful tugs in the fleet between the wars and in great demand on the river with the large liners of the day. *Muria* also towed the *Cutty Sark* on her last sea voyage from Falmouth to Greenhithe in 1938 where she joined the *Worcester* as a training ship.

Under the command of Captain James Walker, *Muria* was fortunate with salvage, one of note being the US steamer *Hybert* ashore on the Goodwin Sands in 1931. *Muria* with *Arcadia* and a number of other tugs got her afloat, the *Muria* getting a special mention and an award of £1,700 for her efforts.

Muria with stanchions fitted

© A. Duncan, Gravesend, Kent

Muria towing *Cutty Sark* in 1938 on her last sea voyage

Muria escorting *Dominion Monarch* outward bound passing *Worcester* and *Cutty Sark* at Greenhithe

Muria

Rumania as *Dreadful*

With the outbreak of World War Two the *Muria* was requisitioned by the Royal Navy in 1940 and stationed at Harwich as a rescue tug. In November 1940 the *Muria* was bound from Harwich to Ramsgate to be refitted. She had put into Sheerness to land a crew member and was outward bound through the Princes Channel and struck a mine off North Foreland on 8th November in position Latitude 51° 26.5' N. Longitude 001° 27' E with the loss of all on board. Naval standing orders for rescue tugs stated when proceeding to a casualty, take the most direct route, at all other times use the swept channels. The *Muria* was lost using the swept channel.

Rumania 1920 -1923

Official No. 131148
Call sign GJKB
Gross tons 285.58
Net tons nil
Dimensions 118.5ft x 25ft 2ins Draft 15ft Speed 11 knots

Designed by James Pollock & Sons Co. Ltd, Shipbuilders and Engineers of Faversham, Kent. Ship No. 436 and built by Hepple and Co., South Shields for Canadian owners at Vancouver in 1912 and named *Dreadful*.

Powered by a 1,000 ihp, 74 rpm, three-cylinder triple-expansion engine by Hepple and Co. Ltd, South Shields, with pistons of 15ins, 23½ins and 38ins with a stroke of 30ins.

Steam supplied by multi-tubular boiler 15ft x 12ft with a working pressure of 180 psi. Bunker capacity 130 tons. Coal consumption 10 tons per 24 hours

Her delivery voyage was via Cape Horn as the Panama Canal was not completed at that time. She was built in the North American style with a large deckhouse and a short after towing deck, as against the long towing deck of a European tug. She was fitted with electric light and a towing winch, not many if any British tugs were fitted with these luxuries in 1912.

During World War One with the relentless U boat campaign there was an acute shortage of rescue tugs and the *Dreadful* was requisitioned by the Royal Navy on 9th May 1917 and sailed across the Atlantic Ocean and stationed at Queenstown (now Cobh) Ireland. The Navy purchased her on 9th May 1918 and in 1920 she was transferred to W. Watkins Ltd as a compensation for the loss of the *Oceana* in Scapa Flow during November 1918.

When the *Dreadful* arrived in the Thames the crews soon nicknamed her 'The Something Awful'. Watkins renamed her *Rumania* under the command of Capt. George Wood OBE from the *Hibernia* and based her in the Downs on salvage station and for any sailing ships that required a tug. This work was insufficient for her to make her pay and her design was not found suitable for work in European waters and in consequence she was laid up in Ramsgate and was sold 11th November 1923 back to her original home port of Vancouver, Canada to Pacific Coyle Navigation Co. Ltd and renamed *Pacific Monarch*.

Disappeared from register early 1950s.

Rumania as *Pacific Monarch*

Palencia 1920 – 1939

Official No. 127528
Call Sign
Gross tons 95
Net tons 4
Dimensions 75ft 6ins x 18ft 1ins x 10ft 2ins draft 10ft 9ins
Coal consumption per 24 hours 4 tons
Bunker capacity 35 tons.
Speed 10 knots

Built 1916 by Abdella & Mitchell, Queensferry, Flintshire for the Alexandra Towing Co. Liverpool as the *Sloyne*. Powered by a 350 ihp compound engine with pistons of 15ins and 31½ins with a stroke of 24ins.

Steam supplied by a 10ft x 11ft multi-tubular boiler by J. Neilson & Son, Glasgow with a working pressure of 130 psi.

Palencia and ***Fabia*** **laid up at Ramsgate between the wars.** ***Gondia*** **under refit**

Requisitioned by the Royal Navy soon after completion and later brought outright by them. In 1920 transferred to W. Watkins Ltd as a replacement for losses sustained during the war and renamed *Palencia*.

Used as a river tug and when the extension and new entrance lock was being built in the twenties at Tilbury Dock, *Palencia* was used towing the mud hoppers to the spoil ground. With the depression in the thirties affecting world trade, the *Palencia*, along with other tugs in the fleet, was laid up in Ramsgate Harbour. In1939 sold to James Towing Co. Southampton.

Requisitioned by the Royal Navy September 1939 to January 1946 as harbour tug. In 1946 sold to Shell Oil Company, and stationed at Gibraltar. In service until late 1960s.

Palencia   © *J.E. Wilkins, Grays, Essex*

Watkins tugs on buoy 1921. *Simla, Hibernia, Badia, Palencia, Vincia, Scotia, Doria, Java* **and Pilot Cutter**

Palencia in Shell Oil Co. colours

Fabia 1920 – 1946

Official No. 144445
Call sign MJXP
Gross tons 151
Net tons 12
Dimensions 85ft x 20ft 9ins x 11ft 4ins Draft 10ft 6ins
Consumption of coal per 24 hours 4 tons
Bunker capacity 45 tons,
Speed 9½ knots

Built in 1919 by Edwards & Co Millwall, London as *H.S. 85.* Renamed *Wendy.* 1919 transferred from the War Department to Royal Navy and renamed *HMS Early* in 1920.

Powered by a 450 ihp 2-cylinder compound engine by Plenty & Son, Newbury, with cylinders of 15ins and 32ins and a stroke of 24ins.

Steam supplied by a cylindrical multi-tubular boiler by S. Hodges & Sons with a working pressure of 150 psi.

April 1920 surplus to requirements and offered for sale.

Acquired by W. Watkins Ltd and renamed *Fabia*. Placed in Watkins upriver fleet where she was the crack tug and had a cock on the truck of her mast for a time. During the depression of the 1930s the *Fabia* was laid up in Ramsgate Harbour.

In 1938, liners started running to the Upper Pool during the summer months and the *Fabia* got underway to attend on these ships and then to lay up again during the winter, but with the threat of war looming, it was decided to keep her underway.

She was requisitioned by the Royal Navy in 1939 and placed on the Dover patrol with *Kenia, Java, Vincia* and *Sun VII*. During the evacuation of Dunkirk, the *Fabia* was sent to search for the hospital ship, *Paris*, which had been bombed. Unfortunately, she had sunk before finding her.

After Dunkirk, *Fabia* was stationed at Sheerness for about a year

Fabia towing **Fairplay One** to Ramsgate after grounding on the Goodwin Sands

Fabia

© *A. Duncan, Gravesend, Kent*

Fabia as *Moorcock*

under the RAF victualling barrage balloon vessels in the Thames estuary. She then towed the coal hoist *Biddenden* from the Thames to Lowestoft handing it over to the *Danube VII*, which towed it onto Inverness. *Fabia* ran light to Inverness and was engaged towing barges through the Caledonian Canal for approximately two weeks. These barges were being transferred to the River Clyde from the River Thames. The *Fabia* then towed the *Biddenden* from Fort William to Londonderry and was stationed there under Naval control along with the *Java* and *Cervia* attending the needs of the Fleet of Corvetts that were based there. The *Fabia* and *Cervia* were relieved by the Navy tugs *Sparkler* and *Exploiter* on 5th December 1945 on being returned to Watkins. The *Fabia* had a tow from Birkenhead to Southampton and was sold in 1946

at Southampton to Hemsley Bell & Co. Southampton for £7,500 and used towing bunker barges around the port.

In 1947 she was sold to Liverpool Screw Towing Co. Liverpool and renamed *Moorcock*. She was also used for towing fuel barges in the enclosed dock system.

On 12th April 1956 she was sold for scrap to T. Ward, Preston.

Kenia 1927 – 1964
Official No. 149891
Call Sign GQCX
Gross tons 199.52
Net tons Nil for towage 65.88 for passenger carrying
Dimensions 100ft x 25ft 1ins x 11ft 8ins, Draft 13ft 3ins aft. 8ft 6ins fwd.

Built 1927 by Cochrane & Sons Selby. Powered by a 761 ihp three-cylinder triple-expansion engine by Crabtree & Co Limited, Great Yarmouth with cylinders of 14ins, 23ins and 38ins with a stroke of 27ins.

Steam supplied by a multi-tubular boiler 15ft x 11ft with a working pressure of 180 psi. Bunker capacity 80 tons – coal consumption per 24 hours 10 tons

1929 fitted with a wireless along with her sister Gondia the first Thames tugs to be fitted.

Dutch tanker *Phebos* salvaged after being mined

Kenia in Gravesend Reach

Kenia being launched into Ramsgate Harbour after refit   © A. Duncan, Gravesend, Kent

Passenger Licence for 200 passengers.

The *Kenia* was used in all parts of the company a very useful addition to the river and coastal towing and had a good share of salvage, in 1928 she assisted the *City of Lancaster* in collision at the Nore and beached her on the West Oaze, the *Kenia* was pumping to try and keep buoyancy in the ship.

In 1939 she towed the *Vindicatrix* to Sharpness from Gravesend for use as a training ship for cadets starting their career at sea. August 1939, she was requisitioned by the Royal Navy and placed on examination service in the Dover Strait. After Dunkirk, *Kenia* was sent to Devonport and sent to St. Nazaire with *Atlantic Cock* to tow a half-built destroyer to England, this was refused by

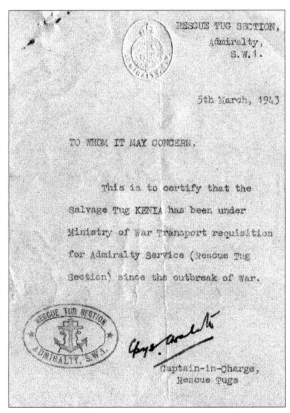

Letter from the Admiralty informing that the *Kenia* had been requisitioned as a rescue tug

***Kenia* assisting war casualty**

the French and she returned to Falmouth, she then returned to the Thames and joined *Muria* at Harwich as a rescue tug given pennant No. W47. She assisted numerous vessels such as the *Dashwood* 2,154 tons which had grounded on the Longsand on 22nd March 1941. Both were attacked by a German aircraft being

***Kenia* assisting Norwegian tanker *Mexico* loaded with 3,823 tons of fuel oil which sank 9 cables from south east Shipwash buoy off of Harwich**

bombed and machine gunned while passing her towrope.

After the war *Kenia* and *Gondia* were used towing surplus naval craft, many to breakers yards around the south and east coasts and near continent.

1st February 1950 transferred to Ship Towage (London) Limited combining the fleets of William Watkins Limited, the Elliot Steam Tug Co. (1949) and Gamecock Tugs.

The *Kenia's* passenger license was frequently used transporting Powder Monkeys (Dockers that loaded and unloaded explosives) from Gravesend to the explosive anchorage at the Chapman and Lower Hope. The tug would stand by the ship and return the Powder Monkeys back to Gravesend when loading was completed.

Each year on the occasion of the Thames Sailing Barge match, the *Kenia* would rig her canvas awnings and Mr Watkins and his guests would follow the progress of the race from the comfort of the tug.

On 12th October 1964 while undocking the *Maashaven* from Tilbury dock new entrance, the *Kenia* was in collision with the ship and was pinned by the bow of the ship to the pier head. The bow penetrated the engine room but the crew managed to scramble onto the pier head before she sank. She was raised by the P.L.A.'s salvage department and beached at Northfleet Hope, where the hole was patched. Refloated, *Kenia* was placed alongside the coal hulk *Artemis*.

Sold to Metal Recovery (Newhaven) Limited it was rumoured she was to be used in the channel tunnel project, this failed to materialize and she was towed from Gravesend on 12th November 1964 by the tug *Sunnyside* and scrapped by Lacmots Limited, Sheerness.

Newhall Hills docking Tilbury Dock new entrance. On 30th September it was towed to Southampton by *Kenia, Cervia* and *Empire John*

Kenia off Gravesend towing the tanker *Newhall Hills* after the collision and explosion which broke her in two, May 1947

Kenia off Gravesend

Kenia beached in Northfleet Hope after being lifted.

© A. Duncan, Gravesend, Kent

Kenia inward bound in Gravesend Reach with passengers after leaving the Royal Terrace Pier

Kenia sinking at Tilbury

Gondia 1927 – 1966

Official No. 149941
Call Sign MDWJ
Gross tons 199.52
Net ton – nil for towage, 65.88 for passenger carrying
Speed 10 knots
Dimensions: 100ft x 25ft 1ins x 11ft 8ins, Draft 13ft 3ins aft, 8ft 6ins fwd.

Built 1927 by Cochrane and Sons, Selby. Powered by a 768 ihp

three-cylinder triple-expansion engine by Crabtree & Co. Ltd, Great Yarmouth. Cylinders of 38ins, 24ins and 14ins with a stroke of 27ins – 103 revs per min.

Steam supplied by a multi-tubular boiler 15ft x 11ft by C.F. Palmer, Newcastle with a working pressure of 180 psi. Salvage pumps 450 tons per hour. Bunker capacity 80 tons. Coal consumption per 24 hours 10 tons.

Bollard pull as of September 1952 6¾ tons.

In 1929, fitted with wireless along with the *Kenia*, the first Thames tugs to do so. The *Gondia's* radio was transferred to the *Muria* in 1931. Board of Trade license for 200 passengers.

In 1940 the *Gondia* was requisitioned by the Royal Navy and stationed at Dover. During the evacuation of Dunkirk she was sent to Boulogne and narrowly escaped being bombed by a Heinkel III which was shot down 100 yards from the *Gondia* as it bombed *SS Groningen* outside of Boulogne harbour.

Gondia was assisting ships in the harbour on 21st May 1940, evacuated personnel and equipment from Gate Mouchoir and sailed at 21:20 with over 100 troops and officers under fire from the shore. It was low water and *Gondia* was trailing the ground and slid by the *Northtown*, which was grounded. A towrope was passed and towed her into deep water. The ship was loaded with ammunition and both ship and tug were under fire. *Gondia*

Gondia in attendance with *Grantully Castle*

arrived at Dover at midnight and landed her troops. On 23rd she sailed for Calais in company of *Foremost 87* but when 1½ miles off were ordered back by destroyers who were shelling and being shelled from the shore. During the rest of the evacuation, *Gondia* assisted the numerous ships to berth and unberth at Dover. In June 1940, the *Gondia* transferred to Milford Haven with *Java* relieving the *Atlantic Cock* on harbour duties. In 1942, she was transferred to Iceland arriving on station 23rd April near Reykjavik, attending convoys forming up, bound for Russia.

In 1944 *Gondia* had returned to the Thames and was supplying steam to the munitions ship *Richard Montgomery*, which had grounded on Sheerness, middle sands and broke her back. 2,500 tons of explosives were salved; the ship was abandoned and lies to this day off of Sheerness. In 1946 the *Gondia* was returned to the owners from the Royal Navy.

After the war, she was used on the east and south coasts, towing numerous surplus naval craft from ports in the UK, and continent, a large number of them to the scrap yards. With the return to normality the *Gondia* settled back in the routine of towage on the Thames with the occasional coastal tow or salvage in the estuary.

The tanker *Newhall Hills* broke in half in the channel in May 1947 and the stern half was towed to Sheerness by *Gondia* and *Kenia* on 24th and 25th.

On 1st February 1950, Ship Towage (London) Ltd, formed by William Watkins Limited and the Elliot Steam Tug (1949) Limited, combining and acquiring Gamecock Tugs Limited. The tugs retained their colours until 1965 when the Ship Towage funnel and house flag was introduced.

A collision occurred in Gravesend Reach when the tanker *San Florentino* struck the Norwegian ship *Hoegh Bell*, loaded with pulp, on her starboard side flooding the engine room on 13th May 1953. She was beached off the canal entrance by five tugs, *Gondia* and *Muria* from Watkins, from where she was patched and refloated.

Hoegh Bell beached at Gravesend 13th May 1953

The *Gondia* assisted by *Kenia* and *Java*, towed the *Cutty Sark* from the East India dock on 10th December 1954 to her permanent berth at Greenwich, this was carried out free of charge.

With her passenger license *Gondia* and her sister *Kenia* covered any passenger carrying such as crew changes on ships in the anchorages or carrying the Powder Monkeys to load explosives on ships in the lower reaches. Explosives not being allowed to be loaded in the enclosed docks, only at designated explosive anchorages.

Gondia with wireless fitted

Gondia approaching Royal Terrace Pier

Gondia and **Watercock** laid up alongside coalhulk **Artemis** July 1966   © *Arthur O'Pollard Jnr, Gravesend, Kent*

Gondia with passenger awning set

Gondia **in Ship Towage colours**

In February 1956 the Greek Hellenic Line ship *Germania* was in collision in the channel off Beachy Head and beached in Pevensey Bay by the *Gondia*, *Water Cock* and the Newhaven tug *Foremost 22*. After patching she was to be towed to Bremen by the *Rumania* but with her loss the *Vanquisher* carried out the tow.

Gondia was laid up on the coal hulk *Artemis* at Gravesend on 24th March 1966 and was sold for scrap to Scrappings S.A. Belgium and left in tow of *Moorcock* on 4th July 1966 to Antwerp.

Germania **with** *Gondia* **and** *Foremost 22*

Gondia **and** *Watercock* **under tow to scrapyard**

Rumania (ii) 1928 – 1935

Official No. 145733
Call sign MPDN
Gross tons 148
Net tons 3
Dimensions 86ft 2ins x 21ft x 10ft 4ins Draft 10ft 9ins
Speed 10 knots

Built 1919 by Philip & Son, Dartmouth, ship No. 499 as *HS79* for Inland Water Docks and Transport.

Powered by a two-cylinder compound engine with cylinders 15ins and 32ins with a stroke of 24ins. Steam supplied by a multi-tubular boiler 10ft 6ins x 13ft 6ins by Lindsay Burnett Govan, with a working pressure of 150 psi. Bunker capacity 50 tons – coal consumption 5 tons per 24 hours.

1921 sold to Crichton Thompson & Co. Limited, London.

1923 sold to W. J. Guy & Sons, Cardiff, and renamed *Welsh Rose*.

June 1928 acquired by William Watkins Limited and renamed *Rumania*.

Used by Watkins mainly as a river tug but was not long in their ownership. 14th May 1935 sold to Nash Dredging and Reclamation Co. for £4,500.

August 1935 boiler converted to burn oil fuel.

1940 sold to Government of Trinidad and renamed *St. David*.

1954 deleted from register.

Rumania

Tanga

Tanga 1931 – 1969

Official No. 162531
Call sign MPYN
Gross tons 208.18
Dimensions 100ft x 25ft 3ins x 11ft 7ins Draft 8ft fwd. 13ft 3ins aft.,
Speed 12 knots

Built 1931 by Messrs. Philip & Son Ltd, Dartmouth.

Powered by an 850 ihp three-cylinder triple-expansion engine by Earles Shipbuilding Co., Hull, with cylinders of 14½ins, 24ins and 40ins with a stroke of 27ins steam supplied by a multi-tubular boiler 15ft x 11ft by Palmers Ltd, Hebburn with a working pressure of 200 psi. Bollard pull 8 tons. Bunker capacity 80 tons coal, 71 tons after being converted to burn oil in October 1969. Fitted with a steam capstan on the after deck.

When the Second World War broke out on 3rd September 1939 the *Tanga* was on the Thames, she sailed six days later on 9th September for Devonport, meeting up with the *Java* there. Both tugs sailed from Devonport to Brest arriving on 12th September; from Brest they were sent to Lorient and then on to St. Nazaire arriving on 16th September. *Tanga* and *Java* worked at St. Nazaire until 30th October, both tugs returning to Devonport arriving on 1st November. The *Tanga* sailed from Gravesend to tow a disabled ship from the Downs to Blyth on 31st January 1940. Underway at 06:00 the following morning and all went well until 22:00 on the 4th when the towrope parted in a severe easterly

gale. The *Tanga* put into Grimsby and after sailing found the ship in tow of a trawler, the ship had lost her anchors in the storm. The *Tanga* towed the ship to Grimsby for replacement anchors and completed the tow with the aid of the *Arcadia* arriving on 16th February. On her way back to the Thames the *Tanga* assisted in the refloating of the *Royal Crown*, which had been bombed and was ashore off Lowestoft.

Tanga bound for Dunkirk 2 June 1940 passing hospital ship *Paris* later sunk by bombs

On 29th May 1940 with the evacuation of Dunkirk gathering pace the *Tanga* sailed from the Thames with the barges *Snowdon* and *Saladin* in tow for Ramsgate. On 31st May she was anchored off Ramsgate and four Lewis guns and two gunners were put aboard. Lt. Cmdr. Sherwood RNR joined and at 14:00 she sailed

Tanga swinging P&O liner *Moldavia* off Tilbury
© *Pamlin Prints, Croydon*

Tanga at Reykjavik, Iceland

Tanga, Cervia, Sun XVI refloating *Sovak Radiant*

for Dunkirk with six boats in tow. When approaching Dunkirk, the *Tanga* had some near misses from air attack, the boats were slipped six miles east of the harbour entrance and 160 troops were ferried off. She then picked up eight men from a boat abeam of the harbour, these were the only survivors from a crew of twenty-five from the naval tug *St. Fagan*, which had been bombed and sunk. *Tanga* then took in tow the auxiliary barge *Pudge* with four onboard and returned to Ramsgate and landed the troops and survivors at 9:00 1st June; she sailed again at 16:00 with four boats in tow for Dunkirk, on arrival 90 British and 80 French troops were put onboard. Ordered back to Ramsgate and landed the troops at 08:00 on 2nd June. She returned to Dunkirk for a

Tanga and *Ocean Cock* refloating a Trinity House vessel at Harwich **1967**

third time on the 3rd June and was ordered alongside the pier with three other tugs to get aboard as many troops as possible, 37 troops had embarked when she was told to clear out and run for it. These troops were landed at Ramsgate making a total of 367 troops evacuated.

In October 1940 she was stationed at Reykjavik, Iceland attending on Russian convoys and salvage duties on the hostile Icelandic coastline. Apart from returning to UK for refits the *Tanga* stayed in Iceland until 20th October 1943 when she sailed in convoy for Loch Ewe, after refitting *Tanga* worked on the River Clyde until the end of hostilities.

Tanga assisting *Port Pirie* in Royal Albert Dock

Tanga docking Australia Star *in King George V dock*

After the war *Tanga* spent most of the time as a river tug with the occasional coastal tow and salvage, such as refloating of the tanker *Sovac Radiant* with five other tugs from the South Foreland on 14th January 1952.

In 1969 the *Tanga* became surplus and she was towed to Antwerp by the *Moorcock* on 25th February and scrapped by Scrapingco S.A. Belgium at Klein, Willebroek.

Doralia 1937 - 1938
Napia 1938 – 1939
Official No. 136661
Call sign MFDC
Gross tons 155
Net tons 3
Dimensions 90ft 3ins x 10ft 7ins Draft 10ft
Speed 10 knots

Built 1914 by J. P. Reynoldsson & Son, South Shields, as the *Doralia* for the Gravesend United Steam Tug Co.

Powered by a 550 ihp two-cylinder compound engine with cylinders of 18ins and 40ins with a stroke of 26ins.

Steam supplied by a multi-tubular boiler with a working pressure of 120 psi.

Coal consumption per 24 hours towing 6 tons.

During World War One the *Doralia* served at Le Havre for the Army.

1929 fitted with fire pumps.

June 1937 Gravesend United Steam Tug Co. (Ring Tugs) and its tugs acquired by William Watkins Limited, the tugs keeping their names and funnel colours until June 1938 when the tugs were renamed, *Doralia* became *Napia*. The Watkins colours were also adopted at this time.

6th December 1939, the Royal Navy requisitioned the *Napia*. On 20th December 1939 she struck a mine in the Ramsgate Channel and was lost with all hands.

Tamesa 1937 – 1938
Cervia 1938 – 1946
Official No. 148586
Call Sign MNLG
Gross tons 157.05
Net tons 1
Dimensions 90ft x 22ft x10ft 6ins, Draft 11ft
Speed 10 knots

Built in 1925 by J. P. Reynoldsson and Son, South Shields for Gravesend United Steam Tug Company as *Tamesa*.

Powered by a 550 ihp two-cylinder compound engine with

Doralia

© A. Duncan, Gravesend, Kent

Napia

© *A. Duncan, Gravesend, Kent*

cylinders of 18ins and 40ins with a stroke of 26ins.

Steam supplied by a multi-tubular boiler with a working pressure of 120 psi.

Bunker capacity 45 tons. Coal consumption per 24 hours 6 tons.

The Company and its four tugs were acquired in June 1937. The tugs keeping their colours and names until June 1938 when the *Tamesa* was re-named *Cervia* and painted in Watkins colours.

22nd May 1939 the *Cervia* beached the coaster *Dicky 507/01* after the *Valparaiso 4979/17* struck her inward bound in Erith Reach. *Cervia* was one of the fleet of tugs that took part in the evacuation of Dunkirk during May-June 1940, under the command of Capt. W. Simmons. The *Cervia* towed the sailing barge *Royalty* loaded with stores and water from Dover and beached at Port Malo, 1 mile east of Dunkirk. She returned towing the sailing barge *Tollesbury* with a cargo of 270 troops, many badly injured.

9th June 1940, the *Cervia* was returning barges and lifeboats to London after Dunkirk when she went to the assistance of the *Empire Commerce 3857/28*, which had struck a mine near the N.E. Spit Buoy, the *Cervia* beached her on the Margate sands. The *Cervia* then carried on to London.

Requisitioned by the Royal Navy, July 1940, she left London 31st July in convoy for Methil in the Firth of Forth where she was

Empire Commerce **under tow of** *Hibernia* **which was beached by** *Cervia*

stationed from 2nd August 1940.

In July 1942 an aircraft on a training flight came down in the sea west of the Isle of May, Firth of Forth. It was recovered by *HMS Victoria* who was used for mock attacks having a target painted on her funnel, the planes having cameras on the gun sights. *HMS Victoria* laid the plane on the after deck of *Cervia*, wings overhanging and landed at Methil Dock.

In June 1943 she was transferred to Londonderry, Northern Ireland, where she attended convoy escorts until December 1945. She sailed on 9th December to Belfast for a refit.

Tamesa

Tamesa at Ramsgate and *Palencia* laid up

Cervia as *Lady Hazel*

Cervia in wartime grey

On 24th May 1946 she was sold to Ridley Tugs, Newcastle upon Tyne for £11,000 and re-named *Monty*.

1954 sold to J. H. Pigott, Grimsby and re-named *Lady Elsie*.

1962 renamed *Lady Hazel*.

1963 sold to Arie Rijsdijk Boss & Zooms, Holland and scrapped at Hendrik Ido Ambact.

Denderra / Racia (ii) 1937 – 1967

Official No .162492
Call Sign MDLX
Gross tons 163
Speed 11 knots
Dimensions 95ft x 24ft 1ins x 11ft 2ins, Draft 11ft 5ins

Built 1930 by Cochrane & Sons Limited, Selby as *Dilwara* for the Gravesend United Steam Tug Co.

Powered by an 850 ihp 3-cylinder triple-expansion engine with cylinders of 15 ½ins, 25ins and 40ins with a stroke of 27ins. Steam supplied by a multi-tubular boiler with a working pressure of 120 psi 7 ¼ tons bollard pull July 1953. Coal consumption per 24 hours 8 tons.

1935 name changed to *Denderra* to leave name clear for British India Liner *Dilwara* being built on the River Clyde.

June 1937 William Watkins Limited acquired the Gravesend Steam Tug Co. and four tugs became part of the Watkins fleet without change of name or Ring tug colours as *Denderra*, until June 1938 when she was renamed *Racia* and the Watkins colours adopted.

Dilwara at builders' yard

Dilwara off Greenwich

At the outbreak of the Second World War the *Racia* was working on the river. In 1940 when the B.E.F. was evacuated from Dunkirk the *Racia* made two trips during May and June. On 30th May the *Racia* took in tow twelve ships lifeboats from Tilbury to Ramsgate, these were provisioned at Southend.

At Ramsgate on 31st May a naval commander came on board and two Lewis guns were fitted on the bridge wings.

The *Racia* left for Dunkirk at 14:30 and arrived off the beaches at 21:30 and the boats were used to ferry troops to the tug. At 01:30 on 1st June she hove anchor and returned to Ramsgate arriving 07:00 and landed the troops by motorboats. 3rd June the lifeboats were handed over to tug *Sun* and *Racia* left for Dunkirk, she put her head on the Mole at 01:00 on 4th June and took onboard French troops, at 02:30 moved out of the way for a destroyer and assisted it to berth, they then left for Ramsgate picking up the crew and a wounded soldier from a disabled M.L. A passing destroyer hailed them and told them to make best speed out of the area. They arrived off Ramsgate at 06:50 and troops were landed by boat.

The *Racia* was credited with landing 423 troops all told.

The *Racia* then returned to the Thames until late 1940 when she towed a barge to the River Clyde and stayed there, joining a growing number of London tugs already working there. While on the Clyde the *Racia* suffered mine damage, which was repaired. During 1944 – 1945 the London tugs gradually returned south as London and the other southern ports re-opened to shipping and *Racia* assisted with the towage of the different components that made up the Mulberry Harbour, many being built on the Thames.

In July 1946 the *Racia* had a Lloyds Open Form salvage agreement with the steamer *Samuel Very*, which had a broken cylinder head cover when near the Rough Towers off of Harwich and towed her to London. In September the American liberty ship *Helena Majeska* grounded on the Goodwin Sands, *Racia* was one of six tugs trying to re-float her, but she broke in half despite the ship being unloaded to reduce her draft. The two halves were re-floated later and scrapped.

Racia was more fortunate on the next ship the *Fort Vermillion* that grounded two weeks later and re-floated on 5th October by five tugs after jettisoning 2,000 tons of iron ore.

Racia also assisted to extinguish a fire in the *Ferriby* loaded with pulp at Swanscombe Buoys with three other tugs in July 1947. The *Racia's* reward was £750.

From the late 1940s the *Racia* was based at North Woolwich with the *Muria*, *Java* and *Simla*, the upriver docks and wharfs being very busy at this time.

On 31st July 1967 sold for scrap to Van Den Bossche & Co Belgium and demolition commenced 2nd August 1967 at Boom.

Racia in tow of *Moorcock* for scrap in Belgium

Racia

Racia 1958

Racia on slip at Ramsgate June 1960

Racia and a Cock tug docking a Natal Line ship into the SW India dock

Racia and *Muria* locking out of King George V dock

Dongara 1937 – 1938
Persia 1938 – 1946
Muria 1946 – 1967

Official No. 162684
Call Sign MLNF
Gross Tons 165
Net Tons Nil
Dimensions 95ft x 24ft 1ins x 11ft 2ins, Draft 11ft 5ins
Speed 11 knots

Dongara being launched 1932

Built 1932 by Cochrane & Sons, Selby as *Dongara* for Gravesend United Steam Tug Company.

Powered by an 850 ihp three-cylinder triple-expansion engine by Earles Shipbuilding and Engineering Co. Ltd, Hull with cylinders of 15^1/$_2$ ins, 25ins and 40ins with a stroke of 27ins. Steam supplied by a multi-tubular boiler with a working pressure of 180 psi. Bunker capacity 60 tons, coal consumption per 24 hours 9 tons. Bollard pull January 1953 7^1/$_4$ tons.

Dongara

June 1937 The Gravesend United Steam Tug Co. was acquired by W. Watkins Ltd, the tugs kept their names and colours until June 1938 when the *Dongara* was re-named *Persia* and Watkins livery was adopted.

January 1940 *Persia* towed a barge from Falmouth to Glasgow, on her return she re-floated the *Permuda* from the Goodwin Sands and towed her to Purfleet.

Persia

Persia took part in operation Dynamo arriving off Dunkirk on 31st May 1940 under the command of Captain Aldrich, towing the sailing barges *Lark* and *Glenway* loaded with stores for inside Dunkirk Harbour. The *Persia* then made fast to the destroyer *Ivanhoe* that had been disabled by dive bombers and towed her to Sheerness.

Persia then towed a Polish destroyer with extensive bow damage with the *Foremost 87* from Dover to Portsmouth, she then went to Newhaven to assist in the evacuation of St. Valery-en-Caux. From there *Persia* and *Tanga* went to Brest to assist British ships to sail and then patrolled outside of Brest turning ships away.

9th April 1941 *Persia* and *Ventorous* were shifting the tanker *Lunula* loaded with 8,500 tons of spirit from anchorage to No. 4 Jetty Thames Haven. Being dead ship, she had no steam so her degaussing coils were not working. As she approached the berth the *Lunula* set off a magnetic parachute mine. The *Persia* was covered in blazing oil and burnt out. Over sixty lives were lost in this incident including all of the *Persia's* crew. Declared a constructive total loss, she was towed to Ramsgate and rebuilt. She returned to work in 1943.

With the build up to D-Day in 1944 *Persia* was one of the tugs towing the Mulberry Harbour blocks from the London docks to Tilbury for on towage to France.

1946 re-named *Muria*

Muria was based at Woolwich after the war with the *Racia*, *Simla* and *Java*, the upper docks being very busy during the fifties and sixties.

11th April 1967 she was towed to Antwerp by *Ionia* for scrap by Scrapping co S.A.

Muria approaching King George V dock

Muria in Woolwich Reach

Muria, Napia, Tanga and *Cervia* docking *Arcadia* into Tilbury Dock New Entrance 1954

Napia

1946 – 1971
Official No. 169087
Call Sign MLSV
Gross tons 261
Net tons nil
Dimensions 105ft 8ins x 30ft 1ins x 12ft 5ins, Draft 16ft
Speed 11 knots

Launched May 1943 by Goole Shipbuilding and Repairing Co. Ltd, Goole and completed July 1943.

Powered by a 1,200 ihp, three-cylinder triple-expansion engine by McKie & Baxter Ltd, Paisley with cylinders of 16½ins x 28½ins x 47ins with a stroke of 30ins. Steam supplied by 16ft x 11ft 6ins coal-fired multi-tubular boiler with a working pressure of 200 psi. Bollard pull 12 tons.

Completed for Ministry of Shipping as *Empire Jester* of the modified warrior class July 1943 under the management of United Towing Ltd.

1946 acquired by William Watkins Ltd for £23,250 and re-named *Napia* on 20th May 1946, used as a river tug but carried out coastal towing and salvage when required.

She was reputed to be a hard tug to steam, her boiler being converted to burn oil at Ramsgate by Claxtons in 1950; she had

Napia **with Federal Line vessel she had undocked from King George V Dock**

an open bridge at this time, this was enclosed with an open flying bridge about 1956.

January 31st 1948 the *Freetown* 5,853 gross tons grounded in Northfleet Hope. *Napia* was one of six tugs that re-floated her on 1st February and docked her in Royal Albert Dock but not before *Freetown* had collided with *Corcrest* 2,373 gross tons at Erith on her way up river.

1st February 1950 William Watkins Limited, The Elliot Steam Tug Co. (1949) Ltd joined forces and acquired Gamecock Tugs

Napia **with open bridge**

Napia, Cervia, Rumania and *Contest* with concrete block that formed the base for No.3 Coryton Jetty at the Mobil Oil Refinery 1950

Napia, Cervia, Rumania and *Contest* with concrete block that formed the base for No.3 Coryton Jetty at the Mobil Oil Refinery 1950

Ltd and traded as Ship Towage (London) Ltd. The tugs operating under their original colours and house flags until September 1965 when the colours were combined.

The Danish ship *Astoria* 4,454 had engine trouble in the Dover Straits at Varne on 30th October 1950, the *Napia* towed her to Copenhagen via the Skagerrak and the Kattegat, arriving 5th November. The *Napia* returned to Gravesend via the Kiel canal. 1951 towed two coal hulks of William Cory from Erith, one in the spring to Terneuzen and the second in the summer to Boulogne. In November 1952 the *Napia* and *Rumania* towed Ben Lines, *Benvorlock* from London to the Tyne.

The BP tanker *British Builder* had been towed from Australia by another BP tanker and was handed over to the Hull tugs *Masterman* and *Tradesman* in November 1954 off of the Isle of Wight for on towage to BP's Isle of Grain refinery. It was decided to use the Princes Channel as there was more room than towing through the North Edinburgh Channel. The weather was atrocious, the South Goodwin Lightship had broken her moorings the night before and was lost after grounding on the Goodwin Sands. The ship took a shear and grounded at the South-East Girdler on 27th November 1954. One of the Hull tugs also grounded and the seas were breaking right over her. The other Hull tug stood by her. The *Napia, Rumania, Contest* and BP tug *Zurmand* went to her

Napia and *Fossa* undocking a ship from King George V dock in Ship Towage (London) Ltd colours

Napia with enclosed bridge and flying bridge

assistance. As the tide started to make, the *Napia* and *Contest* got hold of aft and the *Zurmand* forward. Two of *Zurmand's* crew were injured and she returned to the Medway to land them. *Napia* and *Contest* refloated the ship, *Rumania* got hold of the bow and the three tugs towed her to safety in the River Medway. BP gave £500 bonus on top of the salvage award to each tug, as they were so pleased with the job done.

July 1955, she re-floated the tanker *Cygnet* from Deal after the *Vanquisher* and *Rumania* had beached her there, after a collision in the channel. *Napia*, *Crested Cock* and *Vanquisher* towed her to Sheerness.

27th January 1969 W. H. J. Alexander Ltd (Sun Tugs) and Ship Towage (London) Ltd joined forces under the banner of London Tugs Ltd.

Napia was laid up on 4th July 1971 and sold December 1971 for £7,800 to John G. Efthinou Piraeus and re-named *Tolmiros*. Sailed from Gravesend towing *Astromitos* ex *Culex*, which had also been sold to the same owner. *Tolmiros* lost tow in Bay of Biscay, which she was unable to find. *Astromitos* later found by a trawler and towed to Northern Spain.

1973 sold to Locus G. Matsas Piraeus without change of name.

19th February 1986 sold to M. Tzonis & Co. and scrapped at Perama.

Cervia (ii) 1946 – 1973
Official No. 180997
Call Sign GDPM
Gross tons 233
Net tons 75.99
Dimensions 112.96ft oa 105.2ft bp x 27.1ft x 11.7ft
Draft 12ft 6ins

Built by Alexandra Hall & Co. Aberdeen as *Empire Raymond* of the Foremost Class, launched 21st January 1946, completed May 1946 for Ministry of War Transport. Sold December 1946 to William Watkins Ltd for £36,000 and re-named *Cervia* 1947.

Powered by a 900 ihp triple-expansion engine by the shipbuilder with cylinders of 16ins, 25ins and 40ins with a stroke of 27ins.

Steam supplied by a 16ft x 11ft 6ins three furnace oil-fired multitubular boiler with a working pressure of 190 psi. Bunker capacity 73 tons oil. Consumption per 24 hours 7 tons. Speed 10 knots. Bollard pull 10¼ tons 27th January 1954.

Cervia was used mainly as a river tug but was used coastal towing and salvage when required. On 1st February 1950 William Watkins Ltd and the Elliot Steam Tug (1949) Ltd, joined forces and acquired Gamecock Tugs Ltd, trading as Ship Towage (London) Ltd the tugs keeping their original funnel colours and house flags until September 1965 when the ship towage funnel and house flag was introduced.

1950 the *Cervia* with *Rumania* towed the tanker *Francine Clore* from Purfleet to Rotterdam for repair she had been towed to Purfleet for discharge after having engine failure in the channel off Beachy Head.

1951 towed the British India Steam Navigation Company Ltd (BI) liner *Kenya* from Greenock to Falmouth with *Rumania*, taking five days in bad weather.

Cervia **with BI Liner** *Kenya* **to berth on Tilbury landing stage**

25th October 1954 the *Cervia* was undocking the P&O Line Liner *Arcadia* stern first from Tilbury dock new entrance. The *Cervia* was on the starboard quarter when the ship went ahead on her engines and the *Cervia* got caught in the wash of her powerful steam turbine engines and was girted and capsized in seconds with the loss of five crew members. Her Master Capt. W Russell MBE, Mate, Leading Hand, One Fireman and the Cook. The two Deckhands and Second Fireman being rescued by the *Challenge*, which had been the port quarter tug. Raised by the P.L.A. Salvage Department, she was beached at Grays, pumped out and was taken to Gravesend. On 2nd November 1954 was towed to Ramsgate by *Gondia* for repairs and refurbished and returned to work March 1955.

11th January 1965, *Cervia*, *Crested Cock* and *Napia* beached the *Medicine Hat* in Long Reach just above Stoneness after being in

Cervia **running out of Tilbury Dock new entrance**

Cervia towing replica of *HMS Bounty* from Ramsgate inner harbour

Cervia

Cervia with training ship *Worcester* in tow

Cervia passing Bow Creek with *Sir Joseph Rawlingson* in tow

collision with *Esso York*.

During May 1966 *Tanga* assisted in the salvage of the LCC sludge vessel *Sir Joseph Rawlingson* which had been sunk by the mud hopper *Black Deep* in fog under tow of the *Danube VIII* on 28th September 1965 in the vicinity of the Redsand Towers in the Thames Estuary. When she was raised she was towed to the Nelson Drydock at Rotherhithe for repair by the *Cervia*, *Challenge* and *Crested Cock*.

25th – 29th January 1967 *Cervia* with a number of other tugs re-floated the American victory ship *Fenn Victory* ashore Shotley Spit, Harwich Harbour, grounded inward bound for Ipswich.

12th – 13th October 1967 *Cervia* with another ten tugs re-floated

the large tanker *Statue of Liberty* in the North Edinburgh Channel, which had grounded inwards for Thames Haven.

27th January 1969 Ship Towage (London) Limited and W. H. J. Alexander Ltd (Sun Tugs) joined forces and traded as London Tugs Ltd.

18th May 1971 laid up.

7th December 1972 sold to be preserved for £3,250 but in 1973 was returned to commercial towing by International Towing Ltd Sittingbourne.

1983 sold to East Kent Maritime Trust and preserved at Ramsgate in William Watkins Ltd Colours.

Empire Winnie 1944 – 1946
Zealandia (ii) 1946 - 1952

Official No. 169177
Call Sign MGRS
Gross tons 479
Net tons 34
Dimensions 136ft x 30.1ft x 15.3ft
Draft 17.6
Speed 11 knots

Built 1943 by Clelands (Successors) Ltd, Willington Quay, River Tyne, YN 68. Powered by a 1,275 ihp, three-cylinder triple-expansion engine by George Clarke (1938) Ltd, Sunderland, with cylinders 16½ins, 27ins and 46ins with a stroke of 30ins. Steam supplied

© A. Duncan, Gravesend, Kent

Zealandia at Gravesend 1947

Zealandia as *Yuna*

from a multi-tubular oil-fired boiler 16ft 6ins x 12ft 6ins with a working pressure of 215 psi. Bollard pull 15 tons. Bunker capacity 300 tons. Oil consumption per 24 hours towing 9 tons.

Completed as *Empire Winnie* of the Englishman Class 31st December 1943 for Ministry of Shipping. William Watkins Ltd appointed managers, under the command of Watkins Master Capt. J.E. Fryer.

31st May 1944 *Empire Winnie* sailed from Oban with ships known as 'Corncobs' for the channel. These ships were sunk off the invasion beaches to make a harbour for supply ships to unload until the Mulberry Harbour was built. The *Empire Winnie* positioned the first ship sunk the *Alynbank* on 7th June the day after the invasion.

She then worked taking tows from tugs from the U.K. and positioning the ships, three or four a day. The *Empire Winnie* worked off the invasion beach until she returned to the Solent on 6th July to be dry-docked at Southampton, from then until the end of the war she was coastal towing.

1946 acquired by William Watkins Ltd and re-named *Zealander* 1947. January 1947 towed Navy sloop ex *HMS Sheldrake* from Portsmouth to Algiers where she handed it over to *Rumania* for on towage to Shanghai. She then towed a liberty ship from Ceuta, Morocco to Naples; another liberty ship from Gibraltar to Genoa, then to Lisbon for a ship known as Hitler's Yacht to

Genoa, returning to Falmouth for a re-fit then coasting.

June 1948 towed two barges from Thames to Suez then two L.S.T.'s from Suez to Mombasa in conjunction with the groundnut scheme that was being implemented at that time.

1st February 1950 William Watkins Ltd, and Elliot Steam Tug (1949) Ltd, joined forces and acquired Gamecock Tugs Ltd, and traded as Ship Towage (London) Ltd, tugs keeping own colours and house flags until 1965.

1950 ran from Gravesend to Leningrad to tow a tug to Constanza, put into Harwich with condenser trouble. Tug broke adrift in Bay of Biscay, which was picked up by Spanish fishermen and taken to Santander. *Zealander* put into Ferrol then Santander for tug but was refused permission by Spanish to take tow. Laid in Corruna over New Year and January 1951 took over tow of L.S.T. from *Rumania* at Lisbon and towed it to Genoa.

1952 sold to Adelaide S.S. Co. Ltd, Australia and re-named *Yuna*.

1971 Sold to Coral R. Rotondella, Australia

1972 Sold to M. C. & A. Michela, Australia

1973 Stripped and reduced to a barge.

1974 scrapped at Bunbury Harbour, Western Australia.

Zealandia **taking over tow of the four masted Barque** *Pamir* **from the** *Kenia* **on 30th April 1948 at the Chapman Buoy, Sea Reach with** *Cervia* **alongside for towage out of the estuary**

In 1947 a poem was written by a crew member about life onboard the *Empire Winnie*. The author is anonymous except that he refers to himself in the final line as a Geordie from Willington Quay.

"The Life of a Tuggy

On a cold and frosty morning
I make my way down
To start my days' work
On a riverside town
At six in the morning
Big Ben I will hear
As I walk down Harmer Street
Towards the Terrace Pier

Now the "Empire Winnie's"
A jolly good ship
As there's a good crowd aboard
From the boy to the skip
And I'll tell you this
Before it's too late
MacCurdy's the Skipper

And George Allen's the Mate

When we get aboard
We let go from the buoy
This jolly old Skipper
Handles this tug like a toy
He stands on the bridge
Square rigged and clean shaven
He sings "Our first job
Is down at Thames Haven"

He'll turn her around
And make way downstream
And He'll shout down the voice pipe
"What about some more steam"
It's easy to see
That towing's no play
For that's how a tuggy
Starts his day

When we get down to the Haven
We take hold of a ship
With the rope on the hook
Already to slip
The pilot shouts out
"Pull her midstream"
And we pull away
As the winds on our beam

The ship shears off
As our rope comes tight
For the "Empire Winnie"
Is using her might
When in mid-channel
Our whistle's will blow
Then the Mate he will shout
"Let your rope go"

Now by this time
It's half past ten
So back we go
On the buoy again
The Skipper says
"That's finish for the day"
So up to the office
We go for our pay

Now up to the "Crown"
We will go
As all these tuggies
Have plenty of dough
And when they get
A few pints of best beer
They are either Jimmy Wilde
Or else Carpentier

So just life up your glasses
And drink this toast with me
Here's good luck to one and all
From a lad from Willington Quay"

Empire Susan 1944 – 1947
Rumania (iii) 1947 – 1956

Official No. 169185
Call Sign MDFC
Gross tons 592
Net tons 66
Dimensions 137.1ft x 33.1ft x 15.1ft
Draft 17ft 6ins

Built 1944 by Clelands (Successors) Limited, Willington Quay, River Tyne as *Empire Susan* for the Ministry of War Transport of the improved Larch Class.

Powered by a 1,150 ihp, three-cylinder triple-expansion engine by Ailsa Shipbuilding Co. Ltd, Troon with cylinders 16ins, 26ins and 43ins with a stroke of 30ins.

Steam supplied by an oil-fired multi-tubular boiler 16ft 1ins x 11ft 3ins with a working pressure of 215 psi. Bunker capacity 330 tons oil, consumption per 24 hours towing 11 tons. Speed 11 knots.

Bollard Pull September 1952 12¼ tons.

Launched 19th July 1944 and completed 9th October 1944 and put under the management of William Watkins Ltd. Her Master, Capt. H. Griffiths, had transferred from *Empire John* and was lying at Southend on 7th November 1944 proceeded to assistance of *Abraham Baldwin* ashore on Goodwin Sands. Ship re-floated

9:00 on 11th November by *Empire Susan* and Dover tugs *Lady Brassey* and *Lady Duncannon*. *Empire Susan* was employed with various tows to and from south coast ports to the near continent until the end of hostilities.

March 1946 acquired by William Watkins Ltd, for £35,000. First tow was a Saint Line ship loaded with sugar from Port of Spain, Trinidad to Charlton Buoys, River Thames, she then towed two L.S.T.'s from Appledore, Devon to Rio de Janeiro sailing on 21st September 1946 bunkering at Las Palmas and the Cape Verde Islands, arriving at Rio on 3rd November. *British Mariner* from Freetown, West Africa to Lagos with torpedo damage, then towed French tug *Abeille 10* towing a dredger which had boiler trouble to Funchal Madeira, award £2,500. She then towed a lifting lighter from Azores to Birkenhead after towing a L.S.T. to Flushing she re-fitted at Grimsby, fitted with new masts, funnel and a motor lifeboat. Her name changed to *Rumania* at this time.

On 29th January 1947 she sailed to Southampton, bound Shanghai, towing *Tuck Loonex* ex *HMS Sheldrake*. *Zealandia* had sailed towing *Tuck Shing* ex *HMS Kittiwake* to Algiers where she handed it over to the *Rumania*, sailed Algiers towing both ships in tandem 120 fathom rope to first tow and 90 fathom rope between the first and second ship. Bunkered Port Said, through Suez Canal down Red Sea, bunkered Aden and while bunkering received a distress call from a French ship 200 miles west of Aden, agreed Lloyds Open form and towed to Aden, award £8,000. Proceeded with tow bunkering at Colombo and Singapore arriving Shanghai May 1947.

Rumania **leaving Sydney with** *Canberra* **in tow September 1947**

A record of crew's antics in Shanghai

Rumania then towed a coaster from Formosa (Taiwan) to Hong Kong. Boiler clean at Singapore then ran light to Sydney, Australia. Sailed from Sydney on 8th September 1947 towing Howard Smith Interstate liner *Camberra*, which had been sold to Greek owners. Australian run crew onboard to Singapore bunkering off Cape York from ship 200 tons fuel oil had been put in 40-gallon drums. At Singapore, Greek run crew took over but ship was not steered and sheered badly for rest of tow. Bunkering at Columbo, Aden and Port Said, delivering *Camberra* at Genoa January 1948. Rumania was then chartered by the British Government to tow eight converted L.C.T.'s and two small tugs to East Africa in conjunction with the groundnut scheme. She first towed a Naval pontoon to Haifa from Port Said, she then towed two L.C.T.'s and one tug from Suez to Dar-es-Salam. The small tugs tail end leaked and the tug sunk off the African coast.

She then took two L.C.T.'s and a tug from Suez to Mombasa. While bunkering at Aden received a mayday from *Gladys Moller* with engine failure, in the mouth of the Persian Gulf. On arrival ship was ashore on the coast of Yemen, re-floated on 11th March 1948 and towed to Aden at the speed of four knots, award was £15,000.

Rumania with *Gladys Moller* in tow to Aden March 1948

Rumania then carried on to Mombasa with her tows. She then escorted a coaster south towards Durban, after three days she was released and returned to Suez connected to two L.C.T.'s for Mombasa, told this was her last tow as *Zealandia* towed the last two. She returned to the UK after delivery of tows at Mombasa

DISTANCES AND STEAMING TIMES.
FROM
PORT TO PORT

Rhumania

PORTS			DAYS STEAMING	TIME (HRS)	SPEED	MILES
SOUTHAMPTON	TO ALGIERS	TOWING HMS SHELDRAKE	11	21.0	5.4	1554
ALGIERS	PORT SAID	HMS KITTIWAKE " " SHELDRAKE	12	00.0	5.3	1520
3 TIMES THROUGH SUEZ CANAL.						261
PORT THEWFIK	ADEN	"	15	3.0	5.4	1325.5
ADEN	COLOMBO	"	15	12.0	5.65	2114
COLOMBO	SINGAPORE	"	11	19.0	5.54	1605
SINGAPORE	SHANGHAI	"	14	8.0	5.4	2304
TWO RUNS	SHANGHAI TO WHANGPOO	"				30
SHANGHAI	SINGAPORE	(LIGHT)	11	3.0	8.5	2218
SINGAPORE	SOURABAYA	"	4	0.9	8.1	811
SOURABAYA.	SYDNEY	"	14	0.5	8.4	3543
SYDNEY	THURSDAY ISLAND	TOWING SS.CANBERRA	18	13.58	4.54	2013
THURSDAY I	SINGAPORE	"	23	10.16	4.4	2521
SINGAPORE	COLOMBO	"	16	13.0	4.1	1614
COLOMBO	ADEN	"	14	6.0	5.0	2146
ADEN	SUEZ	"	12	2.0	4.5	1320
SUEZ	PORT SAID	"				90
PORT SAID	GENOA	"	14	3.14	3.54	1469
GENOA	PORT SAID	(LIGHT)	6	16.34	9.1	1460.5
PORT SAID	SUEZ	"				90
SUEZ	ADEN	(TOWING 2 L.C.Ts.)	9	23.09	5.5	1316
ADEN	DAR-ES-SALAAM	"	13	23.54	5.28	1444
DAR-ES-SALAAM	ADEN	"	9	15.05	4.05	1433
ADEN	BACK TO ADEN	16.26N 62 36 E TOWING (GLADYS MOLLER)	4	18.37	5.42	1064
ADEN	SUEZ	(LIGHT)	6	13.10	8.36	1315
SUEZ	ADEN	(TOWING TWO L.C.TS) + TUG "WITCH"	11	21.47	4.62	1321
ADEN	MOMBASA	"	16	22.03	4.02	1635
MOMBASA	DAR-ES-SALAAM	(TOWING 1 LCT)	1	21.55	4.00	183
DAR-ES-SALAAM	ADEN	LIGHT	4	13.13	9.42	1442
ADEN	SUEZ	"	6	21.08	4.95	1313
SUEZ	PORT SAID	"				90
PORT SAID	GRIMSBY	"	18	0.56	4.48	3342
			233	14.3		46.840.

Distances and steaming times from port to port compiled by L. Smith, Fireman on this trip

Baron Douglas beached at Fairlight

Canberra under tow of Rumania

and arrived Grimsby 19th July 1948. She had been away nineteen months and steamed 47,000 miles, 38,000 towing.

Rumania's next tow was a new oil survey ship from Portsmouth to Bahrain August 1948 taking fifty days, she then towed a British India Steam Navigation Company Ltd ship from Karachi to Bombay, taking nine days. She then returned through Suez Canal and took in tow a Greek ship in sinking condition off of Sicily and towed to Naples. *Rumania* lost her starboard lifeboat and some vents on foredeck owing to bad weather during the salvage. She then towed a Norwegian ship from Samos Island to Carthagena, Spain. She was chartered by the Navy at Malta for six weeks as a rescue tug; she towed a L.S.T. to Cyprus, a lifting Lighter to Genoa and then relieved a Naval tug of a L.S.T. at Aden and towed it to Milford Haven.

Her next long tow was two hoppers from Amsterdam to Piraeus, and then through the Suez Canal. Had major boiler trouble and sixty boiler tubes were replaced, it was nine weeks before repairs were completed. She then ran down the Red Sea and assisted three Navy tugs with a dry dock to Malta then a L.S.T. from Malta to Milford Haven.

Rumania had various tows around Northern Europe during 1950 including sections of the dismantled Mulberry Harbour, which

Rumania

were to be towed to Iceland. Towing one to Iceland and seven to Amsterdam where they were made seaworthy and towed to Iceland by Dutch tugs. Also many salvages, including tanker *Francine Clore*, engine failure off Beachy Head to the Thames and then to Rotterdam, award £14,000 and re-floating *Generton* from Red Sands, Thames Estuary with *Kenia, Napia, Challenge*. £16,000 award.

In January 1951 she was contracted to tow six new ferries, two at a time from New Orleans to Rio de Janeiro, bunkering at Trinidad and Recife a distance of 5,200 miles. She sailed on 16th February from New Orleans with the first two and delivered the last two at Rio on 25th October.

The *Baron Douglas* and the Yugoslav ship *Korenica* collided in the channel. The *Baron Douglas* had major damage and was beached on 14th June 1952 by the *Rumania* and *Sun XVI* at Fairlight near Hastings. She was patched by the naval salvage craft *Uplifter* and *Kimbrace*. Refloated by *Rumania, Sun XVI* and *Sun XVII* and with the salvage craft moored alongside pumping, she was towed to London and berthed in Tilbury Dock.

In June 1953 *Rumania* and *Gondia* represented the company in the Queen's Coronation Spithead Revue.

Rumania was stationed at Dover on salvage station and had numerous tows and salvages until 10th February 1956 the Brazilian Freighter *Loide Honduros* grounded on the North Longsand in the Thames Estuary, the *Rumania* left Dover and arrived at the ship in the early hours of the 11th, it was blowing a gale Force 8, N.E. gale and snowing, a salvage agreement was agreed and the *Rumania* anchored to await the flood tide. *Rumania* dragged her anchor and grounded herself and began taking water with the pounding on the sands. She sent a Mayday at 5:00 and the crew attempted to launch the starboard lifeboat but the seas smashed it. Fortunately, she had sailed with only ten crew, half her normal complement and they were clinging to the handrails of the Focsle. Two Whirlwind helicopters based at RAF Martlesham Heath, Suffolk, rescued them, eight in the first and the remaining two in the second. The *Rumania* was a total loss.

Rumania **wrecked on North Longsand February 1956**

Empire John 1943 – 1944
1945 - 1951
Official No. 169171
Call Sign MQVJ
Gross tons 479
Net tons 42
Dimensions 136ft x 30.1ft x 15.3ft
Draft 15ft

Built 1943 by Clelands (Successors) Ltd, Willington Quay, River Tyne for Ministry of War Transport, and placed under the management of William Watkins Limited.

Powered by a 1,275 ihp, three-cylinder triple-expansion engine built by Swan Hunter & Wigham Richardson (Newcastle) Ltd, with cylinders of 16½ins, 27ins and 46ins with a stroke of 30ins. Steam supplied by multi-tubular oil-fired boiler with a working pressure of 215 psi. Bunker capacity 340 tons.

Sailed from Oban 29th May 1944 with convoy of ships known as *Cob II*. These ships were to be sunk off the Normandy coast after the invasion to make a rudimentary harbour until the Mulberry Harbour was built. Anchored Poole Bay 5th June. Underway 16:00 6th June heading for Arromanches, *Empire John* positioned first ship of her group No. 558 and ship was sunk 12:45 8th June. She then assisted various ships to their allotted position until completed 15:00 10th June. She then returned to Lee-on-Solent and completed three tows from the UK to the invasion beaches.

From 23rd June *Empire John* was re-floating various British and American L.C.T.'s from the beaches until 26th July when she returned to Lee-on-Solent. In late 1944 she was placed under the management of Lawson-Batey Tugs Ltd, Newcastle until 1945 when management was returned to William Watkins Ltd. In 1946 Watkins took *Empire John* on long-term charter and in early 1947 sailed from Plymouth with a dredger in tow for Piraeus, when off Vigo the dredger capsized and sunk, *Empire John* returned to Gravesend.

Empire John

Towed stern half of tanker *Newhall Hills* from Gravesend on 30th September to Southampton with *Kenia* and *Cervia*. The ship had been in collision off the Goodwin Sands in May and broke in half. The *Doria* and *Vinci* had been sold to Italian owners and left Ramsgate under tow of the *Empire John* 29th November 1947 bound Genoa and re-named *Euro* and *Eolo*. When crossing Gulf of Lions, she had problems with her fuel oil and hurricane force winds forced her to seek shelter in Puerto Selva. She delivered the tugs at Genoa on 1st January 1948.

The British Government in conjunction with the groundnut scheme that was being implemented then chartered the *Empire John* to tow four barges from Suez to Lindi in Tanganyika. She delivered two barges at Lindi and went to the assistance of the Italian tanker *Olterra* loaded with 8,000 tons of crude oil and on fire and abandoned at Port Taufiq in the Suez Canal. The *Empire John* put out the fire, shifted the ship to safe anchorage off Green Island and traffic resumed in the canal.

She sailed from Suez with *L.C.T. 7021* and *L.C.T. 536* on 16th March 1948 for Lindi. On delivering the L.C.T.'s she ran light to Genoa picked up a run crew and returned to Port Said to tow a liberty ship to Venice. The ship had a broken back and was strapped together in the middle. A storm was encountered en-route and the ship broke in half again. The *Empire John* slipped the tow and picked up the run crew from a lifeboat. Picked up her

tow wire and towed the bow section to Taranto. When entering Taranto, the trailing towrope fouled a wreck. She then returned to Grimsby light tug via Algiers.

In 1950 *Empire John* and *Rumania* were to tow dismantled sections of the Mulberry Harbour from Arromanches to Iceland. Problems were had with the tows and they couldn't keep the schedule and the Dutch got the contract. Watkins part was to tow the blocks to Amsterdam where they were made good for towage to Iceland.

1st February 1950 to Ship Towage (London) Limited.

1951 Returned to Ministry and sold to Dominion Coal Co. Ltd, Montreal, Canada without a change of name or British Registry.

1965 sold to Commonwealth Metals Inc. Canada for scrap.

Resold to Cia Espanola De Demolicion Naval, Madrid.

26th November 1965 arrived Bilbao in tow of the tug *Praia D'Adraga*.

Dhulia

Dhulia 1959 – 1980

Official No. 300982
Call sign GFJA
Gross tons 272
Net tons 75.07
Dimensions 113ft 7ins x 28ft 9ins x 12ft 6 ½ins
Draft 15ft 6ins aft. 10ft fwd.

Built 1959 by Henry Scarr Limited (Richard Dunston Limited) Hessle at a cost of £132,813 2s. Powered by a 1,280 bhp, 8-cylinder Atlas Polar M48M two-stroke engine manufactured by British Polar Limited, Glasgow with cylinder of 13.39ins with a length of stroke 22.44ins. These polar engines being direct drive to the shaft, the engine being reversed when going astern. Speed 12 knots. Bollard pull 17½ tons.

Arrived Gravesend from builders on 2nd September 1959.

On 1st February 1950, William Watkins Limited and Elliot Steam Tug (1949) Ltd, joined forces and acquired Gamecock Tugs Ltd, trading as Ship Towage (London) Ltd. The tugs keeping their funnel colours and house flags until September 1965 when they were combined. The *Dhulia* was registered as owned by William Watkins Limited with Ship Towage (London) Ltd as managers.

Built to replace the ageing steam tugs and with the rapid increase in the size of tankers more modern and powerful tugs were needed. In 1960 Ship Towage (London) Ltd won the contract to supply two firefighting tugs twenty-four hours a day at the oil refinery at Thames Haven, Coryton and Canvey Island. The *Dhulia*, *Moorcock* and *Vanquisher* had their fire equipment improved to be able to supply foam. The *Vanquisher* and *Moorcock* were mainstays of this with the *Dhulia* as backup for breakdowns and refits.

The *Dhulia* assisted in the positioning of oilrigs in the North Sea in the early days of exploration there. Amongst numerous tows undertaken by *Dhulia*.

May 1964 escorted Fred Olsen Lines *Bencomo* from Tilbury to Gothenburg with extensive bow damage, the *Bencomo* had been

Dhulia escorting *Bencomo*

in collision with the *Esso Cardiff* in the Thames Estuary on 18th April.

September 1965 towed paddle steamer *Medway Queen* from the Thames to the River Medina, Isle of Wight where she became a floating restaurant.

Dhulia towing *Medway Queen*

June 1967 towed Ferry *St. Andrew* from Holyhead to Antwerp.

21st January 1969 Ship Towage (London) Limited and W. H. J. Alexander Ltd (Sun Tugs) joined forces and traded as London Tugs Limited.

The Paddle tug *Reliant* was towed from Seaham Harbour to the Thames in June 1969, taken to Cory's barge yard at Charlton, *Reliant* was cut up into sections and rebuilt in the Neptune Hall of the National Maritime Museum as the main exhibit.

June 1971 towed trawler from Fleetwood to Hull. *Dhulia* also participated in numerous salvages such as *Erne*, which had a fire in the engine room on 16th March 1965 when berthed at No. 1 Jetty, Thames Haven. *Dhulia* and four other tugs attended, award £5,000.

25th – 29th January 1967 re-floated *Fenn Victory* with *Cervia*, *Challenge* and Naval tugs aground in Harwich Harbour, award £5,582.

Dhulia was one of eleven tugs who re-floated the large tanker *Statue of Liberty* aground in North Edinburgh Channel in outer Thames Estuary 12th – 13th October 1967, award £12,500.

Dhulia ran over to the Danish coast to tow the *Marmofjell* with engine problems off Esberg to Felixstowe in October 1968 and berthed her in Felixstowe Dock. When cargo work had been completed *Dhulia* towed her to London and with the assistance of a Sun tug from Gravesend berthed her in the South West India Dock.

1975 London Tugs Ltd was acquired by the Alexandra Towing Co. Ltd, Liverpool and traded on the Thames as the Alexandra Towing Co. (London) Ltd.

A violent storm hit the south east of England on 12th January

Dhulia

Dhulia

P&O Line *Strathardel* being welcomed at the end of her maiden voyage in 1967 by *Hibernia, Avenger, Dhulia, Burma* and *Ionia*

Dhulia towing *Marmofjell*

1978 and the gas tanker *LNG Aries* of 83,646 gross tons started to break her mooring at the North Thames Gas Board Jetty at Canvey Island and called for tug assistance. The *Sun Essex* was duty tug and *Sun London* was inward bound in Sea Reach. Both tugs went to the ship and were pushing to keep her alongside the berth. *Dhulia, Moorcock, Sun XIX* and *Sun XXI* ran down from Gravesend and were all pushing. Even with the combined power of the six tugs a violent gust broke her adrift. The ship then

grounded on the Kent shore breaking adrift the collar barges of Egypt Bay barge roads, one of the barges spinning in the air. She was refloated by the six tugs. The *Sun London* and *Sun Essex* managed to get hold of forward with great difficulty and with the four tugs pushing, refloated her. The ship then made her way to the Warps anchorage off of Southend, with the two tugs towing forward. With the severity of the weather the tugs had to lengthen their towropes and this was achieved by passing a towrope through the escape hatch from the after hold into the engine room and up the engine room ladder and onto the deck and shackled onto the towrope. It wasn't possible to open the

Dhulia dressed overall with passengers

Dhulia **towing dredger** *Afrika* **from Gravesend to Southampton April 1977** © *J.E. Reynolds*

hatch to the after hold in the conditions prevailing at the time. Award £87,353. During the early hours of the next morning 13th January 1978, the *Thordrache* broke adrift from Swanscombe Buoys and grounded. *Dhulia* refloated her and she was remoored to the buoys.

16th June 1980 transferred to Great Yarmouth, replacing *Canada*. At that time A.T.C.L. had a tug stationed at Great Yarmouth and a crew from Felixstowe would man it when required.

April 1981 until April 1983 spare tug at Felixstowe

April 1983 sold to General Marine Enterprises (Antwerp) Ltd and re-named *Dhulia S* under the Panamanian flag.

December 1985 sold for scrap to Arie Rijsdijk Boss and Zoonen at Hendrik-Ido-Ambacht.

Dhulia **and** *Moorcock* **towed tanker** *Panaghia A* **from Gravesend to Rotterdam 28th February 1977** © *J.E. Reynolds*

Dhulia in Ship Towage colours

Dhulia and Great Yarmouth port tug *Hector Read* towing barge into Great Yarmouth

Ionia

Ionia 1960 – 1987

Official No. 301193
Call Sign GHGX
Gross Tons 187
Net tons Nil
Dimensions 99ft 9ins x 26ft 2ins x 11ft 7ins

Built 1960 by Henry Scarr Limited, Hessle (Richard Dunston Ltd) Powered by a 6-cylinder British Polar Atlas two-stroke diesel, 960 bhp, 1,200 ihp with pistons of 13.39ins with a length of stroke of 24.44ins. Bunker capacity 56 tonnes. Bollard pull 12 tons, post 1973 22 tons.

Built for Ship Towage (London) Ltd's Woolwich base the *Ionia's* hull was extremely strong to withstand the knocks from pushing through docks full of barges.

April 1966 *Ionia* undertook a coastal tow of a pontoon from London to Dawlish, Devon and on 11th April 1967 towed the *Muria* from Gravesend to be scrapped at Antwerp. These coastal tows were unusual for the *Ionia* as she spent most of her time on the Thames as a river tug, with the build-up of Felixstowe as a container port; the *Ionia* was transferred to Harwich/Felixstowe July 1967. On 27th January 1969 Ship Towage (London) Ltd and W. H. J. Alexander Ltd (Sun Tugs) joined forces and traded as London Tugs Ltd.

Ionia **laying on the Navy Yard at Harwich**

15th March 1969 returned to the Thames from Felixstowe.

October 1969 fitted with Westinghouse bridge control, which enabled the complement of the engine room to be reduced from four to two.

Ionia and *Ocean Cock* **assisting** *Monte Ulia* **outward bound through Tower Bridge**   © *Pollard, Gravesend, Kent*

With the size of ships increasing it became necessary to increase the pulling power of tugs in the fleet. On 1st June 1973 she went to the River Tyne where she was fitted with a gearbox, a fixed Kort nozzle and three Towmaster rudders by the Tyne Dock and Engineering Co. This increased her bollard pull from 12 tons to 22 tons. The *Ionia* arrived back on the Thames after her conversion on 1st October 1973 and on 31st October 1973 was again transferred to Harwich/Felixstowe until mid-1974 when she returned to the Thames. Amongst the many salvages *Ionia* took part in was one of eleven tugs re-floated the tanker *Statue of Liberty*, ashore in North Edinburgh Channel 12th – 13th October 1967 award £12,500.

4th – 5th June 1968 re-floated *Hermar* from South Shipwash Sands with Ocean Cock, award £1,525

17th January 1976 re-floated *Golar Nishu* ashore on Mucking. Four tugs and the same ship from same place this time six tugs were required on 2nd April 1978.

1st January 1975 London Tugs Ltd was acquired by The Alexandra Towing Co. Ltd (Liverpool). The Thames fleet trading as Alexandra Towing Co. (London) Ltd.

25th May 1976 transferred to Alexandra Towing Co. Ltd, Southampton, until 25th September 1976 when she returned to the Gravesend fleet.

10th August 1987 laid up on buoy at Gravesend.

24th November 1987 sailed from Gravesend to Falmouth after being sold to Falmouth Towing Co.

1988 re-named *St. Mawes*

Ionia in Alexandra Towing Co. colours

Ionia as *St. Mawes*

© *D.J. Lynch, Newport, Gwent*

Ionia laid up at Bideford. Engine room casing has been removed

© *J.E. Reynolds*

Sold September 2001 to Mr. A. Anderson.

17th September 2001 grounded Pole Sands, River Exe towing *Dawn Monarch*. Tug arrested by M.C.A. due to irregularities with crew qualifications and charts.

2005 laid up at Bideford.

April 2007 re-named *Ionia*.

2010 still laid up at Bideford, possibly being converted to a floating café. 2014 Still extant.

Hibernia 1963 – 1987
Official No. 304415
Call Sign GKTA
Dimensions 111.2ft x 30.1ft x 12ft
Draft 16ft 6ins
Gross Tons 293
Net tons Nil
Speed 12 Knots
Bunker Capacity 75 tons
Bollard Pull 18 tons, from 1975 35 tons

Built by Cochrane & Sons Limited, Selby 1963 at a cost of £141,522 8s.

Powered by a 9-cylinder British Polar 1,800 bhp, 2,250 ihp two stroke, single acting diesel engine with cylinders 13.39ins with a stroke of 22.44ins.

A large fire tug built to service the fire contracts at Thames Haven. Two fire pumps driven by Rolls Royce engines supplied water or foam from four fire monitors high up the main mast.

Soon after arriving at Gravesend from the builders the death occurred of the joint Managing Director of Ship Towage (London) Ltd. Mr J. R. Watkins on 20th August 1963. His ashes were scattered into the River Thames from the deck of the *Hibernia* on 27th August 1963 at the Nore.

When built the *Hibernia's* engine was driven manually, as were all the Polar engined tugs in the fleet. The tugs were gradually modernized and in August 1971 were fitted with Westinghouse bridge control, which reduced the engine room complement from four to two. With the size of ships increasing drastically, the bollard pull of 18 tons was now not sufficient and the *Hibernia* entered the dry-dock at Sheerness in September 1975 where a

Hibernia being launched

© *F. Harland, Selby, Yorkshire*

Hibernia   © *K.W. Wightman*

Hibernia in dry dock at Sheerness

towmaster Kort nozzle, three rudders and a Berg variable pitch propeller were fitted by the Medway Dry Dock & Engineering Co. Ltd. These improvements increased her bollard pull to a useful 35 tons.

The *Hibernia* and her sister tug *Avenger* maintained the fire contract at the oil refineries until Ship Towage (London) Ltd, joined forces with W. H. J. Alexander Ltd (Sun Tugs) on 27th January 1969 to form London Tugs Ltd. This increased the number of fire fighting tugs by three, the *Sun XXV, Sun XXVI* and *Sun XXVII,* with this increase in tugs to cover the fire contract the *Hibernia* was available to participate in coastal towing when required.

The *Hibernia* assisted in various incidents, her firefighting gear being used on numerous occasions. On 16th March 1965 the tanker *Erne* had a fire in the engine room while berthed at Thames Haven, the *Hibernia* attended and on 2nd September of the same year the coaster *Vauban* caught fire and was abandoned in the vicinity of the East Tongue Buoy, north of Margate. The *Hibernia, Vanquisher* and *Kestrel* (J. P. Knight) and the fire brigade extinguished the fire and she was towed to Lime Kiln Dock, London.

On 17th November 1973 the *Cap San Antonio* caught fire ten miles south of Hastings in the midship accommodation at 01:53. The *Sun XXVI* was close by and took the ship in tow towards Dover. The Dover Tug *Diligent* and German Tug *Hermes* arrived

Cap San Antonio on fire 1973   © *Skyfotos, Ashford, Kent*

Hibernia and *Kestrel* fighting fire on the *Vauban*

Hibernia fighting fire on *Portal III*. Author of this book can be seen on the fire platform of the *Hibernia*

Hibernia **off Shell Haven**

and assisted with the fire fighting. The *Hibernia* arrived at 10:30 after the ship was anchored off Dover with the fire brigade and extra pumping gear. The ship had developed a 10° list to port and the *Hibernia* and *Sun XXVI* were pumping to clear the build-up of water. At 19:30 on 18th November the fire was extinguished and the *Hibernia*, *Diligent* and fire brigade were stood down, leaving *Sun XXVI* and *Hermes* in attendance. Four crew and two passengers lost their lives in this incident.

On 27th November 1979 the barge *Portal III* caught fire while building an extension to Tower Wharf at Northfleet. A broken fuel pipe was feeding the fire and gas bottles were exploding and shooting across the river. The *Hibernia* was close by and began fighting the fire and *Sun XXVI* arrived soon after with the fire brigade. The fire was controlled and extinguished soon after.

On 19th December 1969 the *Lizzie Terkol* had engine problems in the Dover Strait at the Varne and was towed to Bremerhaven by the *Hibernia*.

On 30th March 1971 the tanker *Panther* grounded on the Goodwin Sands, the *Hibernia* was one of a large number of tugs from London and the continent fighting to stop the Goodwin's claiming another ship. It was the 6th April before she was re-floated.

The large tanker *Statue of Liberty* grounded in the North Edinburgh Channel in the Thames Estuary in October 1967 and

was re-floated by the *Hibernia, Moorcock, Dhulia, Ionia, Cervia, Sun XIX, Sun XX, Sun XVII, Sun XXII, Sun XXV* and *Sun XXVI*, award £12,500.

1st January 1969 Ship Towage (London) Ltd and W. H. J. Alexander Ltd merge and traded as London Tugs Ltd.

1st January 1975 London Tugs Ltd acquired by Alexandra Towing Co. Ltd, Liverpool and operated on the Thames as Alexandra Towing Co. (London) Ltd.

10th August 1887 laid up on buoy at Gravesend.

21st August 1987 towed to Sheerness for dry-docking prior to being sold to Ahilleuss II Shipping Co., Thessaloniki, Greece and re-named *Atrotos*.

24th September 1987 sailed from Sheerness in tow of *Sauria*, of the Alexandra Towing Co. (Felixstowe) Ltd also sold to the same owners and arrived Pireaus mid-October.

1992 sold to Stravos Karapiperis, Perama, Greece and re-named *Karapiperis X*.

2006 sold to Katakolon Tugboat Service Shipping Co., Katakolon, Greece and re-named *Alfios 2007*.

Hibernia as Alfios

Fossa 1965 – 1977

Official No. 302599
Gross Tons 98
Bollard Pull 12 tons
Dimensions 85ft 9ins x 21ft 6ins x 10ft 9ins
Draft 7ft fwd. 11ft 6ins aft.

Built 1961 by Henry Scarr Ltd, Hessle for Gaselee & Son, London and powered by a 1,000 bhp, 8-cylinder Deutz engine.

Fossa was the last and most powerful tug built for Gaselee & Son. On the 1st March 1965 she was sold with the *Culex, Rana* and *Vespa* to William Watkins Ltd, Ship Towage (London) Ltd. Managers with all the ship towage contracts of Gaselee & Son on the rivers Thames, Medway and Swale.

The *Fossa* was painted with the red band of Watkins soon after and with the introduction of the Ship Towage combined funnel colours introduced in September 1965, all the tugs being painted in the new colours as they were re-fitted. The *Fossa* had her tall drop funnel removed and replaced with a short fixed one and was the last tug in the Watkins colours.

The *Fossa* had her share of salvages, on 20th November 1967 one of six tugs re-floated tanker *Esso Westminster*, aground lower Gravesend Reach. 22nd March 1968 pulled Flatiron Collier, *Dulwich* stuck under Wandsworth Bridge with the *Rana*, award £1,500.

Fossa **in Ship Towage colours locking in the South West India Dock**

20th March 1972, Fossa was one of five tugs that assisted *Sugar Refiner* that collided with *Artagan* moored at Samuel Williams jetty, Dagenham. The *Sugar Refiner* was outward bound.

Fossa **in Gaselee colours** © *Arthur O'Pollard Jnr, Gravesend, Kent*

Fossa

Fossa and *Rana* assisting *Dulwich* stuck under Wandsworth Bridge

Dulia taking over tow of the *Medway Queen* from *Fossa* in Gravesend Reach bound for the Isle of Wight. Author is on the deck of the *Fossa*.
© *Arthur O'Pollard Jnr, Gravesend, Kent*

Fossa as *Mamba*

Fossa **in Alexandra Towing colours locking in the South West India Dock**

3rd January 1975 re-floated *Nemeo* ashore in Long Reach with six other tugs, award £19,416.

27th January 1969 Ship Towage (London) Ltd, and W. H. J. Alexander Ltd (Sun Tugs) merged and traded as London Tugs Ltd. On 1st January 1975 Alexandra Towing Co. (Liverpool) acquired London Tugs. The Thames fleet trading as Alexandra Towing (London) Ltd.

The *Fossa* worked successfully the whole length of the river from Fulham to Ridham Dock on the Swale, but with new tugs being delivered and the run down of the upper river and docks, the *Fossa* became surplus and was laid up in the King George V Dock for a short period, before being sold on 24th June 1977 to Darling Import Export Services Ltd for £71,500 and re-named *Kilda*.

1987 sold to Bennett Bros. and re-named *Mamba*, the company later trading as Medway Lighterage Co.

2002 sold and converted into a houseboat and moored at Hoo, St. Werburgh Marina, River Medway.

Vespa 1965 - 1975
Official No. 163552
Gross Tons 72
Dimensions 75ft 6ins x 18ft 1ins x 9ft 6ins
Draft 6ft 2ins fwd. 9ft aft.

Built 1934 by Alexander Hall & Co., Aberdeen and powered by an 8-cylinder Mirrlees, Bekerton & Day Ltd, 500 bhp engine, for Frederick Leyland & Lighterage Ltd, London, as *Evelyn Brodstone*.

1946 sold to Gaselee & Son Ltd, and renamed *Vespa*. On the 24th November 1953 the *Vespa* with a tow of six barges was in collision with the *Malmo* of the Wilson Line in Gallions Reach. The *Malmo*

inwards bound, struck the *Vespa* on her port quarter and sank her. The Gaselee tug *Tayra* was laying at the Albert Dock, she observed the incident and quickly got underway and rescued the crew from the river and got hold of the drifting barges. The *Vespa* was raised by the P.L.A. Salvage Department and when being refurbished was re-engined, her old Mirrlees being replaced by a 7-cylinder 525 bhp, British Polar Diesel that had been in the coaster *Petrel* of the General Steam Navigation Co.

On 1st March 1965, she was sold to Ship Towage (London) Ltd, along with the *Fossa*, *Rana* and *Culex* as well as all the ship towing contracts of Gaselee & Son Ltd.

Vespa **in Gaselee colours**

In September 1965, the new Ship Towage funnel colours were introduced and the *Vespa* was painted in these colours when she was refitted, also her tall drop funnel was replaced with a short fixed one. Hydraulic steering gear was also fitted. The *Vespa* had hand steering up to this time as did most of the Craft tugs, but as she was only used for ship towing it was now necessary to have it powered as it was very difficult to move or hold the helm when being dragged with the weight of water on the rudder.

In August 1965, it was decided to station a tug at Ridham Dock on the Swale, and as the *Vespa* was rather small for most of the

Vespa **laying at Sheerness**

Vespa assisting ship through Kings Ferry Bridge, River Swale

Vespa as *Wendy-Ann* in Harry Rose (Towage) colours

Wendy-Ann in Poole Harbour Commissioners colours

shipping in London, she was chosen and attended all the pulp and log ships that ran to Ridham Dock and the colliers that berthed at Grovehurst Jetty. She also towed occasionally on the River Medway and once berthed a ship at Snodland Paper Mill five miles above Rochester Bridge.

On 21st January 1969, Ship Towage (London) Ltd, and W. H. J. Alexander Ltd, merged and traded as London Tugs Ltd.

In 1969, *Culex* replaced the *Vespa* at Ridham Dock, the *Vespa* being laid up at North Woolwich.

In July 1970, she was sold to Harry Rose (Towage) Ltd, Poole for £5,000 and re-named *Wendy-Ann*, she was towed to Poole from London on 6th July by the *Sun XXVI*.

In 1974, she was re-engined with a 600 bhp Mirrlees Blackstone Engine and in 1981 she was transferred to Poole Harbour Commissioners when Harry Rose (Towage) Ltd ceased trading. In June 1996, she was sold to Laxey Towing, Douglas, Isle of Man.

Culex 1965 – 1971

Official No. 187697
Gross Tons 97
Dimensions 80ft 3ins x 21ft 6ins x 10ft
Draft 11ft 7ins

Built 1958 by F. Schichou, Bremerhaven, West Germany.

Powered by a 660 bhp, 825 ihp, 8-cylinder Deutz engine.

Cost to build £59,720.

Built for Gaselee & Son Ltd, London who were engaged in craft (barges) and ship towage on the River Thames and Medway and to Lloyds Paper Mill at Ridham Dock on the Swale.

The steam tug *Serviceman* of United Towing Co., Hull, towed *Culex* to London from her builders in Bremerhaven.

1st March 1965 William Watkins Ltd (owners) and Ship Towage (London) Ltd as managers acquired *Culex* for £51,884 along with the *Fossa*, *Rana* and *Vespa* and all the ship towing contracts of

Culex in Gaselee colours assisting *Alice Bowater* in frozen River Swale. Winter 1963

Culex in Gaselee colours

Culex in Watkins colours at North Woolwich Pier alongside *Rana* and *Vespa*

***Culex* in Ship Towage colours**   © *Arthur O'Pollard, Gravesend, Kent*

Gaselee & Son which included Mac Andrews, General Steam Navigation Co., Lloyds of Brazil and all the pulp and log ships to Ridham Dock and colliers to Grovehurst Jetty on the Swale.

When acquired by William Watkins Ltd, the *Culex* funnel was painted with the red band of Watkins until September 1965 when she was refitted and her tall drop funnel was replaced with a short fixed funnel in the new Ship Towage (London) Ltd funnel colours, which combined the colours of Watkins, Elliot and Cock and a new house flag with the Elliot flag with a red border replacing the individual house flags of the three companies.

27th January 1969 Ship Towage (London) Ltd and W. H. J.

***Culex* in London Tugs colours**   © *Arthur O'Pollard, Gravesend, Kent*

Alexander Ltd (Sun Tugs) joined forces and traded as London Tugs Ltd. The funnel colours were changed but the house flag stayed the same.

The *Culex* was employed mainly in the upper reaches and docks until 1969 when she replaced the *Vespa* at Ridham Dock, but with the gradual rundown of the upper docks and wharfs the *Culex* became surplus and was laid up on 16th July 1971.

December 1971 sold to John G. Efthinou, Piraeus, Greece for £14,150 and re-named *Astromitos*. She sailed from Gravesend in tow of *Tolmiros*, ex *Napia* who had also been sold. Crossing the Bay of Biscay, the tow wire parted and the *Tolmiros* was unable to find *Astromitos*. A Spanish trawler found her and towed her to a Northern Spanish Port. Later being delivered to Greece.

1985 sold to Pelion Maritime Co. Volos. Later known as Volos Tugs.

Rana 1965 – 1975
Official No. 184541
Gross Tons 98
Dimensions 80ft 3ins x 21ft 6ins x 8ft 6ins
Draft 7ft 9ins fwd. 11ft aft.

Built 1951 by Cochrane & Sons Ltd, Selby, and powered by a 750 bhp, 5-cylinder British Polar diesel for Gaselee & Son Ltd at a cost of £41,166.

Built as a craft (barge towing) and ship-towing tug, *Rana* was one of the large tugs of the Gaselee fleet. 1st March 1965 sold to William Watkins Ltd (Ship Towage (London) Ltd, managers) for £29,856, along with the *Fossa*, *Culex*, *Vespa* and all the ship towing contracts of Gaselee & Son. The *Rana*, as the other three had also, when being refitted had her tall drop funnel removed and fitted with a short fixed one in the new Ship Towage (London) Ltd colours that had been introduced in September 1965.

With these low air draft tugs, the company was able to offer a towage service above London Bridge for the first time since Watkins first screw tug the *Era* was built in 1869. This work entailed the occasional collier that required a tug to Fulham or Battersea power stations or the gas works up river. On 22nd March 1968 the *Rana* and *Fossa* assisted the South-Eastern Gas Board flat iron collier *Dulwich* jammed under Wandsworth Bridge on a rising tide. Considerable damage was done to her engine room skylight before she was pulled clear.

27th January 1969 Ship Towage (London) Ltd and W. H. J. Alexander Ltd (Sun Tugs) merged and traded as London Tugs Ltd.

September 1974 the *Rana* was transferred to Gaselee (Felixstowe) Ltd, her funnel being painted with the Gaselee three red rings again, she did not stay at Felixstowe for long, being returned in November and laid up at North Woolwich pier.

Rana in London Tugs colours

1st January 1975 London Tugs Ltd, was acquired by The Alexandra Towing Co. Ltd, Liverpool and the Thames fleet traded as The Alexandra Towing Co. (London) Ltd.

5th March 1975 the *Rana* was transferred to the Alexandra Towing Co. Ltd, Swansea.

August 1979 sold to Humphrey Grey (Lighterage) Ltd, London for £32,500 and towed from Swansea to the River Medway by the *Sun London*, arriving 5th August. Re-fitted at Strood and fitted with a new wheelhouse and in September was renamed *Redrift* and used craft towing on the Thames. Humphrey Grey had a number of

Rana in Ship Towage colours

© *Arthur O'Pollard, Gravesend, Kent*

Rana and *Tayra* in Gaselee colours assisting *Loide Coloumbia* in Woolwich Reach to the Surrey Commercial Docks 1953

Rana **being towed from Swansea to River Medway by** *Sun London*
August 1979

large barges built for the transshipping of grain from the Tilbury
Grain Terminal to the Mills that were still in the Victoria Dock.
Redriff was ideal for these heavy grain barges being larger and
more powerful than most of their fleet at that time.

1984 sold to Alan G. Bennett and re-named *Rana* giving her old
name back. Bennett's naming policy was to give units of the
fleet either family names or names of snakes and reptiles from

the Gaselee fleet. The *Rana* being used on Bennett's various
civil engineering contracts. Bennetts later trading as Medway
Lighterage Ltd.

2006 sold and converted to a houseboat at Hoo, St. Werburgh
Marina, river Medway.

Rana **sold to Alan Bennett 1984**

Rana **as** *Redrift*

Burma 1966 – 1989

Official No. 309861
Call Sign GWJA
Gross tons 165.71 Speed 11 ½ Knots
Dimensions 92.4ft x 24.5ft x 8.5ft
Bollard Pull 14.6 Tonnes

Built 1966 by Richard Dunston (Hessle) Ltd for William Watkins Ltd, (Ship Towage (London) Ltd, managers) and powered by an 8-cylinder 4 stroke, 1050 bhp, 1,360 i.h.p Ruston and Hornsby 4-stroke engine with cylinders diameter 10¼ins with a stroke of 14 ½ins.

The *Burma* along with her sister tug *Watercock*, were built for the upriver base at North Woolwich to replace the ageing steam tugs *Muria* and *Racia* which were scrapped the following year.

The *Burma* was very old fashioned in appearance with a large tall funnel and an open bridge. Motovators, Gravesend, made a fiberglass bridge top November 1971, which improved her looks and comfort of the crew. *Burma* was exceedingly well built to take the knocks that were part and parcel of the job of a tug pushing through the numerous barges that were in the enclosed docks loading and discharging their cargoes.

On the 27th January 1969, Ship Towage (London) Ltd and W. H. J. Alexander, joined forces and traded at London Tugs Ltd. With the sale of the ex Gaselee tugs, the *Burma* and *Watercock*,

Burma **being launched**

Burma **on her builders' trials**

Burma

Burma in London Tugs colours with enclosed Wheelhouse

Burma being scrapped at Sheerness

Burma assisting *Sekondi* with steering problems to Anchorage Southend

supplemented by the smaller class of Sun tugs, were used for the towage needs on the Swale to Ridham Dock.

On 1st January 1975, the Alexandra Towing Co. (Liverpool) Ltd acquired London Tugs Ltd, the Thames operation trading as Alexandra Towing Co. (London) Ltd. With the run down and closure of the docks and wharfs in the upper river and the introduction of more modern multi-directional tugs the *Burma* became surplus and was laid up on the buoy at Gravesend on 19th September 1988.

On 8th June 1984 the Elder Demster Co. container ship *Sekondi* had steering failure and grounded inside the Ovens Buoy at the lower end of Gravesend Reach. It took the combined power of the *Burma* and five other tugs to refloat her. She then assisted down river to the Southern Anchorage in the Warps.

On the 19th November 1989, the *Burma* and her sister the *Watercock* were towed to Sheerness by the *Sun London* and scrapped by the Medway Dry-dock (Engineering) Co. Ltd.

Burma on tug moorings at Gravesend

2. Tugs Chartered World War One

With the outbreak of World War One, the Government requisitioned numerous tugs from William Watkins leaving them short of tugs to cover the work on the river Thames. Watkins chartered five tugs to plug the gap while their own tugs were on war service. Three from East Coast Ports the *Liberia*, *Glen Rosa* and *Nestor* and two Belgium tugs that had escaped from Antwerp when the German army invaded. The *Thames* and *Schelde* belonging to Societe Anonyme de Remorque A'Helice.

Liberia

Chartered 1914 – 1918.

Official No. 120612
Call Sign HDPM Later MCGY
Gross tons 128   Net tons 6.21
Dimensions 94ft x 19.6ft x 10.95ft
Draft 12ft
Bunker capacity 50 tons

Steel screw tug built 1905 by Cochrane & Sons, Selby.

Powered by a 500 ihp three-cylinder triple-expansion engine with cylinders of 13ins x 21ins x 34ins with a stroke of 24ins. Steam supplied by an 11ft 3ins multi-tubular boiler with a working pressure of 160 psi.

Built for William Watkins and transferred to River Tees in 1911 when Watkins went into partnership with Mr G. Petrie of Middlesbrough, the company trading as Watkins, Petrie & Co., Middlesbrough.

January 1913 Tees Tug Co. Ltd acquired the interests of Watkins, Petrie & Co.

Chartered by William Watkins Ltd early part of World War One for work on River Thames, returned to owners at the end of hostilities.

30th July 1920 sold to Tees Towing Co. Ltd.

25th June 1930 sold to Newport Screw Towing Co. Ltd.

1937 scrapped.

While on charter the *Liberia* had numerous salvages of ships, many with damage caused by enemy action.

Glen Rosa

Chartered 1914 – 1918.

Official No. 105174
Gross tons 110
Net tons 2
Dimensions 96ft x 18.5ft x 9.7ft

Steel built 1895 by J. Shearer & Sons, Glasgow.

Powered by a 2-cylinder compound engine with cylinders 19ins,

38ins with a stroke of 24ins 400 ihp.

Built for Guthrie, Heywood & Co, Cardiff.

1901 sold to Cardiff Steam Towing Co.

1904 sold to G. Robinson, Middlesbrough

1909 sold to Tees Tug Co. Ltd.

1926 sold to Hughes Bolckow Ship breaking Ltd Blythe for scrap.

1914 chartered by William Watkins Ltd., returned to the river Tees after the Armistice in 1918. While on the Thames she was commanded by her Middlesbrough Master Capt. Rounce, once he had familiarized himself with the Thames. She had numerous salvages while on the Thames; one notable salvage was the *Ayrshire* in 1916 with the *Nubia, Iona* and *Schelde*.

Nestor

Chartered 1915 – 1917

Official No. 84878
Gross Tons 122
Dimensions 100ft x 19.8ft x 10.1ft

Iron built 1883 by Sir W. G. Armstrong, Mitchell & Co. Ltd, Low Walker, Newcastle.

Powered by a two-cylinder compound engine with cylinders 21ins x 38ins with a stroke of 24ins, 600 ihp.

Completed as the steam trawler *Africa* for C. Dyble, North Shields.

1891 sold to C. Hooper, Swansea.

Nestor

1896 sold to Africa Tug Co. Ltd, Swansea and converted into a tug.

1903 sold to Lawson Steam Tug Boat Co. Ltd, Newcastle.

1906 re-named *Nestor*.

1915 – 1917 chartered by William Watkins Ltd, London.

February 1918 – December 1918 requisitioned by Royal Navy and re-named *Velmar*. On return to owners, name returned to *Nestor*

1920 to Lawson-Batey Tugs Ltd.

1937 Scrapped by Clayton & David Ltd, Dunstan.

Schelde

Chartered 1915 – 1918.

Gross tons 91
Dimensions 82ft x 20ft x 10ft
380 ihp

Built 1904 for Societe Anonyme De Remorque A'Helice, Antwerp, Belgium.

When the German army overran Antwerp during World War One the *Schelde* escaped and took refuge in London. She was chartered by W. Watkins Ltd in 1915 and manned by a British crew.

Although not very powerful for a ship-towing tug and quite small, she had numerous salvages of war-damaged ships in the Thames Estuary.

In 1916 she assisted in the salvage of *Ayrshire* with *Glen Rosa*, *Nubia* and *Iona*.

At the end of the hostilities she was returned to her Belgium owners.

1939 hired by Royal Navy as a minesweeper and renamed *Solitaire*.

1941 purchased by Admiralty.

20th June 1944 capsized off Normandy coast in storm and became a total loss.

Thames

Chartered 1915 – 1919.

Call sign OOEB
Gross tons 144
Net tons 31
Dimensions 93.5ft x 21.2ft x 11.6ft

Built 1904 by A. Vuijk Cappellea/D, Yssel, Holland for Societe Anonyme de Remorque A'Helice, Antwerp, Belgium. Powered by a three-cylinder triple-expansion engine with cylinders of $12^2/_5$ins, $20^1/_{10}$ins and $33^1/_{10}$ins with a stroke of 24ins. 525 ihp, 54 nhp, supplied by Amblasserdam Msch. Fab.

Thames escaped from Antwerp, packed with refugees, before the Germans occupied the city and was then laid up in London.

Chartered by Watkins in 1915 as most of their fleet was on war service. Capt. J. Cole from *Nubia* was put in command with her Belgian crew.

She was fitted with large fire and salvage pumps, which were used to good effect pumping out damaged ships. She was sent to Chatham Dockyard after battle of Jutland, pumping on the many damaged warships. She had fourteen salvages during her charter. On 1st June 1916 the *Parkgate* was mined two miles from The Sunk. The *Thames* took the tow over from a P.L.A. Hopper and towed it stern first and beached it on the Mucking Flats. She also assisted on the *Polglass Castle* with, *Simla*, *Scotia* and *Nubia*.

April 1919, she was returned to her owners.

During World War Two she was under German control and was lost at Le Havre, June 1944 during an air raid.

Dandy

3. Tugs Managed for P & O Line

Dandy
1921 – June 1921

Official No. 142781
Call Sign VRXT
Gross Tons 468
Net tons 168
Dimensions 141.8ft x 29.1ft x 14.9ft

Built 1919 by E. Finch & Co (1916) Ltd, Chepstow, as a rescue tug for the Royal Navy.

Powered by two three-cylinder triple-expansion engines with cylinders of 15ins, 23½ins, 26ins with a stroke of 24ins. 204 nominal horsepower.
This twin-screw tug had come into one of the various companies owned by the P&O Line and they approached Watkins to manage it for them. She was tried on the Thames but was too large for river work. *Dandy* was sent to Falmouth on salvage station.

June 1921 sold to Government of Nigeria and re-named *Lagos Vulcan*.

1948 Under same name and ownership.
No information after this date.

4. Tugs placed under the Management of William Watkins Ltd by Ministry of War Transport during World War Two

Security/Stoke
1939 – 1944

Official No. 118084
Call sign MNTC
Gross Tons 188
Dimensions 102ft x 23.1ft x 12ft

Built 1904 by J. P. Rennoldson & Sons, South Shields as *Kingfisher* for Liverpool Steam Tug Co. Ltd.

Powered by a 700 ihp three-cylinder triple-expansion engine with cylinders of 16ins, 26ins and 43ins with a stroke of 27ins by the Shipbuilder.

22nd March 1906 sold to the Admiralty and re-named *Diligence*.

1914 re-named *Security*.

Security

8th February 1927 sold to Elliot Steam Tug Co.

30th August 1939 requisitioned by the Royal Navy and put under

Security towing two barges from Antwerp 1936

management of William Watkins Ltd and stationed at Southend Pier.

24th November 1939 at 06:30 departed Southend with first east coast convoy. The tug allocated to a convoy would normally escort it as far as Great Yarmouth and return with a southbound convoy.

May 1940 *Security* with *Sun III* was sent to Rotterdam from Southend to assist clearing the port. While on passage in the North Sea a destroyer sent them back to Harwich as Rotterdam had fallen to the German Army. *Security* then refitted at Mills and Knights dry dock at Rotherhithe.

June 1940 towed two barges from London to Southampton and was then stationed at Portland Naval base.

13th June 1940 the tanker *British Inventor 7101/26* loaded with 10568 tons of fuel and diesel oil struck a mine 5 miles from St. Albans Head, *Security* and Navy tug St. Martin beached her in Weymouth Bay the ship well down by the head.

30th June 1940 ship broke in half, the stern half towed to Portland Harbour. Towed to Southampton, arriving 31st July. Ship scrapped.

May 1943 re-named *Stoke*.

11th August 1944 Management returned to owners.

Security alongside Royal Terrace Pier, Gravesend

January 1946 re-named *Security*.

8th December 1946 sunk in storm towing tanker *Kelletta 7434/29* with *Contest* and *Watercock* from Falmouth to River Tyne, twelve miles from Anvil Point on the Dorset coast. *Watercock* picked up survivors from the sea in extremely bad conditions. But four were lost including her Master Capt. A. Pattison and his son, who was deckhand.

Foremost 22
1939 – 1945

Official No. 147740
Call Sign GFJM
Gross Tons 195
Built September 1924
Dimensions 100.4ft x 27.2ft x 12.2ft

Built by J. Meyers Shipbuilding Co. Zalt-Bommel, Holland, powered by a 110-nominal horsepower 900 ihp three-cylinder triple-expansion engine by H. Beardmore & Co. Ltd, Coatbridge with cylinders 15ins x 25ins x 40ins with a stroke of 27ins

Built for James Dredging, Towage & Transport Co. Ltd Southampton.

1924 sold to Newhaven Harbour Co., Newhaven.

1926 sold to Southern Railway Co. & stationed at Newhaven.

Foremost 22

August 1939 requisitioned by Royal Navy and placed under management of William Watkins Ltd.

During Dunkirk evacuation *Foremost 22* was ordered to tow the fleet minesweeper *HMS Sharpshooter* that had been in collision with the Channel Islands ferry *St. Helier* on 30th May 1940 to Dover.

2nd June attempted to tow ferry *Rouen* out of Dunkirk Harbour but tide had dropped and tug grounded also but managed to get back into deep water.

9th June sailed from Newhaven towing fishing boats to Le Havre to evacuate troops from there.

10th June put injured man on hospital ship *Worthing* off Le Havre.

1945 returned to owners.

1948 to British Transport Commission.

1961 sold to Canter Nav. Santa Maria S.P.A. La Spezia, Italy and re-named *Terranova*.

1978 sold for scrap.

Lynch
1940 – 1946

Official No. 148512
Call Sign MNQY
Gross Tons 211
Built October 1924
Dimensions: 100.4ft x 27.2ft x 12.2ft

Built by J. Myers Shipbuilding Co. Zalt-Brommel Holland.

Powered by a 650 ihp three-cylinder triple-expansion engine with cylinders of 15ins x 25ins x 40ins with a stroke of 27ins by H. Beardmore & Co Ltd, Coatbridge. Steam supplied from a coal-fired boiler at 180 psi.

1924 built as *Foremost 23* for James Dredging, Towing and Transport Co. Ltd, Southampton.

1925 sold to Falmouth Docks and Engineering Co. Falmouth and re-named *Lynch*.

1931 sold to Falmouth Towage Co. Ltd.

1940 requisitioned by Ministry of War Transport and placed under management of William Watkins Ltd, and used for coastal towing. After the invasion of June 1944, towed whale unit from Solent to Mulberry A. Late 1944 harbour tug at Boulogne.

1945 Harbour tug at Dieppe.

April 1946 returned to owners Falmouth Towage Co. Ltd.

October 1968 sold to Haulbowling Industries Ltd for scrap at Cobh.

Lynch

Lynch **in Falmouth Towage Co. colours**

Fairplay One
1940 – 1945

Official No. 166573
Call Sign MSRD
Gross tons 162   Built 1911
Dimensions 103.4ft x 22.6ft

Built by Schiffsw A. G. Hamburg.

Powered by a three-cylinder triple-expansion engine by the shipbuilder for Fairplay Schlepp-Dampfsch Reed, Hamburg as *Fairplay X*

Fairplay One **in colours of Fairplay Towing and Shipping Co. Ltd**

1938 transferred to Fairplay Towing & Shipping Co. Ltd, London and re-named *Fairplay One* and worked at Avonmouth. Requisitioned by the Royal Navy 1939 and placed under the management of William Watkins Ltd from 1940. During evacuation of B.E.F. from Dunkirk, *Fairplay One* made four trips; on 29th May she towed the *Claude* loaded with fresh water to Dunkirk. On 31st May she towed the sailing barge *Barbara Jean*, loaded with ammunition and stores, one of fourteen tugs to reach Dunkirk that evening.

1st and 2nd June made two trips searching for anything that needed assistance. 12th June towed lifeboats to St. Valery-en-Caux to assist in evacuation there. Landed beach party and came under fire from shore, when returning across the channel she warned the *Persia* to be careful entering port as Germans were closing in. On the 19th October sailed from London with *Atlantic Cock* towing P.L.A. heavy lift floating crane *Atlas* to Scapa Flow.

12th November 1944 when shifting a ship in Ostende Harbour set off a mine causing extensive damage to her aft, her propeller was blown off and the after cabin set on fire, towed to Grimsby by *Empire Jester* December 1944. *Empire Jester* was to become Watkins *Napia* after the war.

When *Fairplay One* was being dragged up slip for repairs she fell off the blocks and had to be lowered gently back into the water listing heavily. Her Master was heard to comment 'This tug seems determined to kill us all, one way or another'.

April 1945 management transferred from William Watkins Ltd.

1950 returned to Fairplay Hamburg and re-named *Fairplay XX*.

1951 rebuilt and fitted with a 970 bhp Deutz engine and re-named *Fairplay 1*.

6th September 1954 sank after colliding with *Italia 16,777/28*.

2nd February 1959 sank assisting *Solfonn 19,810/56*.

1964 sold to Augustea Impresa Maritime Spa, Palermo, Sicily and re-named *Duro*.

1968 sold to Italian ship breakers at La Spezia.

Foremost 87
April – August 1940

Official No. 164503
Call Sign MPKP
Gross Tons 163   Built 1935
Dimensions 88.4ft x 24.6ft x 9.6ft

Built by Scott & Sons Ltd, Bowling.

Powered by a 500 ihp three-cylinder triple-expansion engine with

cylinders 13ins x 21ins x 35ins with a stroke of 24ins by Aitchison & Blair Ltd, Clydebank.

Steam supplied by a coal-fired boiler with a working pressure of 185 psi.

Ordered and named by James Contracting & Dredging Co. Southampton and sold before delivery to London & North Eastern Railway Co. Ltd, and stationed on River Humber.

April 1940 requisitioned by Royal Navy and placed under William Watkins management, under the command of Watkins Master J. Fryer.

22nd May 1940 *Foremost 87* was lying in Dover Harbour and ordered to Calais as the port was being bombed and ships were trapped in the docks. On arrival told to clear jammed lock gate, she smashed the lock gate by ramming for about one hour. When gate cleared sufficiently she entered the dock and towed *Katowice 1553/25* full of refugees through the lock and out of the harbour. 23rd May assisted *City of Christchurch 5659/15* and *Williamstown 797/37* out of Calais both ships full of troops, nurses and civilians.

30th May 1940 sailed from Dover with *Lady Brassey* with salvage officer onboard to find *HMS Bideford*, missed her in fog and carried on to Dunkirk. *Foremost 87* ordered to assist beaching barges at Malo, then assisted ferry *Prague* loaded with 1,019 troops with Dover tug *Lady Brassey* to re-float her, as she was

Foremost 87

hard aground in the harbour. Master commended for work carried out off beaches and in the harbour. 31st May both tugs ordered back to Dover.

2nd June towed Hastings lifeboat and Pool & Bournemouth lifeboats from Dover to Dunkirk. On reaching the position given to cast off lifeboats and given coxswains courses for Dunkirk. They heard explosions as German aircraft bombed hospital ship *Paris*. On arrival at position found lifeboats full of survivors, she took on board ninety-five survivors some badly injured. She picked up another boat close by with thirteen Spaniards on board, unable to find out where they were from, headed for Dover and arrived 03:30 on 3rd June and landed survivors at Admiralty Pier. Her Master Captain J. Fryer awarded D.S.O.

After the Dunkirk evacuation, *Foremost 87* and *Persia* towed a Polish destroyer with major bow damage from Dover to Portsmouth, stern first; not an easy tow and as the destroyer sheered badly.

August 1940 returned to owners and based at Hull.

1949 to British Transport Commission.

January 1965 to British Transport Docks Board.

1969 sold for scrap.

Empire Piper
1942 – 1945

Official No. 165836
Call Sign MKZZ
Gross Tons 250
Dimensions 107.8ft x 26.2ft x 12.5ft

Built 1942 by Clelands (Successors) Ltd, Willington Quay, River Tyne

Powered by a 1,000 ihp three-cylinder triple-expansion engine by Swan Hunter & Wigham, Richardson Ltd, Newcastle. With

Empire Piper in Iceland

Renamed *Piper* in John Cooper Ltd colours

cylinders 16.5ins x 27ins x 46ins with a stroke of 30ins. Steam supplied from a coal-fired boiler.

Built for Ministry of War Transport of the Warrior class, completed May 1942 and handed over to William Watkins Ltd as managers. *Empire Piper* served in Iceland while under Watkins management.

1945 Management transferred to Townsend Bros.

1947 sold to John Cooper Ltd, Belfast, re-named *Piper*.

1969 John Cooper became part of R. & J. H. Rea Ltd.

1970 Cory ship towage.

1971 sold to A. P. Papayanis A. E. Greece and re-named *Sotirios*.

1984 sold and re-named *Lalrion*.

1987 scrapped at Rafina.

Empire Wold

Empire Wold
1942 - 1944

Official No. 169021
Call Sign BDQL
Gross Tons 269
Dimensions 107.8ft x 26.2ft x 12.5ft

Built 1942 by J. Crown and Sons Ltd, Sunderland of the Warrior class.

Powered by a 1000 ihp three-cylinder triple-expansion engine built by Swan Hunter & Wigham Richardson Ltd, Newcastle, with cylinders 15½ins x 26ins x 43ins with a stroke of 30ins, steam supplied from a coal-fired boiler.

June 1942 handed to William Watkins Ltd on completion as managers. *Empire Wold* served in Iceland, departed Reykjavik 10th November 1944 to assist tanker *Shirvan* that had been torpedoed. It was believed *Empire Wold* had been sunk by German U Boat U300 but this was not claimed by them and it is now thought she was lost through stress of weather.

Empire Wold

Empire Winnie 1944 - 1946

Official No. 169177
Call sign MGRS
Gross tons 479   Net tons 34
Dimensions 136ft x 30.1ft x 15.3ft
Draft 17ft 6ins
Speed 11 Knots
Bollard Pull 15 tons
Oil Consumption per 24 hours 9 tons
Bunker Capacity 300 tons

***Empire Winnie** laying alongside **Empire John** at Gravesend 1944*

Empire Winnie

Built 1943 by Clelands (Successors) Ltd, Willington Quay, River Tyne, Yard No. 68.

Powered by a 1,275 ihp three-cylinder triple-expansion engine by George Clarke (1938) Ltd, Sunderland, with cylinders 16 ½ins, 27ins and 46ins with a stroke of 30ins. Steam supplied from a multi-tubular oil-fired boiler 16ft 6ins x 12ft 6ins with a working pressure of 215 psi.

Completed 31st December 1943 as *Empire Winnie* of the Englishman Class for Ministry of Shipping and William Watkins appointed managers. Capt. J. E. Fryer D.S.O. appointed Master.

31st May 1944 underway from Oban with ships known as 'corncobs', these ships to be sunk off invasion beaches at Arromanches to make a rudimentary harbour until the Mulberry Harbour was completed.

5th June 1944, sixty vessels anchored in Poole Bay waiting for the orders to open secret orders as to final destination.

6th June 1944 at 16:00 underway to french coast.

7th June 1944 03:00 in mid-channel came across a broken down invasion barge loaded with TNT took in tow and put it to anchor off Port en Bessin. She then rejoined corncobs and then proceeded to Arromanches arriving 14:00 and the *Alynbank* was sunk in position to form a temporary harbour.

8th June, three more corncob ships were sunk, *Empire Winnie* towing the first one *Saltersgate* close to the bow of *Alynbank* and moored to it and *Winnie* holding stern of *Saltersgate* in position until it had been sunk. Two more ships the *Georges P* and *Njecos* were sunk in position that day. On 9th, 10th and 11th June three ships were sunk each day so by the 12th, thirteen ships were in a line making a breakwater. The first Phoenix Unit for the Mulberry Harbour was positioned on 12th touching the stern of the *Alynbank*.

Empire Winnie carried on positioning Phoenix Units and assisting where required until 21st when she had boiler problems, the checks on the boiler had given out, told to moor alongside *HMS Dispatch*, which was moored alongside *Alynbank,* and blow down boiler for repairs. The repairs were completed on 24th and she carried on building the Mulberry Harbour, and assisting what ships and tows required it until 4th July when she was ordered to return to Lee-on-Solent. 6th July anchored in Solent and dry-docked at Southampton 12th July.

After refitting, the *Empire Winnie* was used coastal towing until 1946 when William Watkins Ltd acquired her and re-named her *Zealandia*.

1st February 1950 William Watkins Ltd and Elliot Steam Tug (1949) Ltd joined forces and acquired Gamecock Tugs Ltd and traded as Ship Towage (London) Ltd.

1952 sold to Adelaide S.S Co. Ltd, Australia and re-named *Yuna*.

s.t. "EMPIRE WINNIE".

RECORD OF WORK DONE BY s.t. "EMPIRE WINNIE" FROM 31.5.44.
to 5.7.44.

WEDNESDAY, MAY 31ST, 1944.

Aweigh anchor at OBAN anchorage 0700 with vessels known as
Corncobs for unknown destination, having attended conference aboard
Warship "SUMATRA" and received instructions to this effect. On the
afternoon of JUNE 2ND had occasion to take s.s. "EMPIRE DEFIANCE"
known in Corncob as No. 512 in tow, she having broke down and fallen
out of line.   Towed "512" for 7 hours in Georges Channel while
temporary repairs were carried out, then caught up with rest of convoy
abreast of PENDEEN HO, casting off two rope and letting "512" proceed
independently.   Eventually arrived Poole Bay to anchorage on the
evening of June 5th 1944.

JUNE 5TH.

Lying to anchor with corncobs, 60 in number, awaiting orders
and instructions to open package "A" which had been issued on board
"SUMATRA" at OBAN, package "A" containing final place of call, but
not to be opened until official orders were given.

JUNE 6TH.

Lying to anchor in Poole Bay awaiting the word to open
package "A" and the word "Go".   At 11.00 received signal to open
package "A" and be ready to proceed any minute to sea.   On opening
package found destination to be ARROMANCHES, NORMANDY, FRANCE known
on routes and instructions as "GOOSEBERRY 3".   Mate won sweep he
being nearest to twenty ports and places put into the hat, he having
drawn ISIGNY.   At 16.00 received instructions to weigh anchor and
proceed, cleared Poole Bay 18.00 when abeam of No. 3 Buoy had occasion
to take hold of s.s. "BELGIGUE" known in corncob as "419" who had
tangled buoy up in his propeller.   Cleared same and proceeded on
our way, when abeam of E.3 turning buoy took dummy pontoon in tow
which had nobody on board and towed same clear of convoy route, then
cast same off and proceeded with corncobs.

JUNE 7TH.

Steaming with corncobs towards ARROMANCHES.   At 03.00
weather being fresh wind from S.W. with choppy sea and very dark,
heard some shouting going on, position of corncobs by now being about
mid channel.   At once proceeded in direction of shouting and located
invasion barge which had broken down and was entirely disabled.
Hailed same and asked what the trouble was, and received reply that
they were making water fast withnthe sea going over them, and that
engines had broken down also that the position with them was hopeless.
Ordered towing hawser to be connected to barge and when this was done
for crew of barge, nine in number, to fetch what belongings they had
aboard Tug "WINNIE".   Had difficulty in getting crew out owing to
sea running, but managed after a little damage to stern, then was
informed by senior Officer of crew that he was bound for PORT EN BESSIN,
this being all on our way I proceeded with tow, who by the way was
loaded with T.N.T.   "WINNIE" caught up with corncobs about 4 miles
from French Coast, tow having behaved pretty good and still afloat.
I put them to anchor having made them comfortable with some hot tea
and corn beef sandwiches.   We then proceeded with corncobs to
"ARROMANCHES ("GOOSEBERRY 3") arriving about 14.00.   First vessel
s.s. "ALYNBANK" known as "504" was first vessel to be blasted and
sunk in position to form the Harbour, this operation taking exactly
30 minutes, not too bad.   Not surprising that the "ALYNBANK" was
the first because she had been our commodore ship right from the
start from OBAN.   Very heavy barrage going on ashore and afloat
during these operations with one or two mines along the beach blowing
up, it looks as though things are moving fast.   Jerry doing his stuff
overhead, but not having it all his own way with the barrage which
is being put up.   Seems as though the sky has opened up with pretty
lights.   "ALYNBANK" only vessel planted this day.

Empire Winnie - Master's Report of D-Day

PAGE TWO.
s.t. "EMPIRE WINNIE".

JUNE 8TH 1944.

Lying to anchor ARROMANCHES in attendance on vessels to be planted in building harbour. Heavy barrage being put up, mine laying the object with Jerry but he is sure getting a good reception. At 0700 commenced operations on building harbour, steamed off to s.s. "SALTERSGATE" No. "407" took hold of same and towed her to position of "ALYNBANK" connecting "407" bows to "ALYNBANK" stern, then held same in position while blasted and sunk, blasting shaking "WINNIE" a little being as tow rope holding vessel in position was about 200 feet in length, returned to vessel took maintenance crew off same and transferred them to various other vessels in vicinity. Planted "GEORGES P" No. "331" and "NJECOS" No. "215" this day when operations ceased owing to depth of water not being enough for Tugs and all concerned to carry on, "WINNIE" making herself generally useful transferring crews etc., until 2000 then settled down to the usual din and blasting going on all around.

JUNE 9TH.

In attendance ARROMANCHES building harbour. Commenced operations 0700. A little more navigation to do as small craft in numbers have arrived to commence unloading vessels gradually coming in to anchor. Towed and planted three more vessels to-day as tide suited s.s. "IMMERTON", No. "325" s.s. "VINLAKE", No. "413" and s.s. "FLOWERGATE" 301, transferred crews to various vessels in outer anchorage, jumped one or two obstacles which no doubt have been planted or perhaps submerged wreckage, but one never knows in these parts as things are. Finished making ourselves generally useful about 2300 and settled down to watch the usual firework display. Jerry is certainly trying to plant a few mines but barrage put up is certainly making him a bit wary. One Jerry 'plane just met his doom 23.10.

JUNE 10TH.

In attendance ARROMANCHES building harbour. Operations commencing 0700, banging still going on. Planted usual number of ships to-day 3 in number, s.s. "PARKLAN" No. 216, s.s. "MODLIN" No. 218 s.s. "WINHA" No. 222. Transferred maintenance crews to vessels in outer anchorage. Weather beginning to be a little unkind, fresh breeze from N.E. prevailing, can do without this as it fetches swell right in to where our operations are carrying on. Assisting in directing Tugs and Tows to safe anchorages until 22.00 then settled down to another performance of pretty lights and banging. Our Navy doing its stuff just to Eastward of us, putting shells BAYEAU way.

JUNE 11TH.

Busy at ARROMANCHES building Harbour as tides and weather suit. Weather none too good, quite a fresh wind from N.E. causing choppy sea and hindering work a little, but not stopping it. Planted 3 more ships to-day names and numbers being s.s. "INGMAN" No. 117, s.s. "SIREHEI" 220, and s.s. "ELSWICK PARK" No. 303. Beginning to look like breakwater by now, thirteen ships all in one line and coasters and small craft creeping in behind them and dropping anchor to get shelter from swell, which is just beginning to make itself known. Finished this day's work 19.50. As per usual firework display on in conjunction with barrage, our Man-of-Wars are putting across. Not much sleep these parts.

JUNE 12TH.

Still busy at ARROMANCHES building Harbour and making ourselves generally useful. Planted first Phoenix to-day close up to "ALYNBANK" only westward of same Phoenix touching "ALYNBANK"s stern, this making harbour with ships known as corncobs to eastward and Phoenix to westward. Still a few more ships to plant but depth of

Empire Winnie - **Master's Report of D-Day**

PAGE THREE.

JUNE 12TH (continued).

water and nature of weather does not permit much to be done to Eastward at present. Amphibian doing their stuff getting ammo. ashore, quite interesting to see them loading alongside vessels afloat and withint 30 minutes driving away up over the cliff in the middle of a green feld to unload with mobile cranes, which are ashore for this purpose. They are sure doing a good job of work here, non-stop so far irrespective of weather, which is none too good. Planted three Phoenix to-day, pretty lucky, sustained a little damage owing to swell and position having to be maintained in berthing units. At 0800 received instructions to proceed to Eastward of "Gooseberry 3" to berth corncob "PANOS" No. 205. Took hold of same when holding in position Jerry put bomb right through middle saving trouble of blasting her. Fortunately no casualties, only a few broken windows to wheel house. Finished this day's work 22.30 and settled down for next performance of pretty lights which have already started. Pretty warm tonight.

JUNE 13TH.

Under way early this morning 04.30 day break. Making hay while the sun shines. Several Phoenix arrived during the night lying astern of Tugs at anchor outside. Steamed off and relieved No. 1 of Phoenix berthed and planted same, time taken 1 hour 20 minutes, not too bad. Carried on, berthed six to-day, very good work, can see harbour progressing going on at this rate, something has to be done, weather beginning to get foul and nasty. Now sustained a little more damage to-day underneath but cannot see it. Submerged wreckage of which there is plenty these parts, not telling what is here. Finished to-day 20.50 job to find anchorage in our own harbour now, everything and something creeping in behind corncobs and Phoenix to get as much shelter as possible. Managed to squeeze in between two coasters unloading ammo., bedded down for our usual performance which started 22.45.

JUNE 14TH.

In attendance ARROMANCHES weather unkind, wind from N.E. but not stopping operations, a little difficult carrying on but managing with a little damage. Everybody concerned a little anxious but job has to be done. Broke two springs 16" and 4" wires placing first Phoenix, two more to do before weather gets too bad on account of turn of tide. Managed to berth these by 17.00 and settled down to a bit of splicing etc., ready for more Phoenix when they arrive, weather permitting. Land mines still being blown ashore along the beach. Seems as though the beach is honeycombed with them. Performance of fireworks started on schedule 22.45. A bit stiff tonight.

JUNE 15TH.

In attendance ARROMANCHES building harbour. Commenced operations berthing Phoenix at 06.00 berthed two then received signal to proceed with all speed to N.W. of Manview to assist floating bridges which had broken adrift with crew of soldiers on board. Arrived given position and contacted bridges. Managed to connect towing hawser to same, weather being at this time strong N.E. wind causing heavy swell on to shore. Took bridges in tow towards ARROMANCHES Harbour, entered under the Lee of same about 17.00 anchored with same. At 18.00 sent signal to be relieved by smaller tugs of bridges, as they were labouring heavily astern of me. Advised authorities to have them beached. Relieved of bridges as requested 19.00 by TID Tugs, bridges being towed in towards beach to safer berth. Crew of bridges being more than thankful for assistance given, just one instance of many about these parts. Finished operations and on stand-by from 22.50. Weather getting worse, wind from N.E. increasing. Fireworks display in progress. Jerry about trying to do his best minelaying.

Empire Winnie - Master's Report of D-Day

PAGE FOUR.

JUNE 16TH, 1944.

In attendance building ARROMANCHES harbour. 07.00 berthed and planted Phoenix on East side, on completion of this planting heard explosion to Northward of position where working, at once steamed towards direction of explosion, noticed steamer settling by stern which proved to be Trinity House vessel "ALERT". Assistance of no avail as she was settling pretty fast by stern having caught mine under her stern. "ALERT" only arrived previous morning, her stay at ARROMANCHES being very short. Fortunately no casualties, took about 20 minutes for her to settle on bottom, pity as she was known so well on London River and had done some fine work since beginning of war in Thames Estuary Channels. Returned to ARROMANCHES and made ourselves generally useful helping one and another who had fallen foul of each other, assistance given was just help the nearest and neediest such as we could under the circumstances. Managed to plant another Phoenix on East side under great difficulty, having to use both anchors to hold same in position with help of engines, finishing at 19.00. Harbour by now full of vessels of all kinds trying to get a little lee from swell which is rolling in towards shore, certainly making it difficult for amphibians which are still ploughing away on their sea and land operation. Settled down for firework display 22.40 outside of harbour - no room inside, all berths taken up.

JUNE 17TH, 1944.

Still in attendance at ARROMANCHES. Managed to plant three Phoenix to-day, weather seemed to lull while carrying out this operation but returned with vengeance about 12.00. Standing by awaiting and watching, still listening to mines ashore being blown and watching bunches of trees going in the air away inland, this being caused by barrage from Man-of-War lying just outside us. Have had to put other anchor on the ground to-night, weather getting worse. Tows which apparently were due three hours ago have not arrived yet understood owing to nature of weather. Pulled two WHALES clear which were banging themselves to pieces alongside one another, letting them put their legs down in ground clear of each other. Settled down for next exhibition, this starting on schedule.

JUNE 18TH.

Lying to both anchors outside ARROMANCHES harbour, weather bad, strong wind prevailing from N.E. causing heavy sea right in, two barbadons utilized to form outer breakwater for harbour just broke adrift, looks as though more will go if this weather keeps on. At 09.00 received signal to proceed at once to H.M.L.T. "EMPHATIC" with tow in distress three miles North of "GOOSEBERRY 3" anchorage. At once proceeded to given position and found "EMPHATIC" who had broken down and was drifting helplessly with tow consisting of three sections of bridges towards ships at anchor. At once passed towing hawser which consists of 120 Fathom 16" Manila with 50 Fath. 4" Wire attached on board "EMPHATIC", this being connected from his port bow after great difficulty, owing to heavy sea, then towed same clear of anchorage and in towards Manvieu beach, arriving within two miles of same signalled "EMPHATIC" to anchor with both anchors, as I was doing the same, this being necessary owing to heavy sea and weight of tow. About 19.00 noticed tow astern of "EMPHATIC" was breaking up fast so signalled "EMPHATIC" to cast tow adrift and let it drive ashore as it would be a danger to navigation otherwise. This being done watched damaged bridges blow ashore then took "EMPHATIC" in tow independently to safer anchorage finishing this job of work 20.00 then returned to ARROMANCHES and anchored outside of Harbour, riding to two anchors also steaming slow ahead on engines owing to heavy sea prevailing wind by now gale force, barbadons forming outer breakwater, breaking away from moorings one after the other and

Empire Winnie - **Master's Report of D-Day**

PAGE FIVE.

JUNE 18TH 1944 (continued).

and driving inshore fouling shipping at anchor etc.   One or two
Phoenix beginning to crack and crumple, gunners having been taken off
just previously.   Not much air activity tonight, a little too rough
for Jerry.   On the stand-by from 23.30, case of looking after oneself.
At present sea is 12 to 14 feet high.

JUNE 19TH.

        Lying to both anchors ARROMANCHES, steaming slow ahead sea
is running high gale force from N.E.   At 07.45 received signal to
proceed at once to assist vessel which had blown ashore Eastern end
of Gooseberry 3, arrived given position but unable to get within 1 mile
of vessel owing to shallow water and heavy seas.   Vessel being CORVETTE
stood by but unable and impossible to do anything so signalled "DESPATCH"
to this effect.   Informed to return and on returning steaming slow in
swept Channel struck submerged wreckage "WINNIE" jumping two to three
feet fore and aft, this happening twice, only suggest barbadons having
broken adrift were drifting submerged just below water.   Managed to
reach ARRO Harbour but as per usual no room so anchored outside to
ride it out with both anchors and engines.   At 17.00 took two converted
barges in tow which had broken adrift in harbour and hung them astern
on long 8" ropes, taking care of them until daylight of the 20th.

JUNE 20TH.

        Lying to both anchors outside ARROMANCHES harbour nursing
"WINNIE" as best as weather will allow, gale from N.E. still prevailing.
At 06.00 received instructions by morse lamp to assist anything in
need, this being easy but not too easy to know where to start.   View
of shore this morning doesn't look too good, something of everything
lying high and dry, tugs, bridges, pontoons, beedles and invasion
barges all lying ashore comfortable until the tide makes again to give
them another knocking about.   Managed to shift and re-moor several
barges and other craft to safer place than where they had dragged or
blown, no time to take names or numbers too busy getting things cleared
up a bit, such as we could.   Finished this job of work round about
17.00 and managed a pot of tea, then received signal to proceed to
Western entrance of harbour to assist in bringing in destroyer "FURY"
which had been mined and was in tow of tug.   Closed "FURY" and tug
but impossible to assist in any way owing to sea rolling in.   Tug
and "FURY" had bad luck inside entrance, fell foul of steamer at anchor
causing "FURY" and tug to part company.   "WINNIE" at once closed
"FURY" and connected 16" spring with 5" wire but of no avail, just
simply parted without fuss owing to heavy broken water where "FURY"
had blown, just had to lay and look out for oneself.   "FURY" eventually
fetched the beach with the rest, "WINNIE" steaming around slow ahead
all night, this being safer than anchoring.   While steaming around
found American Tug "OWL" out of commission outside of harbour with wire
wound round his propeller in a pretty bad state.   Connected towing
hawser to him and towed him in amongst those already anchored inside,
a few uncalled for remarks thrown about owing to limited space for
anchoring but just steamed around taking good care to keep clear of
barbadons, which had practically all broken adrift by now and were
very dangerous to navigation.   Jerry had a rub tonight, pretty warm too.

JUNE 21ST.

        Steaming around ARROMANCHES waiting for weather to abate a
little.   About 05.30 informed by Engineer that engine room was full
of steam and boiler checks had given out.   Notified H.M.S. "DESPATCH"
she being parent vessel here and received reply to try to anchor, would
investigate nature of trouble later.   Found anchorage about 06.00 with
both anchors to ground.   Boarded by Engineer from "DESPATCH" 09.30.
At 16.00 received signal to proceed alongside "DESPATCH" she being
moored inside "ALYNBANK" first ship scuttled made fast to same about
17.20 and received instructions to blow boiler down.   Jerry warm
to-night.

Empire Winnie - Master's Report of D-Day

<u>PAGE SIX.</u>

<u>JUNE 22ND 1944.</u>

Lying alongside "DESPATCH" repairing checks to boiler.
Weather eased off a lot, getting better every hour. ARROMANCHES
beginning to look itself again. Beach strewn with miscellaneous
craft, some good, some bad, but certainly small tugs work to pull
them off owing to shallow water. Seven Phoenix crumpled up altogether
not too bad the weather we have had, but still harbour has certainly
been a Godsend here to one and all, in particular to amphibians who
have not stopped, certainly worth their weight in gold on this job.

<u>JUNE 23RD.</u>

Made fast alongside H.M.S. "DESPATCH" undergoing minor
repairs. Nothing to report only weather ever so much better.
Managed to borrow some grub to-day and a dropey. Everybody feeling
a little better in mood now, weather has brightened up. Jerry
getting quite busy early to-day, 16.00 trying his hand, just dropped
a couple on the buildings ashore which have already had it by the
look of things.

<u>JUNE 24TH.</u>

Moored alongside H.M.S. "DESPATCH". Lit boiler up 11.00
expecting to be ready by 18.00. Plenty to get on with when ready.
Phoenix already outside with Tugs waiting to be relieved. At 18.50
steamed off to Tugs relieved nearest of Phoenix and berthed same on
Eastern side. Too dark to do any more so settled down to firework
display which had already commenced.

<u>JUNE 25TH.</u>

Anchored ARROMANCHES, at 06.00 weather being fine but still
a little fresh from N.E. commenced berthing Phoenix. Did three to-day
can see that harbour is nearly completed, all but Units to be planted
close inshore, not enough water for "WINNIE" to get close enough,
smaller Tugs will have to carry on with the good work inside. At
17.00 assisted Tug who had contacted damage and wound wire up round
propeller to alongside "DESPATCH" finishing at 18.20. Received
instructions to relieve American Tug of Phoenix whose bridle and wire
had fouled him at anchor, did this and hung Phoenix with "WINNIE"s
both anchors all night. Jerry having another rub round about 22.00
worse than ever but nothing hit.

<u>JUNE 26TH.</u>

Lying to anchors ARROMANCHES with Phoenix astern. At
06.00 berthed same then carried on berthing remaining two which were
waiting outside. Finished these then assisted three coasting
vessels from Eastern end of Gooseberry 3 to anchorage in Western end,
then took water which was badly needed and settled down. Quietest
day yet since beginning but still on stand-by. At 20.00 Tug in
trouble dragging with "WHALE", relieve Tug of same and hung same to
anchors. Seems as though everybody wants helping when they get here.
Jerry performing overhead, pretty stiff too.

<u>JUNE 27TH.</u>

Lying to anchor with WHALE astern. At 07.00 took same
in and moored to WHALE Pier which had just been completed, then
returned to carry on berthing Phoenix, three again to-day, finished
17.00 then steamed to Northern entrance, took barge in tow which had
broken down right in entrance, towed same to Whale Pier and made him
fast, then returned to anchor. Managed to find a place in the sun
now weather has eased up. Firework display as pretty as ever to-night
lasting well into the next morning. Our Warships still putting
barrage across to well inland.

Empire Winnie - **Master's Report of D-Day**

PAGE SEVEN.

JUNE 28TH 1944.

Lying to anchor ARROMANCHES in attendance with harbour
contruction.   One Phoenix waiting for water to be planted, took
same in tow at 09.00 and planted Western side.   According to
information received will have to wait a while for more, been a
few lost in the crossing during breeze from N.E.   Not surprised
to hear this news.   Finished berthing Phoenix 10.30 then took
"WHALE" in tow and shifted berth with same, then assisted Tid Tugs
with pontoons to position required of them, finishing about 21.30.
Dropped anchor inside harbour for change.   Jerry started his
performance round about 23.15 a bit thick too, mine laying as per
usual, the object has had one or two results with them too by the
look of things to East of Gooseberry 3.

JUNE 29TH.

Underweigh at 08.00 receiving instructions to assist
H.M.S. "DESPATCH" from place where moored to buoys, which have been
laid in centre of harbour.   Finished this job at 09.30 then steamed
off to Unit and connected awaiting water to plant same in towards
beach.   About 14.30 commenced with this operation finishing round
about 17.00.   Couple of amphibians known as ducks just got in
trouble so helped them out with a friendly pull to one of the ships
they are unloading, then received instructions to assist s.s.
"BEN MY CREE" from inside harbour to outside.   Did this finishing
at 19.30 then steamed to anchorage waiting for further small hand
bills.   Jerry commencing round about his usual time getting used
to it now, he has lost about five 'planes all told yet.

JUNE 30TH.

Aweight anchor 07.00 steamed off and relieved Tug of Phoenix
which has just arrived in company with another, planted same at
Western entrance then assisted second one to position, finishing
at 12.00.   Weather being very kind, just slight breeze with no swell
at all, harbour looks as though completed, just wants a touch up
here and there where Phoenix have crumpled up.   At 18.00 received
instructions to assist s.s. "FORT AUGUSTUS" from outside anchorage
to inside harbour mooring buoys, took hold of same at 18.30 and
assisted to buoys as instructed, finishing at 20.10 then returned
to anchor inside harbour 20.30.   Jerry's performance to-night pretty
hot.

JULY 1ST.

Lying to anchor ARROMANCHES awaiting instructions.   At
10.30 received instructions to proceed outside and assist s.s.
"FORT CHIPEWYAN" from outside anchorage to mooring buoys inside
harbour.   Took hold of same at 11.30 and assisted to buoys as
instructed finishing 12.50 then had a look round for coal for galley,
found some with Master's consent in Coaster who gave us couple of
tons then returned to anchor, time being 14.00.   Then at 17.00
received instructions to visit ships which we had planted to see
what wires and ropes we could get, as we were very short.   Visited
vessels and found a couple of good wires but no ropes as they were
too small, so returned to anchor and carried on splicing and knocking
up what we could out of tow ropes etc.   Jerry commencing round
about schedule, lasting about 4 hours.

JULY 2ND.

Aweight anchor at ARROMANCHES 05.00 took Pilot on board at
WHALE Pier and steamed outside.   Took hold of s.s. "EMPIRE PEDRO"
and assisted from anchorage to inside harbour, mooring her to buoys
as instructed, finishing 07.00 then settled down to anchor for awhile.
At 14.00 invited ashore, first time since arrival here on the 7th,
quite interesting place, knocked about a bit but not what one

Empire Winnie - Master's Report of D-Day

JULY 2ND (continued).

expected. Every villa still has it's Rose Garden, the village pumps are still working. Visited the Church up in the Square, R.C. and was shown round by the Priest, then had a stroll to outside Village, visited Cemetery where one and all had been buried. Had picked a nice place an orchard, our soldiers buried to the left and Jerry to the right, passed two or three Signposts marked "MINEN" with skull and crossbones painted on them. Returned to Village and noticed on the way back cattle still grazing in the fields but with padlocks and chains fastened to their hind legs so that nobody would pinch them I reckon. Several of the French villagers just making their way back to start up again, plenty of "Bonjours" knocking about now things have quietened down. On arriving ack in Village invited to Officers' Mess for tea, had a cup of tea and piece of cake, not too bad under the circumstances. About 17.00 made my way back towards beach, stood for five minutes watching amphibians coming out and toing into the water, policemen directing them like a two-way traffic. Took a stroll on to sea wall, noticed gun emplacements (Jerry's) inside of emplacement was painted in colours of area and its buildings it could cover, very interesting I thought. Made my way back to "WINNIE" arriving on board about 19.30 awaiting any further instructions. Jerry very quiet tonight, only lasted about two hours, unusuals for him. Can see the harbour better from the shore.

JULY 3RD.

Lying to anchor ARROMANCHES. At 10.00 received instructions to assist s.s. "EMPIRE SEAMAN" from outside anchorage, took hold of same and assisted to inside, "WINNIE" having on this operation to drop anchor to hold vessel in position, when finished with vessel endeavoured to heave anchor up but found it to be foul of sunken barbadon, so had to slip anchor with 15 fathom of chain, a bit of hard luck after having stuck it out right through. Went to anchor and carried out minor engine repairs. About 23.00 noticed steamer stuck in Northern entrance, knew what was the trouble, he had put himself on one of the Phoenix which had crumpled up at once, steamed to him and passed my towing hawser on board, name of steamer being "VESTRA" repair ship here. I commenced to tow seawards with "WINNIE" clearing "VESTRA" of obstruction about 00.45 on 4th and put her to anchorage outside harbour, then returned to inside harbour and made fast to WHALE PIER. Jerry as per usual performing during these operations.

JULY 4TH.

Made fast alongside WHALE PIER, ARROMANCHES. At 09.00 informed by assistant A.B.O. that we are about to be relieved, not surprised as the harbour has been completed, but for just touching up here and there. Sorry in a way but "WINNIE" certainly does want overhauling, being tried as she has been here jumping over wrecks and barbadons, with a few knocks and bumps berthing ships and Phoenix. I reckon she has a few scars underneath, but she has completed her share towards constructing the harbour from start to finish. At 09.45 received instructions to close H.M.S. "HAZLEMERE" to take on board Army and Navy Personnel, and return with them to U.K. Closed "HAZLEMERE" 09.55 took twelve Army and Twelve Navy, also Six U.S. personnel on board with baggage and commenced our journey back to LEE-ON-SOLENT as instructed, cleared Northern entrance of ARROMANCHES harbour which was not there when we first came, at 10.40. closing H.M.S. "ROYAL ULSTERMAN" lying at Juno, at 12.40 received further instructions and routes from same to proceed at 14.00 towards destination. Dropped anchor in vicinity of "ROYAL ULSTERMAN" about 13.20. Aweigh anchor 14.20 and proceeded as instructed first speaking invasion barge which seemed to be in difficulty but said he could manage, repairs being only about 15 minutes work so carried on, arriving Nab Tower, I.O. Wight 23.30. passing through Spit Head Gate 00.30 on 5th.

Empire Winnie - **Master's Report of D-Day**

PAGE NINE.

JULY 5TH 1944.

Steaming towards Lee-on-Solent, signalled s.s. "ROANCI" at 01.10 in reference to personnel on board to whom we had given passage back. Informed to hold them until later, went to anchor with our one and only, time being 01.40. awaiting instructions. Lying to anchor LEE-ON-SOLENT awaiting instructions.   At 09.20 launch disembarked personnel brought back from Far Shore.   Boarded by one or two Naval Officers for information in respect of things in general then remained to anchor at LEE-ON-SOLENT awaiting Dry Docking etc.

JULY 6TH.

Lying to anchor LEE-ON-SOLENT awaiting Docking and repairs. Received instructions to dock at No. 1 Dry Dock, Southampton on July 12th.

JULY 12TH.

Aweight anchor 14.00 steamed towards Southampton.   Arrived No. 1 Dry Dock at 15.30 entered same at 17.00.   Settled on chocks 19.00, "WINNIE" dry at 10.50.   Viewed damage to bottom, this being four plates on port side under bottom dented, rivets leaking in oil tanks, rolling chock starboard side split in middle and knocked back to ship's hull, small indent on rudder post, not so bad as expected. She hasn't done too badly.

(Sgd.) J.E. Fryer.

Master, "EMPIRE WINNIE".

Empire Winnie - **Master's Report of D-Day**

1971 sold to Coral R. Rotendella, Australia.

1972 sold to M. C. & A. Michela, Australia.

1973 stripped and reduced to a barge.

1974 scrapped at Bunbury Harbour, Western Australia.

Assiduous 1943 – 1946

Official No. 169321
Wartime Pennant No. W142
Gross tons 597
Dimensions 156ft 8ins x 32ft 2ins x 14ft 9ins

Built 1943 by Cochrane and Sons, Selby of the Assurance Class, for the Admiralty and powered by a 1,350 ihp three-cylinder triple-expansion engine with cylinders 17ins x 28ins and 46ins with a stroke of 33ins by Charles D. Holmes & Co., Hull.

Placed under William Watkins Ltd, management as an Atlantic convoy rescue tug.

1944 at Normandy landings towing Mulberry harbour blocks across the channel.

1946 dockyard tug at Singapore.

1947 stationed Trincomalee, Ceylon.

1953 stationed Gibraltar.

1958 sold to J. D. Irvine Ltd, St. John N.B. Canada.

1961 re-named *Irving Tamarrack*.

1969 sold to Canadian ship breakers.

Assiduous   © *World Ship Photo Library*

Empire John
1943 – 1944
1945 - 1946

Official No. 169171
Call sign MQVJ
Gross tons 479   Net tons 42
Dimensions 136ft x 30.1ft x 15.3ft
Draft 15ft
Bunker Capacity 340 tons

Built by Clelands (Successors) Ltd, Willington Quay, River Tyne of the Englishman Class for Ministry of War Transport and placed under management of W. Watkins Ltd, October 1943.

Powered by a 1,275 ihp three-cylinder triple-expansion engine by Swan Hunter & Wigham Richardson (Newcastle) Ltd, with cylinders 16½ins, 27ins and 46ins with a stroke of 30ins. Steam supplied by a multi-tubular boiler, oil-fired with a working pressure of 215 psi.

Empire John sailed at 07:00 29th May 1944 from Oban assisting ships in group Cob II. These ships were to form a harbour off of the invasion beaches. Anchored Poole Bay 19:30 5th June 1944, weighed anchor 16:00 6th June and proceeded in convoy with ships to invasion beaches. In the morning of 7th June picked up broken down invasion craft and towed it into beach at 12:30. On 8th June assisting ships into position for sinking, first ship *No. 558* completed 12:45. *Empire John* assisted the ships into position for sinking under heavy shellfire from the shore and from enemy aircraft. At 15:00 11th June the last ship had been positioned and the rudimentary harbour known, as Gooseberry 1 was complete. *Empire John* then joined a UK bound convoy at 17:15 on 11th June and arrived Lee-on-Solent at 08:00 12th June.

The *Empire John* then made two round trips from 13th June to 18th June from Selsey to Mulberry Harbour A & B. The first tow was a whale roadway, the second a whale buffer. 19th June searching in channel for any drifting tows or invasion craft that needed assistance. She was then sent to Mulberry Harbour A for rescue work, arriving 04:00 22nd June 1944. *Empire John* spent the next month clearing sunken wreckage and re-floating stranded L.C.T.'s. On 24th July she took in tow a whale pier head to be returned to the UK and proceeded independently at 06:00 25th July a N.E. Gale blew up and tow broke adrift 05:00 26th July, recovered tow and proceeded to Lee-on-Solent.

The *Empire John* was highly thought of while working off the invasion beaches as can be seen by the letter from the Commander of the Task Unit. In the latter part of 1944, management of *Empire John* was transferred to Lawsen-Batey Tugs Ltd, Newcastle, until 1945 when management was returned to William Watkins Ltd.

1946 took on long-term charter by William Watkins Ltd.

1st February 1950 to Ship Towage (London) Ltd.

1951 return to Ministry and sold to Dominion Coal Co. Ltd,

***Empire John* during World War Two**

Montreal, Canada without change of name or British registry.

1965 sold to Commonwealth Metals Inc. Canada for scrap. Resold to Cia Espanola de Demolicion Naval, Madrid.

26th November 1965 arrived Bilbao in tow of tug *Praia D'Adraga*

Letter from the Commander of the Task Unit

COPY OF REPORT -   "EMPIRE JOHN".

REPORT DURING INVASION OF CONTINENT.

Received Top Secret orders at Oban the 28th May, also sailing orders for 29th May. Weighed anchor at 0700, 29th May at Oban and commenced to assist Ships of Group Cob.11 as ordered. Completed 1030, proceeded at full speed to take up, position in convoy. Position reached at 1330, proceeding on passage. On 30th May at 1000 it was seen that Ship 405 had to fall out of convoy, proceed to 405 to offer assistance, was asked by Captain of 405 to stand by ship, received signal from Escort that as 405 was not one of my Group to proceed on passage and let "EMPIRE RUPERT" return and look after 405 as ship belonged to "EMPIRE RUPERT's" Group. Proceeded on passage, arriving Pool Bay at 1930 of 5th June. Anchored awaiting further instructions.

Received orders at 1100 on 6th June to open Top Secret and be ready for sea at 1530. Weighed anchor 1600 on 6th June, proceeded to assist ships of Group as necessary to proceed. Completed 1730. proceeded with convoy on passage to Assault Area. On morning of 7th June sighted repair invasion craft broken down, put tow rope on same and continued on passage. Towed invasion craft into beach, arriving at 1230, was then ordered by U.S.Commander of Operations to anchor near ships and to give assistance as necessary. Anchored at 1300, was ordered to shift anchorage at 1630, owing to being in range of enemy shore batteries, anchored again at 1800.

8th June received orders from U.S.Commander to assist ships into beach area for sinking, weighed anchor 1130, proceeded in with first ship No.558 and assisted ship in to position for sinking. Owing to draft of tug being 17 ft. and working in shallow water, handling of tug very difficult, operation completed 1245, proceeded out to second ship, was informed by U.S.Commander that we were to stand by next ship in and that two small U.S.tugs would assist ship into position. Commander afterwards informed me that ship had been sunk in wrong position and that operations would cease for the day and to anchor near next ship in. At 1700 enemy aircraft attacked shipping off beach head, crew at action stations till 1900, Enemy aircraft attacked again at 2230, crew at action stations and intercepting enemy aircraft which dropped bombs close to s.s. Order given to crew to stand down at 0500, 9th June. received orders at 1400 to proceed in with next ship, put tow rope on ships port quarter and proceeded into position. Whilst proceeding in in, came under shell fire from enemy shore batteries. Ships charges were blown and tug and ship came under very heavy shell fire, was ordered to hold ship in position until ship had settled. All other craft ordered out of area. Whilst holding the ship, tug was under very heavy fire and explosions were very close to tug. Held ship till 1545 when ship had settled, had to slip tow rope from tug as crew had left ship. Proceeded out to sea, requested conference with U.S.Commander and suggested that operations should continue during darkness, but U.S.Commander thought that it was not possible to handle ships during darkness. Was informed that operations would cease for that day. Anchored at 1800. Enemy aircraft attack on shipping commenced 2300. crew at action stations till 0400 of 10th June. Commenced operations at 0700 during this day, assisted four ships into position. Whilst assisting fourth ship into position, towing ship from port bow, tug grounded and owing to ship drawing less water than tug, ship came up and collided with "EMPIRE JOHN" on port quarter, doing damage to rubbing belting on "EMPIRE JOHN". Operations were ceased that night at 2230. Whilst proceeding out to anchorage, enemy aircraft bombed ships that had been placed in position that day. Anchored 2300. At 0200 of 11th, enemy aircraft attacked shipping, crew at action stations till 0500, commenced operations at 0900, assisting ship into sinking position. Tow rope on starboard bow. Whilst proceeding tug's propellor hit ground, also striking anchor cable of ship that had previously been sunk in breakwater, damage not known. Operation completed 1200. Received orders from U.S.Commander that owing to draft of tug, to stand by next ship and assist only if ship requested assistance. Was informed at 1500 that whole operation was completed. The whole operation taking place West of Capelle Roadstead and was known as Gooseberry 1.

Proceeded to H.M.S. "CEROS" at Point Perue, arriving at 1615, received orders to proceed at full speed and join Convoy for U.K. Arrived with Convoy at 1715, proceeded on passage to Lee on Solent, arriving at 0800 on 12th June. Anchored, awaiting further instructions. Hove up anchor at 1000, proceeded and took in fresh water, returned to anchor for slight steering engine repairs. Hove up anchor at 1900, proceeded to Selsey, arriving at 2130, picked up tow at 0130 on 13th June, being Whale Roadway, proceeded on passage at 0500, weather - fresh wind, sea heavy swell. Arrived at Mulberry B. beach at 2245, anchored to shorten in tow, enemy aircraft attacked shipping, also dropping mines. Decided to keep at anchor until

(Continued)

Empire John - Report during invasion of Continent

COPY OF REPORT FROM "EMPIRE JOHN". (CONTINUED)

- 2 -

0600 14th June. Proceeded to Mulberry A and delivered tow inside of breakwater, completed 1200, received instructions to return to U.K. proceeded on passage 1230, arriving Lee on Solent at 2315 and anchored.

Weighed anchor at 1645 on 16th June. Proceeded to Selsey, arriving 1900, proceeded in and picked up tow - Whale Buffer. Proceeded off to anchorage to comply with routeing instructions. Weighed anchor at 2145, proceeded on passage, arriving at Mulberry B. at 1615, shortened in tow and proceeded into breakwater, put tow in position alongside Whale 405, received orders to await instructions, received sailing orders at 1715, proceeded on passage to U.K. arriving at Lee on Solent at 0300 on 18th June.

Weighed anchor at 1030 on 19th June, proceeded to sea in search of tows that were adrift, also any invasion craft that needed assistance, searched on routes also as far as Lat. 50 deg. and found nothing, also having no reports from returning vessels, decided to return to Lee on Solent, arriving at 2230 and anchored.

Received orders on 21st June to be ready for sea at 1400, received orders at 1600 to proceed to the Farshore, Mulberry A. for rescue work, proceeded on passage - weather N.E. gale proceeding. Arrived Farshore at 0400, 22nd June, was ordered to anchor to await daylight. At 0500, Chief Wireless Operator, J.Long, reported seriously ill. Proceeded to Hospital Ship and transferred R/O to Hospital, then proceeded to Mulberry A. Reported to U.S. Operations Commander for orders, was told to anchor until weather abated.

Received orders on 23rd June that 17 Bombardons had sunk in main channel and that "EMPIRE JOHN" in company with U.S. Tug "A.T.A.125" was to tow Bombardons clear of Channel to Perue Point - a distance of five miles - and sink same by gun fire. Was engaged in this operation until 29th June, towing 8 Bombardons clear and sinking same by gun fire and was then ordered to beach to assist in refloating landing craft, Owing to draft of ship was unable to get in close and had to use 250 fathoms Tow line, put tow line on H.M.S. L.C.T.735 and commenced to tow full speed. U.S.Landing did not see signal hoisted by "EMPIRE JOHN" and passed between Tug and L.C.T.735 and parted tow line. Operations had to be suspended until a.m. tide 30th June. At 0400 put tow line on H.M.S. LC.T.735 and commenced towing full speed Had been towing until 0500 when slip hook on L.C.T.735 parted. Operations again were suspended until p.m. tide. Made fast to L.C.T. 735 at 1630 and commenced towing until 1930. Buoyed tow line off for next tide, was informed that 735 had moved. On 1st July at 0530 picked up tow line and commenced towing on L.C.T.735. 735 refloated 0700, at 1730 assisted U.S. Tugs in refloating U.S. L.C.T.271 and H.M.S. L.C.T.1166. Operations completed 2030, anchored awaiting further instructions. On 2nd July continued salvage operations on beach head, refloating H.M.S. L.C.T.1002 and assisting her to safe anchorage, also refloated U.S.2008. On 3rd July refloated U.S.L.C.T.2043, and H.M.S. L.C.T.562. On 4th July refloated L.B.V. 239 and H.M.S. 1806. Operations completed 2300. On 5th July whilst proceeding into beach in shallow water, s.s. struck submerged wreckage very hard, reported position of wreckage to U.S.Harbour Master, refloated H.M.S. L.C.T.651 and L.B.Y.22, thus clearing one section of the beach of craft. On 6th July was ordered to another section of beach, whilst proceeding into position s.s. again struck more wreckage very hard, reported incident to U.S. Harbour Master, refloated L.B.V.33. Whilst heaving in towing wire, wire became foul of submerged wreckage and parted and had to suspend operations, commenced operations again at 0015 7th July, refloating H.M.S. L.C.T.2337 and also beached L.C.T.2337 again on different section clear of all operations. Then at 2200 7th July proceeded into beach and took hold of L.C.T.879 which had engines and rudder disabled and towed same to Eastern Breakwater Ships and moored, completed 2400.

On 8th July at 0930 proceeded to beach and connected to two pontoons which were half submerged, towed them clear of beach and to repair section. Owing to falling tide was unable to continue operations on beach but received signal stating that U.S. Tug "CORMORANT" had fouled submerged wreckage and proceed to her assistance. Proceeded to "CORMORANT", connected towing spring and towed "CORMORANT" clear into channel way, completed 1330. Then being too late on tide to continue beach operations. July 10th at 1000 proceeded into beach and connected towing wire to U.S.C.Patrol Boat 1307 and proceeded to tow full speed, 1307 refloated 1430. Anchored and held 1307 alongside until her engines were repaired, then at 1500 proceeded to Perue Point and located floating wreckages dangerous to navigation and disposed of same.

July 11th proceeded into beach to attempt to refloat L.C.T.25 but on inspection of craft decided that it was not advisable to refloat same owing to severe

Empire John - Report during invasion of Continent

COPY OF REPORT FROM "EMPIRE JOHN" (CONTINUED)

- 3 -

damage to stern of vessel and a danger of sinking on refloating, reported matter to U.S.Commander "HUIE", was told to await further instructions.

July 12th proceeded into Blockships and worked on sunken L.C.T.555 putting bridle round L.C.T. and then on the high water towed L.C.T. into shallow water in beach, then proceeded to assist U.S.tug T.34 to tow sunken L.C.T.552 into beach and shallow water, then with T.34 attempted to tow sunken L.C.T.572 into beach, but owing to falling tide was unable to complete operation.   July 13th was ordered with U.S. Tugs T.34, A.R.S.2, to attempt to tow L.C.T.572 into beach, put bridle round L.C.T. and commenced towing with U.S.Tugs. but owing to position of L.C.T., operations were unsuccessful.   July 14th, proceeded into beach and put towing wire on Army Barge, commenced towing full speed.   After towing 1 hour, barge refloated.   Was told to disregard all previous orders as Army Barge was of extreme importance.   July 15th, proceeded into beach, put towing wire into L.C.T. 703, refloated L.C.T. and towed same out to Dry Dock Ship "OCEANWAY" and Dry docked L.C.T.

July 16th, refloated L.C.T.7066 from beach, then passed towing wire to L.C.T.7069, during operation towing wire became foul, submerged wreckage and parted, unable to refloat 7069.   July 17th towing gear repaired, proceeded into beach, put towing gear into L.C.T.7069 and refloated, operations difficult owing to draft of tug. July 18th was ordered to try and tow L.C.T.856 200 ft. further down beach.   Attempted operation but 856 was completely under water at high water and operation was unsuccessful July 19th, proceeded into beach and made towing gear fast to L.C.T.856 and commenced towing full speed, moved 856 further down beach as required.   Operations were held up on 20/21 July owing to strong N.wind and heavy swell.

On 22nd July proceeded into beach to attempt to refloat floating crane but owing to heavy swell was unable to get into beach.   Whilst proceeding to report to U.S.Commander, s.s. came into collision with L.C.T.616 that was underweigh with nobody on the bridge navigating vessel.   After collision proceeded into Blockships and "EMPIRE JOHN's" own crew commenced minor repairs to s.s. below the water line.   Repairs completed 2000, proceeded to anchorage awaiting tow back to U.K. Southampton.   On 23rd July at 0300 heavy air raid on shipping in area.

24th July owing to heavy swell on beach was unable to continue operations on beach, standing by, received orders at 1100 to proceed into beach and take in tow Whale Pier Head for U.K.   Connected to Whale 1250, proceeded to convoy anchorage for instructions   25th July weighed anchor at 0600, proceeded independently on passage to U.K.   Whilst on passage ran into N.E.gale at 2200, proceeding 26th July at 0500 tow parted from tug, picked up tow again and proceeded to Lee on Solent for further instructions.

During these operations, the Officers and men of "EMPIRE JOHN" were at times called upon to work on beach and wrecks and showed great seamanship and devotion to duty.   As Master, I wish to put on record my appreciation to my crew.

(sgd.) H.GRIFFITHS.

Master.

27/7/44.

Empire John - Report during invasion of Continent

Empire Humphrey
1944 – 1945

Official No. 169344
Call Sign MGRG
Gross tons 274
Dimensions 105.2ft x 26.6ft x 12.2ft

Built 1943 by Cochrane & Sons Ltd, Selby of the Hoedic Class.

850 ihp three-cylinder triple-expansion engine by Amos & Smith Ltd, Hull, with cylinders 15ins x 25ins x 42ins with a stroke of 27ins.

William Watkins managers.

May 1944 towed concrete block from Gravesend to Southampton. 1st June 1944 sailed from Oban towing one of the corncob block ships for making temporary harbour at Normandy. 8th June blockship sunk in position. She then run to Southampton towing blocks for Mulberry Harbour to Normandy. Stationed at Cherbourg when harbour was usable berthing ships until November 1944. Returned to Ramsgate for boiler clean then January 1945 harbour tug at Calais.

April 1945 towed crane barge to Antwerp and stayed there working. Returned crane barge to Tilbury, arrived Tilbury on the day the Second World War ended. Run to Heysham as harbour tug, then run to Greenock and towed two barges to Gravesend, then to Ramsgate for a refit.

Transferred to Admiralty and run to East Indies and stationed at Batavier.

1946 sold to Netherlands East Indies Government.

1947 re-named *Suus.*

1950 sold to N.V. Nederland Steenkolen Mandelmaats.

1959 Sold to Indonesian Government.

1961 re-named *Laut Sawu.*

1964 Sold to Surabaya Port Authority.

No further details known.

Empire Betsy
May 1944 – September 1944

Official No. 180248
Call Sign MNNX
Gross tons 274   Built 1943
Dimensions 105.2ft x 26.5ft x 12.2ft

Built 1943 by Cochrane & Sons, Selby of the Hoedic class.
Powered by an 850 ihp three-cylinder triple-expansion engine by

Amos & Smith Ltd, Hull with cylinders 15ins x 25ins x 42ins with a stroke of 27ins. Steam supplied from an oil-fired boiler.

Completed May 1944 for Ministry of War Transport and William Watkins Ltd, appointed managers.

Escorted corncob ships across the channel assisted in positioning them to be sunk making a rudimentary harbour off Arromanches, Normandy for the unloading of supply ships for the invasion forces until the Mulberry Harbours were built. She was coastal towing and on 12th September 1944 she came under Admiralty control.

1946 sold to N.V. de Bataafsche Petroleum Maats Holland, and re-named *Soegio.*

12th February 1948 sunk by mine off Borneo in position 02° 36' S 116° 33' E.

Empire Susan
1944 – 1946

Official No. 169185
Call Sign MDFC
Gross tons 592
Net tons 66
Dimensions 137.1ft x 33.1ft x 15.1ft
Draft 17ft 6ins
Oil Consumption per 24 hours 11 tons
Bunker Capacity 330 tons
Bollard Pull September 1952 12 ¼ tons
Speed 11 Knots

Built 1944 by Clelands (Successors) Ltd, Willington Quay, River Tyne as *Empire Susan* of the Improved Larch Class for the Ministry of War Transport.

Powered by a 1,150 ihp three-cylinder triple-expansion engine by Ailsa Shipbuilding Co. Ltd, Troon with cylinders 16ins, 26ins and 43ins with a stroke of 30ins. Steam supplied by an oil-fired multi-tubular boiler 16ft 1ins x 11ft 3ins with a working pressure of 215 psi.

Launched 19th July 1944 and completed 9th October 1944 and placed under the management of W. Watkins Ltd, anchored at Southend on 7th November 1944 ordered to assist *Abraham Baldwin* 7,176 gross tons ashore on the Goodwin Sands. On passage 13:00 with *Empire Aid*. On 8th November tugs *Empire Susan,* Naval tug *Saucy* and Dover tugs *Lady Brassey* and *Lady Duncannon* made fast to ship and towing ships head was swung. 19:30 tugs let go and anchored. 9th November gale force winds. 10th November two Dover tugs made fast. *Saucy* got towrope in propeller and towed clear by *Empire Aid*. 21:45 tugs let go and anchored. 11th November 07:30 *Empire Susan* and two Dover tugs made fast and she re-floated 09:00.

Empire Susan was used coastal towing during 1945 and to near

Empire Susan as *Rumania*

Empire Susan as *Rumania*

continent, and was acquired by William Watkins Ltd, in 1946 for £35,000.

1946 re-named *Rumania (III)*.

1st February 1950 to Ship Towage (London) Ltd.

12th February 1956 total loss on North Longsand, Thames Estuary anchored waiting to assist *Loide Honduros* which was ashore and dragged anchor and pounded on sands tug began taking water, crew rescued by two Whirlwind helicopters from RAF Martlesham Heath, Suffolk. This was one of the first helicopter rescues.

Empire Spruce
July 1945 – September 1945

Official No. 168780
Call sign BDRB
Gross tons 129
Dimensions 92.5ft x 20.5ft x 8.4ft

Built 1942 by Richard Dunston Ltd, Thorne of the Maple Class. Powered by a 500 ihp three-cylinder triple-expansion engine by McKie & Baxter Ltd, Paisley with cylinders of 12ins x 20ins x 32ins with a stroke of 22ins.

Built for Ministry of War Transport. Burns & Laird Lines Ltd, appointed managers.

July 1943 sunk in collision off Garelock, River Clyde, raised and repaired.

July 1945 William Watkins appointed managers.

Towed two barges from Greenock to Gravesend.

September 1945 at Ramsgate for refit, management transferred to Dover Harbour Board.

March 1947 transferred to Admiralty and re-named *Emulous*.

1958 sold to H. G. Pounds, Portsmouth.

1961 sold to J. D. Irvine Ltd, St. John N.B. Canada and re-named *Irvine Oak* and re-engined with a 16-cylinder General Motors V diesel engine.

1991 scuttled off Newfoundland.

Empire Plane of the same class as *Empire Spruce*

Empire Martha
1945 – 1946

Official No. 180459
Call sign GSQZ
Gross tons 296
Dimensions 116ft x 27.6ft x 12.7

Built 1945 by Cochrane & Sons Ltd, Selby of the Stella Class.

Powered by a 750 ihp three-cylinder, triple-expansion engine by Frankline Machine & Foundry Corp. Providence, Rhode Island, U.S.A. with cylinders 12ins x 20ins x 33ins with a stroke of 24ins.

October 1945 completed and handed over to Watkins as managers.

Her first tow was an oil separator from Hull to Portsmouth. When off the Dugeon they run into bad weather and it was found a weld had been missed on her casing and she was leaking badly. She returned to Hull where it was fixed and completed her tow to Portsmouth. The next three months towing trawlers from Harwich to Grimsby.

Her next tow was an ex. C.P.R. liner from Plymouth with the *Empire Aid*. The ship had been loaded with obsolete munitions etc. The two tugs towed her to Stornoway in the Outer Hebrides where more cargo was loaded, they then towed her to deep water in the Atlantic and she was scuttled.

Empire Martha then ran to Middlesbrough via Scapa Flow and towed six trawlers between Grimsby and Middlesbrough, her next tow was an E-Boat from Sheerness to Milford Haven. She then ran to Dublin and was handed over to James Contracting and Dredging Co. to which she had been sold.

1946 sold to James Contracting and Dredging Co. Ltd, Southampton.

1947 re-named *Foremost 106*.

1949 sold to Remorquage Letzer, Antwerp, Belgium and re-

named *Georges Letzer*.

1964 Converted to diesel power.

1977 Owners restyled as Union de Remorquage et De Salvage S.A. (Towage and Salvage Union Ltd).

1992 sold to Northern Europe Shipping, Antwerp and re-named *Hilde*.

1994 scrapped Brugge.

Empire Stella
1945 – 1946

Official No. 180448
Call Sign GBKK
Dimensions 116ft x 27.6ft x 12.7ft
Gross tons 325

Built 1945 by Cochrane & Sons, Selby of the Stella Class.

Powered by a 750 ihp three-cylinder triple-expansion engine by Franklin Machine & Foundry Corp. Providence, Rhode Island U.S.A. Steam supplied by an oil-fired boiler with cylinders of 12ins x 20ins x 33ins with a stroke of 24ins.

Completed August 1945 for Ministry of War Transport, William Watkins appointed managers.

1st January 1946 *Empire Stella* was inward bound in the Thames Estuary to Gravesend from Weymouth with two barges in tow, when off the Knock John Buoy, she had a serious boiler explosion, which killed four crew-members; two were reported missing and others including her Master Captain Woolnough were injured. She was towed to Sheerness by a Naval vessel. She was towed from Gravesend by *Empire Susan* on 17th February to the river Humber and sold to United Towing Co. Hull in May 1946 for £15,000 and re-named *Serviceman*.

Re-engined with a 750 ihp, three-cylinder triple-expansion engine by Alexander Hall & Co., Aberdeen.

1961 re-engined with a 2,000 bhp 6-cylinder British Polar diesel engine.

1969 sold to Rimorchiatori Sardi S.P.A. Cagkiari, Sardinia and re-named *Poetto*.

Empire Martha as *Georges Letzer* after conversion to diesel

Empire Stella as **Serviceman**   © A. Duncan, Gravesend, Kent

Serviceman converted to diesel   © A. Duncan, Gravesend, Kent

Empire Jean as Matinda III

Matinda III and *Salveda* © *Fotoflite*

Empire Jean
1945 – 1946

Official No. 169193
Call sign MNLQ
Dimensions 137.1 x 33.1ft x 15.1ft
Gross tons 593

Built by Clelands (Successors) Ltd, Willington Quay, River Tyne of the modified Englishman Class.

Powered by a 1,250 ihp three-cylinder triple-expansion engine by D. Rowan & Co. Ltd, Glasgow, with cylinders 16½ins x 28½ins x 47ins with a stroke of 30ins.

Launched December 1944 as *Empire Rosa* but completed April 1945 as *Empire Jean* for Ministry of Transport, William Watkins Ltd, appointed managers.

Coastal towing while under Watkins management.

1946 sold for £40,000 to Metal Industries Ltd, Glasgow, and re-named *Matinda III*. William Watkins Ltd had bid £36,000 for her but lost to the higher bid.

1961 sold to Spanish Navy and re-named *RA3*.

1980 re-named *AR33*.

October 1982 sold for scrap at Cartagena.

Appendix 1 – Masters' statements – Dunkirk Evacuation

Statement re Services Rendered Inside Calais Harbour by Tug "Foremost 87".

Dear Sir,

On the morning of Wednesday May 22nd, 1940, I was made fast inside Dover Harbour. At 8.30 a.m. I received orders and signal to proceed with all speed to Calais Harbour and render whatever assistance I possibly could on arrival. I cleared Eastern entrance of Dover Harbour about 9 a.m. and arrived in Calais Roads at 10.55 a.m. On nearing Calais Harbour I noticed that an air raid was on and bombs were being dropped in and around the Harbour of Calais. I at once steamed into the Harbour and offered my services to Captain in charge who informed me to proceed at once to locks of Inner Harbour and do what I possibly could to free the lock gates which had been seriously damaged and rendered useless. The Captain also informed me that he had a Steamer which proved to be S/S "Katowice" in the inner dock and he could not get her out until the lock gates were got clear. I at once took to this job of work and I noticed that the gates had been badly damaged by enemy bombing which was still in progress, I also noticed that the only way to clear these gates was to charge them with Tug "Foremost 87" and smash them up, being as chains of gates had broken and fouled underneath them causing them to jam. I was instructed by officer in charge to clear them at all costs and to get S/S "Katowice" out of the dock so as she could proceed to sea. I commenced going full speed astern then full speed ahead charging gates with Tug until gates were smashed and cleared enough for me to pass through, this job taking about one hour. I at once steamed to

P.T.O.

Foremost 87 - Statement re services rendered inside Calais Harbour (Dunkirk Evacuation)

-2-

S/S "Katowice" and took hold of same, putting two of my men from Tug
ashore to cast his ropes off from Quay, being as there was nobody
about to do this for him. I commenced towing on S/S "Katowice" who
by the way was also loaded with refugees, about 12.45 p.m. and managed
to tow him clear out through lock and into Calais Roads, clear of all
obstructions, the Captain thanking me for my services, I letting go
my tow rope from S/S "Katowice" at 2 p.m. He then proceeded on his
way, refugees all happy and smiling as he steamed away. I then
returned to Calais Harbour for further orders and instructions.

                    I am Sir,

                    Your Obedient Servant,

                              (Late Master "Foremost 87").

Foremost 87 - **Statement re services rendered inside Calais Harbour (Dunkirk Evacuation)**

Five tugs heading for Dunkirk

DUNKIRK EVACUATION - Tug "JAVA".

Left Ramsgate 29th May at 3-0 p.m. for Dunkirk.   In company with us were three drifters and four motor boats.   Arrived in vicinity of beaches at 1-30 a.m. but owing to darkness anchored till daybreak.   At break of day approached as far into beach as possible, the motor boats could not get into the shore on account of draught, so we lowered our boat and this was manned by the mate and deck-hand, who rowed to and from the beach, working incessantly getting troops into our boat, transferring them to motor boats when they were again transferred either to drifters or our Tug.   After working as hard as we could all the forenoon we proceeded into Dunkirk and went alongside of Mole, then filled Tug and all motor boats and drifters full of troops. While doing this we had a teriffic air attack.   We left Dunkirk and proceeded to La Panne, where we transferred all our troops to H.M.S."CALCUTTA" then returned to Dunkirk beaches again and carried out the same procedure as in forenoon, filling up a sloop with troops as well.   After filling ourselves up again there was no other vessel in the vicinity to transfer these other troops to, so decided it would be best to return to England with them.   (During these operations we had been violently attacked from the air by dive-bombers and machine-guns, attack lasting for 1½ hours.

It was 5-0 p.m. on 30th May when we left Dunkirk, and when five miles off we observed a 'plane in the water.   Had a hard job to prevent troops from firing at it as they took it for granted it was German.   It proved to be British and we succeed-in saving the two airman in her.   After proceeding another mile we ran across troops clinging to wreckage and swimming about. We lowered small boat again and also placed the tug so that some of the men were able to climb on board, the mate and deck-hand also bringing them on board with the small boat.   I remained and did all that was possible, saving everyone that could be saved and then carried on to Ramsgate and discharged troops at 9-30 a.m. on 31st May,.

I would like to mention that all the crew worked as hard as they could and did their very best, having not sleep for sixty hours.   They gave all our stores to the troops, and their clothes to individual soldiers as well, especially V. Smith mate and H. Griffiths deck-hand, who worked without a stop with our working boat on Dunkirk Beach and saved lives from the paddle steamer "WAVERLY" which had been bombed.

On 1st June, H.M.Trawler "JACINTA" became stranded on the wreck of the Moel(?) and was in danger of capsizing.   We transferred the 250 troops on board our Tug and landed them at Ramsgate.

(Signed) W. JONES.

Master of Tug "JAVA".

Java - Master's statement regarding participation in Dunkirk Evacuation

THE SERVICE OF THE TUG "SIMLA" DURING THE

DUNKIRK EVACUATION

AT DOVER.

During the Dunkirk Evacuation, the shipping at Dover Harbour was great, and the tugs were in constant demand to control and assist it.

At Dover Harbour, the main berths for the landing of troops, is at the Admiralty Pier, the western end of the Harbour. It has eight berths for ships like the cross channel boats.

During the busy time, there were as many as sixteen to eighteen ships using the Pier at one time, landing the troops and going to make room for other vessels, to attend to them. They practically all required the assistance of tugs, one or two, whatever the position they were in. Some had to be held off while the inside ship got away, or shifted here and there to allow room for others to berth, for which the tugs "Simla" "Gondia" "Roman" and "Lady Brassey" were ordered to attend them, but also, these tugs had other work to attend to, such as ships for the Submarine Camber Dock, which is at the eastern end of the Harbour, where they go for repairs. Then there is the Granville Dock, the Wellington Dock, and the Eastern Arm.

In the main Harbour, there are forty odd buoys for ships to berth. The oil tanker "War Sepoy" is at one of these, and the ships berth alongside of her with the assistance of tugs for bunkers.

The tugs are also required to convey ammunition and stores off to Destroyers and other Naval vessels in the Harbour.

The fortnight commencing May 20th, 1940. at the time of the evacuation, the tug "Simla" assisted inside and outside of Dover Harbour, 140 odd ships. The crew and myself, were practically on our feet night and day. I have great praise for my crew. Never a grumble, but carrying on with the good work, all longing to help as much as possible, to see our soldiers home safe.

On May 22nd, when attending to harbour work, I received a signal, that a French ship, the s.s. "Themsen" with refugees on board, had been in collision with a British ship the s.s. "Efford" three miles south-west of Dover. On arriving there, the "Efford" had sunk, and the crew of her, were in one of her lifeboats which I picked up. I then found out from the Captain of the"Efford". that all his crew were saved, and that the "Themsen" had cut right into his ship.

Simla - Master's Statement regarding service of tug at Dover during Dunkirk Evacuation

(2)

The tug "Simla" took the s.s. "Themsen in tow, and I went on board of her, while my mate took charge of the tug, for the Captain of her, was in such a nervous condition, that he could not take charge of his ship. He had just come from Dunkirk after being bombed all day, and asked me to take charge of his ship. I anchored her off Dover under Naval orders. I then landed the crew of the "Efford" at Dover.

The tugs had orders to shift two Destroyers from Admiralty Pier on May 24th, in the early hours of the morning to buoys in the Harbour, to make room for other ships to berth. They were the H.M.S. Whitshed and Vimey, but the crews of the Destroyers were so tired and exhausted from there recent experience of Dunkirk, that we let them sleep on, and shifted the Destroyers without them. I expect that when they turned out from their much needed sleep, they were surprised to find their ships in a different position, but were all fresh to go to sea again, and carry on the good work.

During the very dark night of May 24th, the s.s. "Kolistan" 5,884 tons, was outside, waiting to berth at Admiralty Pier. She had about six thousand troops on board. The Naval people wanted her to berth as soon as possible on account of enemy planes coming over. The job of berthing her was not an easy one, for the Harbour was full of other ships, no one being allowed to show any light. The tugs "Simla" and "Lady Brassey" decided to do the best they could. It was just like going into thick fog. You could not see the other ships or buoys in the Harbour, and it was a great worry trying not to hit other ships. First we would scrape along one Destroyer, then just miss another one by a few feet. Well, with great care, I for one, was pleased to get that ship on her berth without any mishap, and to know that the soldiers got ashore safely.

On May 27th, the s.s. "Monas Ashe" was five or six mile off Dover, wanting the assistance of tugs. The "Simla" and "Lady Brassey" went to her, and found she had been bombed by a dozen enemy planes, killing forty soldiers and wounding seventy on her upper deck, also putting the ship out of control. Two Destroyers had gone to her aid, driving the enemy off. The tugs towed her into Dover. Then on May 29th, the Destroyer H.M.S. Montrose was full with troops, and four or five mile off with her bow blown away. The "Simla" went to her and towed her into Dover stern first, with the help of tug "Lady Brassey" berthing her at Admiralty Pier.

Simla - Master's Statement regarding service of tug at Dover during Dunkirk Evacuation

(3)

In the early hours of the morning of May 30th, the Destroyer H.M.S. Jaguar was outside the Harbour, wanting the assistance of tugs. She was bombed and making water. The "Simla" assisted her into Harbour and berthed her at the Eastern Arm.

On the next day, the 31st May, the sloop H.M.S. Bideford full with French soldiers was six miles to the south-east of Dover, being in tow of a gun-boat, but required assistance of tugs. She had been bombed and had her stern blown off, killing twenty five men and wounding others. The "Simla" went out to her, towing her back to harbour, and berthing her inside Submarine Camber Dock with the assistance of tug "Gondia" and on the same evening, H.M.S. Impulsive was three miles outside of Dover with starboard engine out of control. The tug "Simla" towed same into Dover.

On June 1st, the cross-channel ship "Maid of Orleans" was leaving Admiralty Pier and when rounding the Prince of Wales Pier, she came into collision with H.M.S. Worcester, to nearly turn over, throwing some twenty soldiers into the water.

The tugs saved as many as possible, but there were so many in the water that some got drowned. How many we did not know. It was very hard luck for them after getting away from Dunkirk.

MASTER OF TUG "SIMLA"

Simla - Master's Statement regarding service of tug at Dover during Dunkirk Evacuation

COPY OF STATEMENT REGARDING SURVIVORS FROM HOSPITAL SHIP

"P A R I S"

by

s.t."FOREMOST 87"

Wednesday, 5th June, 1940.

Dear Sir,

On Sunday afternoon, the 2nd June, I received orders from Naval Authorities Dover to proceed to Dunkirk. My orders being to take Lifeboats R.N.L.B. "CECIL & LILLIAN PHILCOTT and R.N.L.B. "THOMAS KIRK WRIGHT" in tow to assist in evacuating troops from Dunkirk Harbour and Beach.

I cleared Eastern Entrance of Dover Harbour about 3-50 p.m. with Lifeboats in tow, and on instructions before leaving towed towards given position where I had to cast lifeboats off. I arrived at this position and was giving lifeboat coxwains courses for Dunkirk Harbour, when, on hearing aircraft overhead and several explosions, I noticed to the southward of me a hospital ship which proved to be s.s."PARIS" of Newhaven, in, as I thought, difficulties. I at once altered my course, irrespective of routing instructions, towards said vessel, and on nearing same I noticed several of her lifeboats full of survivors who had survived this bombing and machine-gunning which I was afterwards informed had happened. I at once gave orders to crew to get lines etc. ready to take these survivors on board, some of whom were Sisters who were very seriously injured, also some of crew who'd been badly scalded.

I managed to get all of the 95 survivors out of our boats, some of which were half full of water, on board of "FOREMOST 87", and did everything to make wounded (one of whom passed away on board Tug "FOREMOST 87") as comfortable as I could, and then headed at full speed towards Dover.

I had hardly altered my course when I noticed another boat full of people. I stopped engines and on nearing this boat I found that it had 13 Spaniards aboard. I ordered these to be taken on board and kept apart from survivors of "PARIS" as I was uncertain of their Nationality, and I was unable to gather from them how and when they came to be in the boat I found them in.

I headed for Dover, time being about 10-50 p.m., at full speed. Arriving at Dover Pierheads Eastern Entrance about 3-30 a.m. on Monday, 3rd June, and received orders to proceed direct to Admiralty Pier and land survivors, this I did as soon as possible, everything being ready on shore to assist in this job of work. I kept Spaniards on board until they were escorted ashore by armed guard, who no doubt found out more about them than I could.

I am, Sir,

Your obedient Servant,

(Signed) J. Fryer.

Master of s.t."FOREMOST 87".

Foremost 87 - Statement regarding survivors from hospital ship *Paris* (Dunkirk Evacuation)

Appendix 2 – Fleet List

Monarch 1833 – 1876
Fiddler 1840 – 1847
Lord Warden 1845 – 1853
Punch (1) 1846 – 1850-1
Paul Pry 1847 – 1866
John Bull 1849 – 1878
Uncle Sam 1849 – 1900
John Lee 1850 – 1855 Saucy Jack 1855 – 1862 John Lee 1862 – 1866
Britannia 1852 – 1855
Victoria 1853 – 1906
Punch (2) 1854 – 1895
Don 1855 – 1866
Defiance 1856 – 1871
Toby 1856 – 1862
Napoleon 1857 – 1881
Antagonist 1857 – 1867
Victor 1859 – 1894
Times 1861 – 1886
Annette 1861 – 1869
Britannia 1862 – 1875
Express 1864 – 1880
Anglia 1866 – 1894
Albion (1) 1868 – 1869
Era 1869 – 1882
Cambria 1870 – 1914
Albion (2) 1870 – 1872
Robert Bruce 1872 – 1892
Atlas 1873 – 1887
Hibernia (1) 1874 – 1884
Scotia (1) 1874 – 1891
Titan 1874 – 1888
Renown 1874 – 1903
Pilot 1875 – 1883
India 1876 – 1894
Bristol 1877 – 1898
Fox 1877 – 1878
Canada 1880 – 1936
Australia 1882 – 1908
Zealandia (1) 1882 – 1912
Tasmania 1883 – 1897
Malta (1) 1883 – 1885
Columbia 1884 – 1912
Hibernia (2) 1884 – 1961
Mona 1884 – 1885
Malta (2) 1886 – 1888
Burmah 1886 – 1889
Iona 1886 – 1920
Mercia 1889 – 1895
Burma (1) 1889 – 1904
Oceana 1889 – 1918
Guiana 1889 – 1918
Nubia 1890 – 1935
Cynthia 1892 – 1896
Scotia (2) 1894 – 1935
Arcadia 1895 – 1952 Badia (2) 1952 – 1962
Manila 1895 – 1901
Simla 1898 – 1964
Java (1) 1900 – 1901
Mashona 1902 – 1905
Persia (1) 1902 1908
Liberia 1905 – 1911
Java (2) 1905 – 1965

Doria 1909 – 1947
Badia (1) 1909 – 1947
Vincia 1909 - 1947
Racia (1) 1915 – 1919
Muria (1) 1920 – 1940
Rumania (1) 1920 – 1923
Palencia 1920 – 1939
Fabia 1920 – 1946
Kenia 1927 – 1964
Gondia 1927 – 1966
Rumania (2) 1928 – 1935
Tanga 1931 – 1969
Doralia 1937 – 1938 Napia (1) 1938 – 1939
Tamesa 1937 – 1938 Cervia (1) 1938 – 1946
Denderra 1937 – 1938 Racia (2) 1938 – 1967
Dongara 1937 – 1938 Persia 1938 – 1946 Muria (2) 1946 – 1967
Napia (2) 1946 – 1971
Cervia (2) 1946 – 1973
Empire Winnie 1944 – 1946 Zealandia (2) 1946 – 1952
Empire Susan 1944 – 1947 Rumania (3) 1947 – 1956
Empire John 1943 – 1944 / 1945 – 1951
Dhulia 1959 – 1980
Ionia 1960 – 1987
Hibernia (3) 1963 – 1987
Fossa 1965 – 1977
Vespa 1965 – 1975
Culex 1965 – 1971
Rana 1965 – 1975
Burma (2) 1966 – 1989

Tugs Chartered World War One

Liberia chartered 1914 – 1918
Glen Rosa chartered 1914 – 1918
Nestor chartered 1915 – 1917
Schelde chartered 1915 – 1918
Thames chartered 1915 – 1919

Managed for P & O Line

Dandy 1921 – June 1921

Tugs placed under the management of William Watkins Limited by Ministry of War Transport During World War Two

Security-Stoke 1939 – 1944
Foremost 22 1939 – 1945
Lynch 1940 – 1946
Fairplay One 1940 – 1945
Foremost 87 4-1940 – 8-1940
Empire Piper 1942 - 1945
Empire Wold 1942 – 1944
Empire Winnie 1944 – 1946
Assiduous 1943 – 1946
Empire John 1943 – 1944 1945 – 1946
Empire Humphrey 1944 – 1945
Empire Betsey 5-1944 – 9-1944
Empire Susan 1944 – 1946
Empire Spruce 7-1945 – 9-1945
Empire Martha 1945 – 1946
Empire Stella 1945 – 1946
Empire Jean 1945 – 1946

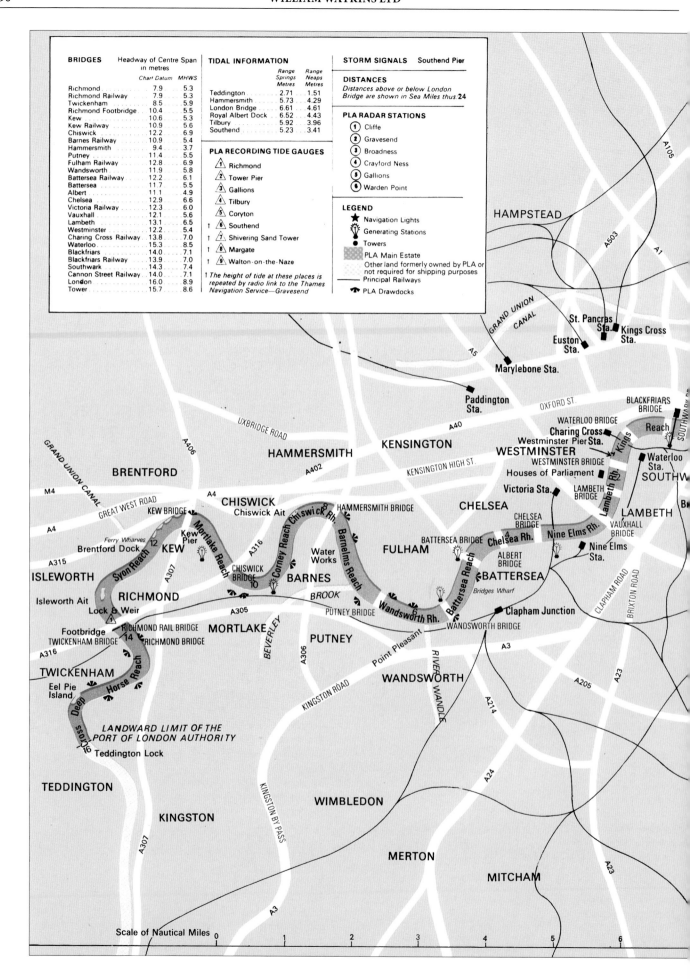

BRIDGES Headway of Centre Span in metres

	Chart Datum	MHWS
Richmond	7.9	5.3
Richmond Railway	7.9	5.3
Twickenham	8.5	5.9
Richmond Footbridge	10.4	5.5
Kew	10.6	5.3
Kew Railway	10.9	5.6
Chiswick	12.2	6.9
Barnes Railway	10.9	5.4
Hammersmith	9.4	3.7
Putney	11.4	5.5
Fulham Railway	12.8	6.9
Wandsworth	11.9	5.8
Battersea Railway	12.2	6.1
Battersea	11.7	5.5
Albert	11.1	4.9
Chelsea	12.9	6.6
Victoria Railway	12.3	6.0
Vauxhall	12.1	5.6
Lambeth	13.1	6.5
Westminster	12.2	5.4
Charing Cross Railway	13.8	7.0
Waterloo	15.3	8.5
Blackfriars	14.0	7.1
Blackfriars Railway	13.9	7.0
Southwark	14.3	7.4
Cannon Street Railway	14.0	7.1
London	16.0	8.9
Tower	15.7	8.6

TIDAL INFORMATION

	Range Springs Metres	Range Neaps Metres
Teddington	2.71	1.51
Hammersmith	5.73	4.29
London Bridge	6.61	4.61
Royal Albert Dock	6.52	4.43
Tilbury	5.92	3.96
Southend	5.23	3.41

PLA RECORDING TIDE GAUGES

1. Richmond
2. Tower Pier
3. Gallions
4. Tilbury
5. Coryton
† 6. Southend
† 7. Shivering Sand Tower
† 8. Margate
† 9. Walton-on-the-Naze

† The height of tide at these places is repeated by radio link to the Thames Navigation Service—Gravesend

STORM SIGNALS Southend Pier

DISTANCES
Distances above or below London Bridge are shown in Sea Miles thus: 24

PLA RADAR STATIONS
1. Cliffe
2. Gravesend
3. Broadness
4. Crayford Ness
5. Gallions
6. Warden Point

LEGEND
★ Navigation Lights
Generating Stations
● Towers
PLA Main Estate
Other land formerly owned by PLA or not required for shipping purposes
— Principal Railways
PLA Drawdocks

Appendix 3 – Port of London Authority – River Thames Maps

The maps on pages 190-200 are reproduced courtesy of The Port of London Authority, Marine House, Denton Wharf, Mark Lane, Gravesend, Kent DA12 2PL and we are grateful to Martin Garside, the PoLA media officer, for facilitating this.

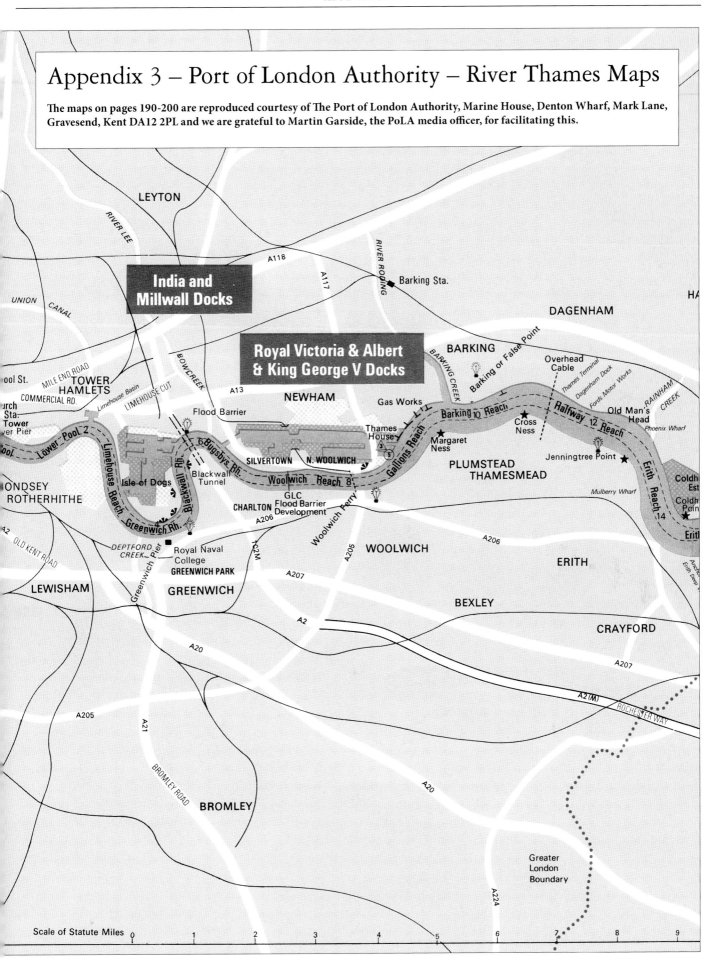

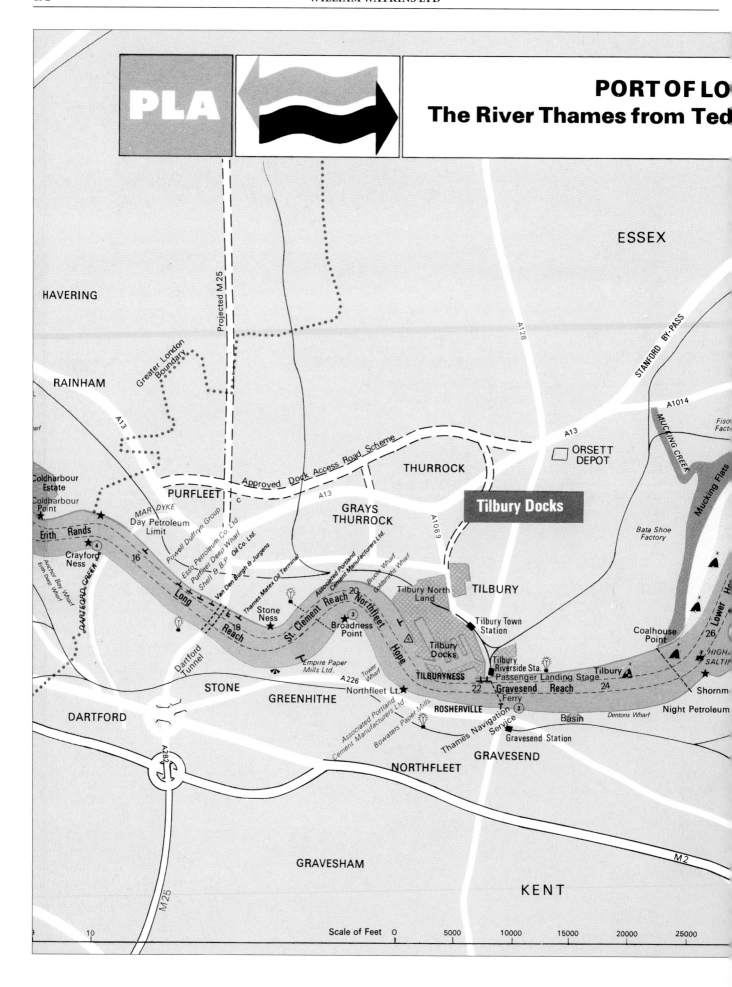

PLA

PORT OF LO
The River Thames from Ted

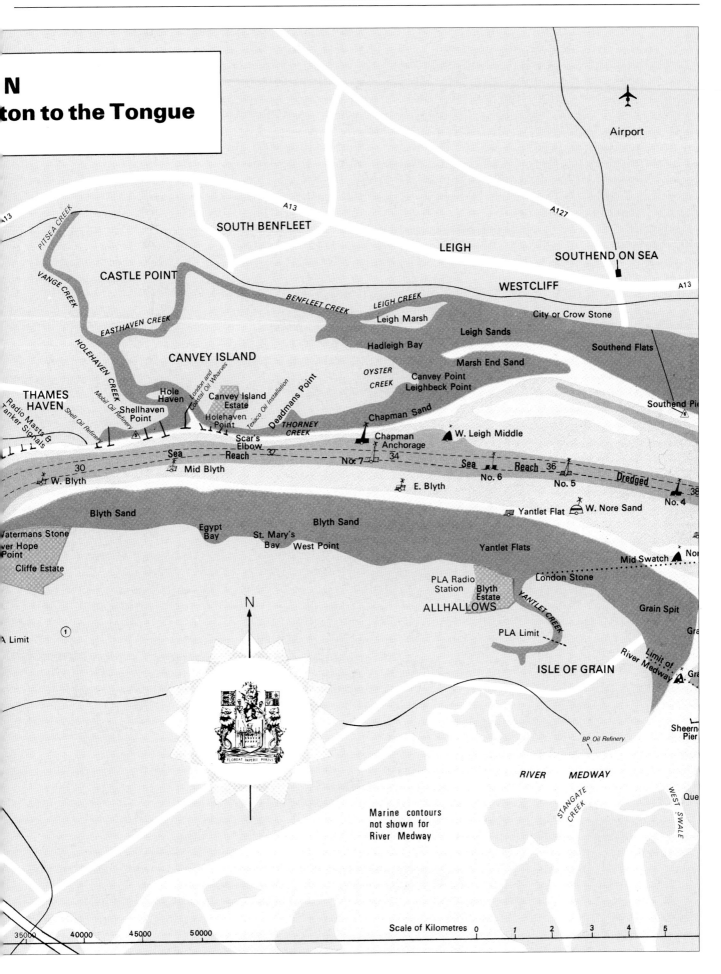

N

ton to the Tongue

A13

SOUTH BENFLEET

LEIGH

SOUTHEND ON SEA

WESTCLIFF

A13

A127

Airport

PITSEA CREEK

VANGE CREEK

CASTLE POINT

EASTHAVEN CREEK

BENFLEET CREEK

LEIGH CREEK

Leigh Marsh

Leigh Sands

City or Crow Stone

HOLEHAVEN CREEK

CANVEY ISLAND

Hadleigh Bay

Southend Flats

Marsh End Sand

OYSTER CREEK

Canvey Point

THAMES HAVEN

Hole Haven

London and Coastal Oil Wharves

Canvey Island Estate

Deadmans Point

Leighbeck Point

Southend Pier

Radio Masts & Tanker Signals

Shell Oil Refinery

Shellhaven Point

Mobil Oil Refinery

Holehaven Point

Texaco Oil Installation

THORNEY CREEK

Chapman Sand

W. Leigh Middle

Scar's Elbow

Chapman Anchorage

Sea — Reach 32

No. 7 34

Sea Reach 36

Dredged

38

30

Mid Blyth

No. 6

No. 5

No. 4

W. Blyth

E. Blyth

Yantlet Flat

W. Nore Sand

Blyth Sand

Egypt Bay

St. Mary's Bay

Blyth Sand

West Point

Yantlet Flats

Mid Swatch

Nor

Watermans Stone

ver Hope Point

PLA Radio Station

Blyth Estate

London Stone

Grain Spit

Cliffe Estate

ALLHALLOWS

YANTLET CREEK

Gra

A Limit

①

N

PLA Limit

ISLE OF GRAIN

Limit of River Medway

Gra

Sheern Pier

BP Oil Refinery

FLOREAT IMPERII PORTUS

RIVER MEDWAY

STANGATE CREEK

WEST SWALE

Que

Marine contours not shown for River Medway

Scale of Kilometres 0 1 2 3 4 5

35000 40000 45000 50000

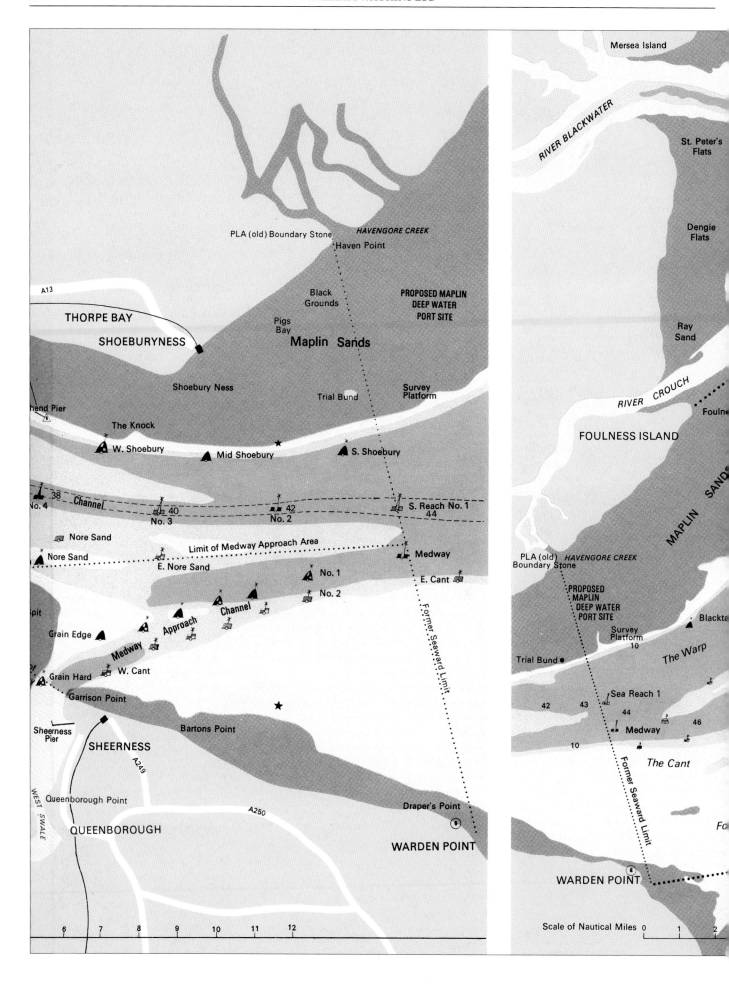

Mersea Island

RIVER BLACKWATER

St. Peter's
Flats

A13

THORPE BAY

SHOEBURYNESS

Dengie
Flats

PLA (old) Boundary Stone

HAVENGORE CREEK

Haven Point

Black
Grounds

Pigs
Bay

Maplin Sands

PROPOSED MAPLIN
DEEP WATER
PORT SITE

Ray
Sand

RIVER CROUCH

Foulne

Shoebury Ness

Trial Bund

Survey
Platform

hend Pier

The Knock

W. Shoebury

Mid Shoebury

S. Shoebury

FOULNESS ISLAND

MAPLIN SANDS

38 Channel

No. 4

40

No. 3

42

No. 2

S. Reach No. 1

44

Nore Sand

Limit of Medway Approach Area

Nore Sand

E. Nore Sand

Medway

E. Cant

PLA (old)

HAVENGORE CREEK

Boundary Stone

PROPOSED
MAPLIN
DEEP WATER
PORT SITE

No. 1

No. 2

Channel

Approach

Survey
Platform

10

Blackta

The Warp

pit

Grain Edge

Medway

W. Cant

Trial Bund

42

43

Sea Reach 1

Grain Hard

Garrison Point

44

Medway

46

Sheerness
Pier

SHEERNESS

Bartons Point

Former Seaward Limit

10

The Cant

A249

Queenborough Point

A250

The Cant

Fo

WEST SWALE

QUEENBOROUGH

Draper's Point

6

WARDEN POINT

WARDEN POINT

6

Former Seaward Limit

6   7   8   9   10   11   12

Scale of Nautical Miles   0   1   2

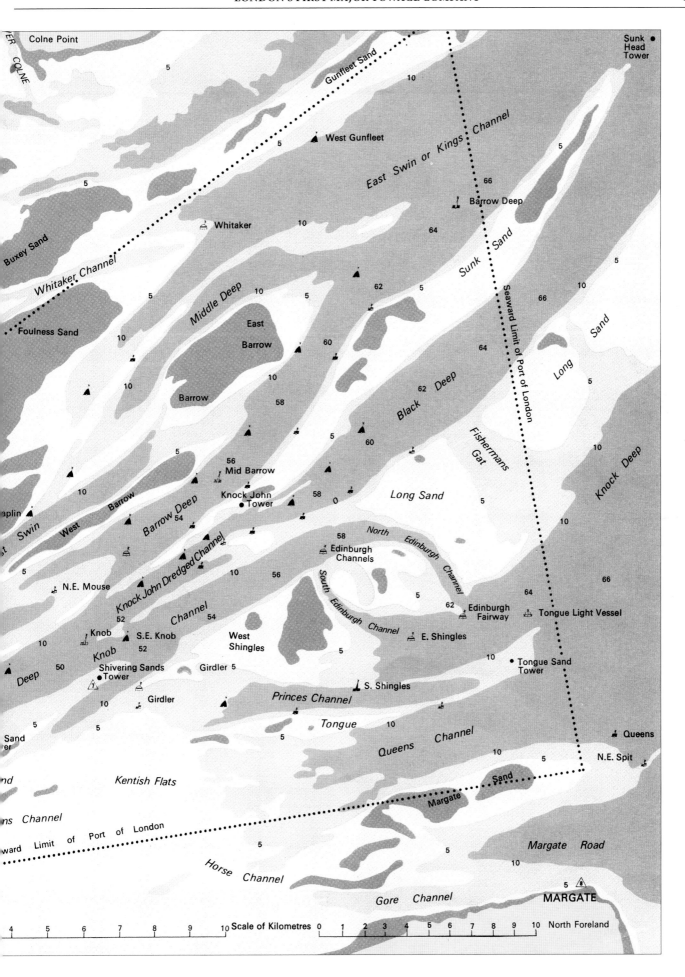

Colne Point

RIVER COLNE

Gunfleet Sand

5

10

Sunk Head Tower

West Gunfleet

5

East Swin or Kings Channel

66

Barrow Deep

5

Buxey Sand

Whitaker

10

64

Sunk Sand

5

Whitaker Channel

5

Middle Deep

10

5

62

5

Seaward Limit of Port of London

66

10

Long Sand

Foulness Sand

10

East Barrow

60

60

64

5

Barrow

10

Black Deep

62

5

Barrow

58

60

5

Fishermans Gat

10

5

Knock Deep

56

Mid Barrow

Long Sand

58

0

5

Knock John Tower

58

West Barrow

North Edinburgh Channel

66

West Swin

Barrow Deep

54

Edinburgh Channels

58

Chaplin

10

Knock John Dredged Channel

10

56

64

Tongue Light Vessel

5

N.E. Mouse

Channel

54

62

Edinburgh Fairway

52

South Edinburgh Channel

E. Shingles

10

Knob

S.E. Knob

West Shingles

5

Tongue Sand Tower

Knob

52

Deep

50

Shivering Sands Tower

Girdler

5

10

S. Shingles

Queens

Girdler

Princes Channel

N.E. Spit

5

5

Tongue

10

Sand

Kentish Flats

Queens Channel

10

Sand

5

Sand

Margate Sand

ns Channel

Seaward Limit of Port of London

Margate Road

5

Horse Channel

5

10

Gore Channel

5

MARGATE

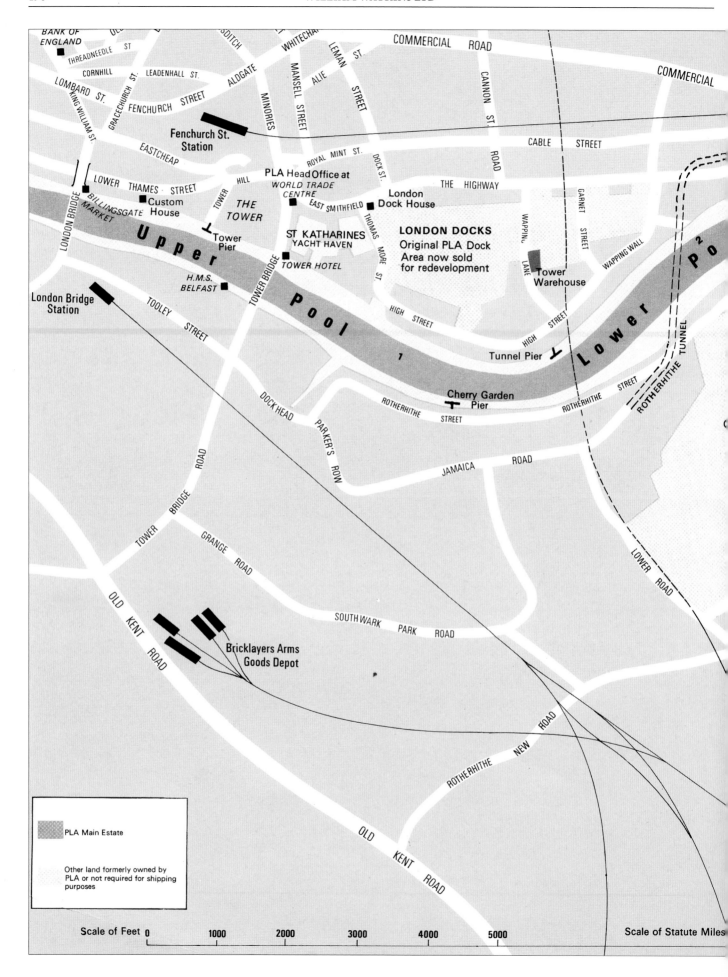

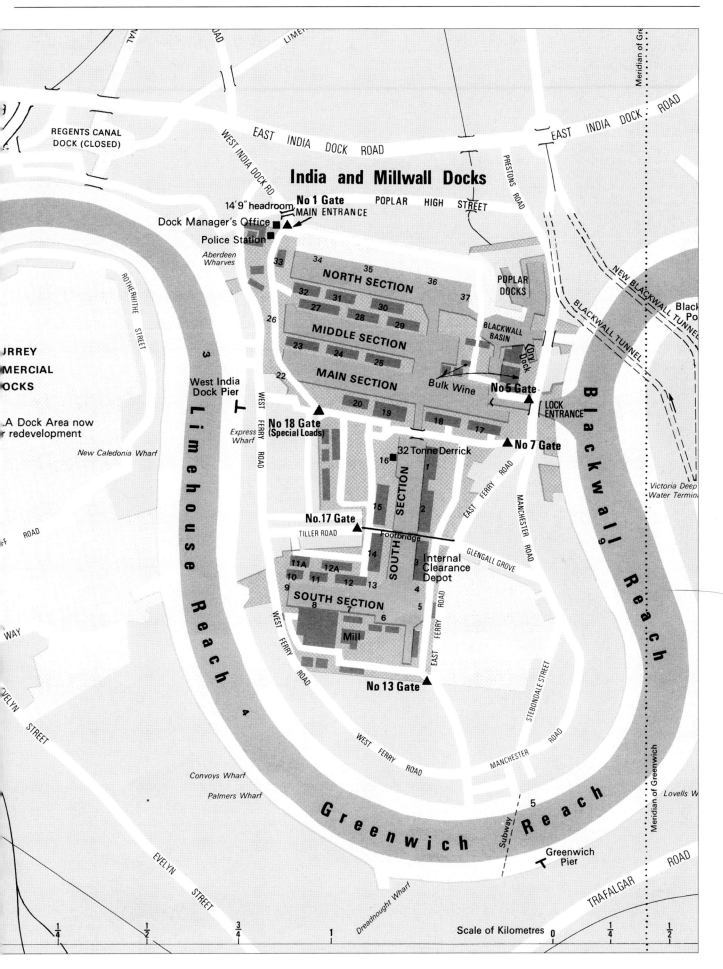

India and Millwall Docks

REGENTS CANAL
DOCK (CLOSED)

EAST INDIA DOCK ROAD

EAST INDIA DOCK ROAD

Meridian of Gr

PRESTONS ROAD

WEST INDIA DOCK RD.

POPLAR HIGH STREET

14'9" headroom

No 1 Gate
MAIN ENTRANCE

Dock Manager's Office ■

Police Station ■

Aberdeen
Wharves

POPLAR DOCKS

NEW BLACKWALL TUNNEL

BLACKWALL TUNNEL

Black
Po

33

34   35

NORTH SECTION

36

37

BLACKWALL BASIN

32 31   30

27 28   29

26

MIDDLE SECTION

23   24   25

22

MAIN SECTION

Bulk Wine

Dry Dock

No 5 Gate

LOCK ENTRANCE

URREY
MERCIAL
OCKS

A Dock Area now
redevelopment

New Caledonia Wharf

ROTHERHITHE STREET

West India
Dock Pier

West India Dock Pier

Express
Wharf

WEST FERRY ROAD

3

Limehouse Reach

20   19

18   17

No 18 Gate
(Special Loads)

No 7 Gate

Blackwall Reach

Victoria Deep
Water Termin

EAST FERRY ROAD

MANCHESTER ROAD

32 Tonne Derrick

16

SOUTH SECTION

1

2

15

No.17 Gate

TILLER ROAD

Footbridge

Internal
Clearance
Depot

GLENGALL GROVE

14

11A   12A

10 11 12 13

9

SOUTH SECTION

8   7   6

Mill

4

5

EAST FERRY ROAD

STEBONDALE STREET

MANCHESTER ROAD

No 13 Gate

ROAD

WAY

EVELYN STREET

WEST FERRY ROAD

Convoys Wharf

Palmers Wharf

EVELYN STREET

Greenwich Reach

Subway

5

Greenwich
Pier

Lovells W

Meridian of Greenwich

Dreadnought Wharf

TRAFALGAR ROAD

Scale of Kilometres   0

1/4   1/2   3/4   1   1/4   1/2

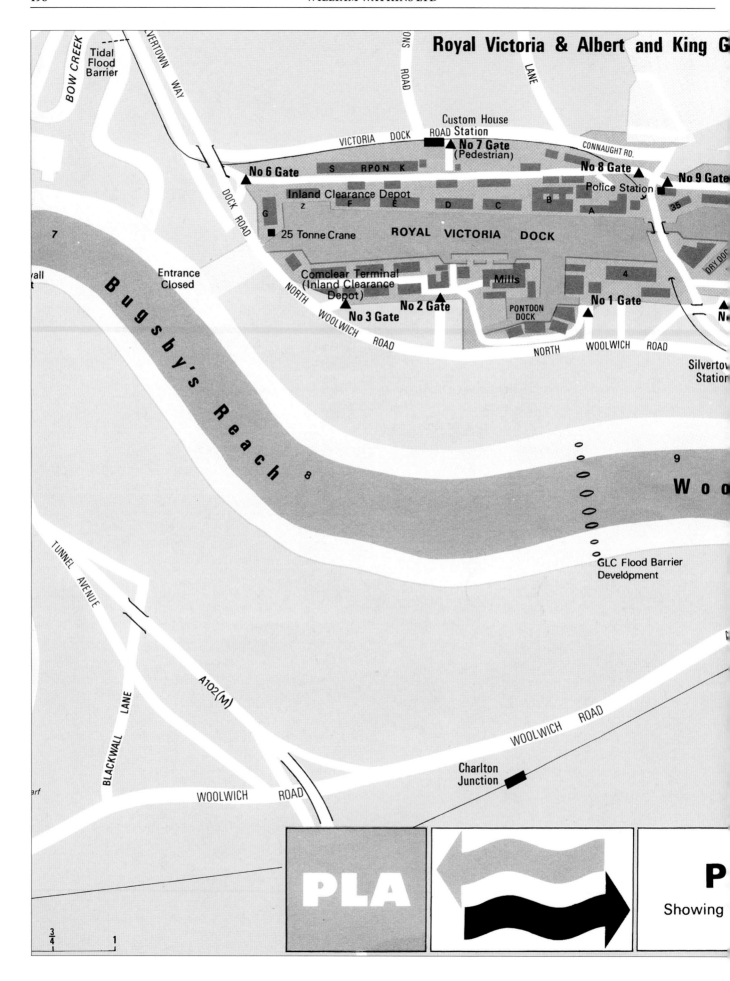

Royal Victoria & Albert and King G

BOW CREEK

Tidal Flood Barrier

SILVERTOWN WAY

VICTORIA DOCK ROAD

Custom House Road Station

No 7 Gate (Pedestrian)

CONNAUGHT RD.

No 6 Gate

S   RPON K

No 8 Gate

Police Station

No 9 Gate

Inland Clearance Depot

G   Z   F   E   D   C   B   A

35

DRY DOC

7

25 Tonne Crane

ROYAL VICTORIA DOCK

DOCK ROAD

Entrance Closed

Comclear Terminal (Inland Clearance Depot)

Mills

4

NORTH WOOLWICH ROAD

No 2 Gate

No 3 Gate

No 1 Gate

PONTOON DOCK

N

NORTH WOOLWICH ROAD

Silverto Station

Bugsby's Reach

8

9

Woo

GLC Flood Barrier Development

TUNNEL AVENUE

A102(M)

BLACKWALL LANE

WOOLWICH ROAD

WOOLWICH ROAD

Charlton Junction

vall

wall t

Wharf

3/4   1

PLA

P

Showing

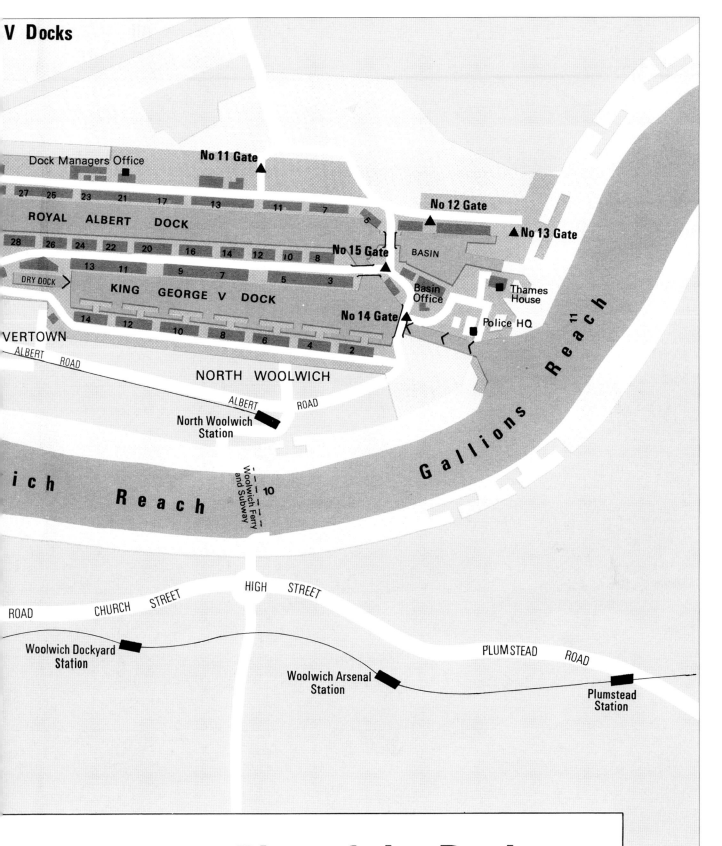

V Docks

Dock Managers Office

No 11 Gate ▲

27 25 23 21 17 13 11 7

ROYAL ALBERT DOCK

28 26 24 22 20 16 14 12 10 8

DRY DOCK

13 11 9 7 5 3

KING GEORGE V DOCK

14 12 10 8 6 4 2

No 12 Gate ▲

▲ **No 13 Gate**

BASIN

No 15 Gate ▲

Basin Office

Thames House ■

Police HQ ■

VERTOWN

ALBERT ROAD

NORTH WOOLWICH

ALBERT ROAD

North Woolwich Station

No 14 Gate ▲

Gallions Reach 11

ich Reach

Woolwich Ferry and Subway

10

CHURCH STREET HIGH STREET

ROAD

PLUMSTEAD ROAD

Woolwich Dockyard Station

Woolwich Arsenal Station

Plumstead Station

# of London — Plan of the Docks

Access, Ships Berths, Warehouses, Transit Sheds, Main Dock Offices, Etc.

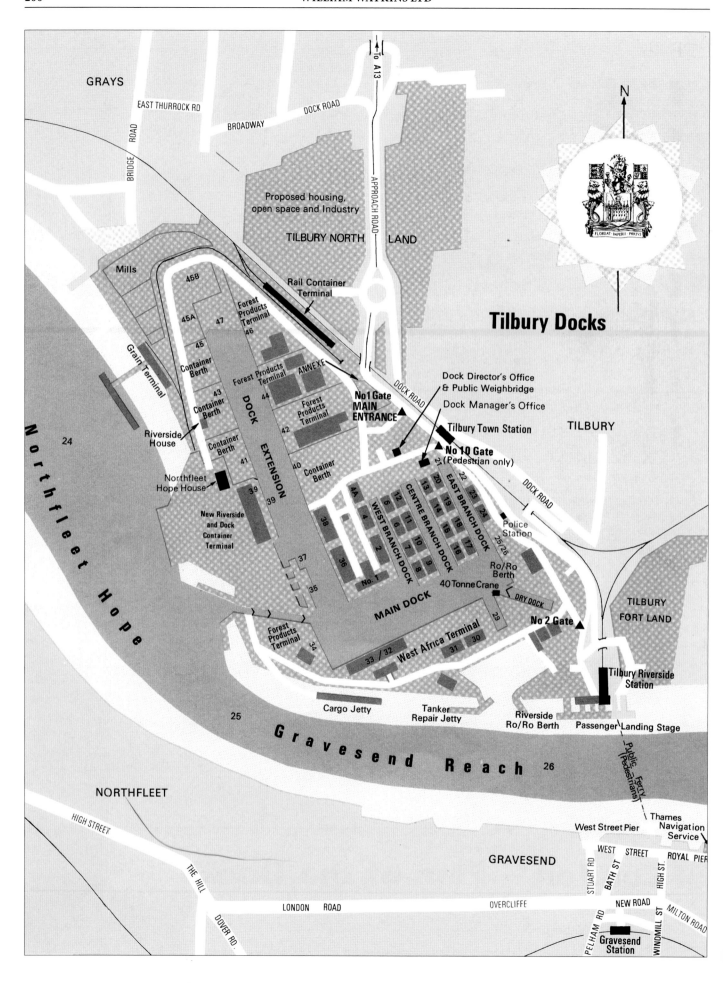

Appendix 4 - Rumania - An account written by Fireman Len Smith

Len Smith in 1949 on board *Rumania* at Ghent

Joined *Empire Susan* in March 1946 at Southampton.

W. Watkins were in the process of buying '*Empire*' *Susan* at this time also '*Empire*' *Jean* and '*Empire*' *Julie* all the same class but the world shortage of tugs created by the war sent prices sky high. It was December 1946 before they eventually purchased '*Empire*' *Susan* and '*Empire*' *Winnie* for £160,000 and got a long charter on '*Empire*' *John*.

The first deep-sea towing job was a Saint Line cargo ship from the Port of Spain, Trinidad, to Charlton Buoys. We left Southampton and bunkered at Las Palmas taking twenty-two days on the voyage out.

On arrival at Trinidad the Skipper was expecting to see a light liberty ship, instead she was loaded with sugar and had been lying there for months, smothered in sea growth. When the Skipper communicated with London they had not taken these points into consideration when making the contract.

We left the Port of Spain for Las Palmas, after ten days of towing in good weather, averaging 100 miles noon to noon, we ran into severe gales. It was then realized that the Steward had underestimated stores for the trip so we had to go on rations, we knew there was plenty of fresh water on tow but the five run crew only had food for a short trip.

We rode out the bad weather for five days, during that time we made only seventy-eight miles headway, we were now at the point

of no return in respect of the fuel position; we had also connected up every bit of towing gear, 350 fathoms out. On the seventeenth day the weather was fine and we came amongst some Portuguese fishing boats so we lowered a boat and bartered blankets, flour and tobacco for fish taking some over to the tow.

On the 26th day and 150 miles from Las Palmas we ran into bad weather again and hove to just making headway for three days. The Master made contact via wireless to Las Palmas for a tug on a normal towing contract but they said they would only attend on salvage conditions.

We arrived in Las Palmas thirty-one days from Trinidad, only ten tons of fuel on board and only a few gallons of fresh drinking water. The tug was bunkered and stored at Las Palmas; all hands in the boats and rafts were used to scrape sea growth off the tow, which took a total of three days.

It took twenty-nine days to reach Southend with bad weather all the way on shortening towrope at the Nore we found it was badly frayed down to the last lay in some places, we were assisted to Charlton Buoys by river tugs, after which we ran to Gravesend and were told we could have a night home before taking the *Rumania* to Grimsby for a major refit and modification which would take two or three months and we would be paid off until the tug was ready.

On arrival on board the next morning we were informed that the company were seeking another tow before the refit so we signed off and those staying signed on two-year articles. Master H. Griffiths then informed us we were to tow two L.C.T.'s from Appledore to Rio-de-Janeiro.

We remained at Gravesend for about a week storing and preparing for the long voyage. The tug left Gravesend and ran light to Appledore, on arrival we found the Dutch tug *Witte Zee* there which was making the same voyage, we prepared the tows together all hands mucking in and we both streamed gear and full away together.

When we were somewhere around Ushant we lost sight of *Witte Zee* astern and ran into bad weather which caused one of our tows to break adrift, we eventually re-connected and arrived at Las Palmas after eighteen days, the tug was bunkered and stored which took a total of three days. On departing and streaming tows the Master became concerned about sheering which had not happened on the way down so we lowered a boat and went around both L.C.T.'s and eventually found that the propellers had been removed by cutting through the shafts, while laying in Las Palmas.

After a week towing in excellent weather we came up and overhauled *Witte Zee* and went into Cape Verde for bunkers (24 hours). When we were three days out from Cape Verde we came upon the *Witte Zee* again, the weather being good we lowered a boat and took fresh fruit, beer and other goodies across to her, we stayed in company for a few hours then slowly hauled away making Rio in twenty-two days from Cape Verde. *Witte Zee* came in 24 hours later, which had run non-stop from Appledore.

Normal repairs were carried out and the stores re-stocked etc. and left Rio after a four day stay, our orders were to proceed to Lagos, West Africa and tow a British tanker which had been torpedoed during the war and had been laying there for two years.

On arrival at Lagos we found that the tow was in a very bad condition and three towing companies had turned the job down, our Skipper made certain conditions in respect of further repairs being carried out to the damaged section and the rudder being centered. We connected steam hoses and got the steering gear and ballast pump working, trimmed the tow down by stern and got bulks of timber and anything possible to shore up where the patch had been placed over the torpedo hole forward. All the hands were working 12 or 14 hours a day for a week, getting the tow ready in temperatures around 98 degrees Fahrenheit.

The tug left Lagos towing the ship stern first, I have never seen a ship sheer and drag so much, we averaged about four knots and must have veered ten or twelve miles each side of our true course. After a week or so it was decided to make for Freetown and further repairs. On approaching Freetown and the shipping lanes, the tow struck Matadi Palm and began making water, we towed to the nearest mud bank and beached her. On arrival in Freetown the port authorities held the tug until the insurance claims were sorted out.

On leaving Freetown we received orders to go to the Azores and on passage came across a French tug *Abelle 10*, towing a dredger to Marseille, he requested our assistance owing to boiler trouble. We towed both into Funchal Madeira and were awarded £2,500.

On arrival at St. Michael's Port, Azores, we took in tow a lifting lighter it was now November and we had extremely bad weather all the way to Birkenhead which took a total of fourteen days, whilst on this trip Deckhand T. George was washed along the main deck and finished up jammed in the rudder quadrant and a severe leg injury, the Fireman A. Birch suffered a severe back injury when struck by a forty-gallon oil drum falling from the storage gratings, both men were treated by the Master until reaching Bar Lightship.

From the Mersey we went to Barrow and towed a Lock Gate to K.G. Docks assisted from South Foreland by *Napia* and *Cervia* and arrived at Gravesend on the 18th December having been away for six months.

It was after this trip we were then told that the *Rumania* was going to Grimsby for a complete overhaul and alterations, and after seven days paid leave we could go up to Grimsby and standby the tug, on pay, which was most unusual at that time, we found out later that H. Griffiths had insisted he wanted to keep the hands together, so we paid off at Grimsby on 21st December 1946.

On the 1st January 1947 we rejoined the *Rumania* at Grimsby, it was so cold we could not live aboard so we had to sleep in the Seaman's Mission which cost 3s 6d per night. The company allowed us 7s 6d a day. At that time the firemen and deckhands wages were £6 16s per week, no overtime, bedding and food provided.

One fireman signed as Donkeyman and received 10s a week extra; a deckhand as Boson who received 7s 6d a week extra. There was never a shortage of food and stores coming aboard. J. R. Watkins told us he would never stint on stores providing there was no waste and all hands from Master down would eat the same. This was OK but then the Steward who was solely in charge, started fiddling with Chandlers and things changed.

It was at this re-fit when *Rumania* received a new funnel and masts and a new motor lifeboat. We had trials off Spurn on the 18th January 1947 and run to Gravesend in snowstorms, which took sixteen hours. We commenced storing up and taking on board as much gear as could be stowed and on the 21st January we signed two-year articles and I don't think anybody signing that day realized they would almost complete those articles in one trip. Our tow was two Navy Sloops *HMS Kittiwake* and *HMS Sheldrake* from Portsmouth to Shanghai.

The *Zealandia* was running light to Naples for a tow to Plymouth so he towed *HMS Sheldrake* to Algiers, which was to be our first bunkering port.

The tugs left Gravsend on 24th January, but on the run down the channel developed engine trouble so we had to go to Southampton, whilst carrying out repairs the *Gondia* bought a tow to us.

We left Southampton on 29th January 1947 and averaged nine knots to Lizards then ran into gales and bad weather until abreast of Lisbon.

The crew for this trip were

H. Griffiths DSO MBE	Towing Master
Captain Snoddy Master F.G	Navigator (homesick Genoa)
R. Rainham	Chief Engineer (homesick Genoa)
F. Boyd	Second Engineer (Chief Genoa)
R. Burns	Third Engineer (lost finger)
J. Warren	Mate
B. Press	Second Mate (homesick Genoa)
C. Blackburn	Marconi Operator
J. Thaites	Cook Steward
R. Gould	A.B. (Boson)
P. Costello	A.B.
C. Pugh	A.B.
K. Gill	O.S.
A. Gulland	O.S.
L. Smith	Fireman (Donkeyman)
A. Gurr	Fireman (3rd Engineer Genoa)
G. Sylvester	Fireman (lost overboard)
A. Ward	Pantry Boy (Officers)
R. James	Galley Boy

Fuel carried 336 tons, fresh water 126 tons.

The tug arrived at Algiers fourteen days from the Solent and found *Zealandia* awaiting our arrival. The three days we spent in Algiers was like a holiday to us after the terrible winter we had left behind, we were assisted clear of Algiers by *Zealandia*, both ships towed as if they were steaming, dead astern in tandem.

During the run to Port Said which took a total of thirteen days in good weather we tried each 24 hours different R.P.M.'s to arrive at the most economical fuel consumption and towing speed which worked out at 10 tons per day, towing speed seven knots up until this time fuel consumption had averaged 12.50 tons daily.

We entered Port Said harbour, secured tows to a buoy and went alongside the quay for fuel and stores, which took a total of two days, we returned to the tows, reversed all the towing gear and entered the Suez Canal at 05.00 on the 4th March assisted by a canal tug and arrived in the Bitter Lakes (Ismailia) at dusk, anchored until daylight and arrived at Port Tewfik (Suez) 16.00. While connecting gear and preparing tows we discovered that both ships still had fuel oil in their tanks.

After a weeks towing in the Red Sea in extremely warm and calm conditions we shortened the tows and extracted about 50 tons of fuel and arrived at Aden twelve days from the Canal.

Whilst we were approaching Aden the 3rd Engineer caught his hand in the main engine and Fireman Sylvester collapsed with heat exhaustion, they were both sent to the Naval hospital while we took on stores and fuel. We received a Mayday call from a ship 200 miles to the west of the Aden, the Swedish salvage tug on station at Aden was in dry-dock and the nearest tug was over a thousand miles away.

On arrival at the ship's position, after agreeing on the radio to Lloyds open form the Master of the ship said he was awaiting another one of his company's vessels to tow him into Aden but if we would accept normal towing rates we could carry out the tow. However, the position he was in and the currents would have put him ashore on Socotra Island within thirty hours. We agreed to stay with him for a few hours and our wireless operator who was listening to the messages notified our Master that Casualty's Consort was at least 60 hours away, the ship was asked if he was happy with its position as we were departing, we steamed away for about two or three hours when the ship called us back and signed a Lloyds open form. We towed him into Aden, the ship was French and had lost its propeller, award to the tug was £8,000.00.

Both the hands who were in hospital returned to the tug, the 3rd Engineer had lost the top of a finger but refused to be left at Aden. The fireman who wished to be left behind was told he was 'swinging

Rumania, Napia, Cervia and *Contest* at **Coryton Jetty**

the lead' and must rejoin the tug. I was really sorry for this man he had no idea about life in a tug, coming straight from the Navy.

The tug left Aden for Colombo in extremely good towing weather conditions, it was very hot on board and all hands were sleeping on deck with awnings rigged, this was a very happy passage, all hands settling down for a long trip. Owing to the heat the refrigerator was only opened twice a day 7.00 a.m. and 6.00 p.m. and we were allowed to put a bucket of fresh water in, so each evening we drew it out and added one bottle of lime juice and one bottle of rum and those off watch had an hour on deck yarning and making rope sandals or hammocks. We all suffered from heat rash but the Fireman previously mentioned was so overcome at times we had to do his watch.

We arrived at Colombo after twenty-three days when shortening in towing gear at each port we used to try and better the time taken. Colombo was the best with a time of twenty minutes, both tows up alongside the tug, 120 fathoms to first tow 90 fathoms to the second tow. We used to reverse all gear at each port, Colombo was also our quickest turn around, we were ready for sea, ten hours after arrival but Griffo allowed us a night ashore and we sailed at 08.00 the next day.

London had notified the Agents to supply us with plenty of fresh fruit, so we left Colombo like a banana boat, but I must mention here the tug herself was like a yacht because the two O.S. were day work, and the three A.B.'s used to work off watch about the deck so when in port they were free of maintenance. The O.S. kept night watches. On passage to Singapore we encountered bad weather and engine problems, taking twenty-one days, on arrival at Singapore we carried out repairs and had a week alongside the quay, which was very nice, while we had cash.

The tug left Singapore on the last leg of the tow and steamed into the China Sea with good weather; somewhere abreast of Hong Kong at about 14.00 hours on a calm very warm day I way laying on deck reading under the starboard lifeboat when I heard the cry 'Man Overboard', we had the boat lowered and away in three to four minutes. I didn't even know we were looking for the Fireman, Sylvester until the 2nd Mate (B. Press) who was in charge of the lifeboat told me he had seen him from the bridge come out of the Engine Room and throw himself over the bulwarks, we searched for over an hour going back over the course and around the tows with no success, of course, this tragedy upset everyone on board.

We continued the voyage but 50 or 60 miles off the Shanghai river (Whangpoo) we received a typhoon warning via the Blue Funnel ship *Eurymedon*. The air became so still and heavy, the clouds so thick I thought this was the end of the world. Whilst shortening in at the river entrance the wind came with such velocity it was almost impossible to stand on deck, we managed to get both tows up fairly short and entered the river steaming head to wind for about 12 hours. The next day the typhoon abated, we steamed up to Shanghai and handed tows over to a ferry company roughly twelve weeks from Southampton, we then had the British Consul on board for a full inquiry into the loss of the Fireman.

We stayed in Shanghai for a week and it was a wild and lively place at that time, the communist were marching from the north and money was worthless, we sold 90 fathoms of 14ins rope for 3 million Chinese dollars at 45,000 to the £1.00, the money was brought on board in suitcases.

We picked up a Fireman from the Seaman's Home (I could fill up three pages on him alone). We left Shanghai on 8th May 1947 to run to Formosa (Taiwan) and tow a Blue Funnel Coaster to Hong Kong, we completed this tow in about ten days. It was while we were in Hong Kong that we were interviewed separately about the Fireman's death.

The tug run light to Singapore, where we were expecting to return towards Europe, but on arrival we were told to have a boiler clean and carry out any repairs necessary. After ten days we were ready for sea and told to sail for Sydney, 4,700 miles, we had a lovely passage down through Islands in very hot weather until abreast of Java (Indonesia) we had engine trouble and put into Serabayo, we had three days carrying out repairs.

We sighted Cape York about four days from Java, it was decided then, that we would sail down inside the Barrier Reef, 1,000 miles. We used to anchor at dusk and heave up at daylight, it was a beautiful sight, hundreds of small un-inhabited islands and coral reefs, with birds and fish of fantastic colours, we had about eight days of this before leaving the Reef somewhere around Brisbane, where we steamed down to Sydney, in very bad weather as it was winter time (August).

On arrival the Pilot took us up to the berth ahead of our tow, which was the Interstate liner *Canberra* 12,000 tons, she had been twenty years on coastal passenger service and had been sold to a Greek company for immigrant trade. She was to have an Australian run crew as far as Singapore but there was a dispute with the Seaman's Union in respect to the manning scale, so we had to wait two weeks before it was settled, it took another week preparing the tow and getting 200 tons of fuel into 40 gallon drums on board the tow and having a trough made to sling over the ships side with four hoses running from it to the tugs bunkers. We also had to deal with a dispute on the *Rumania* over the Steward and the food situation, which had got steadily worse owing to his drinking. We notified the Skipper we would not sail from Sydney with the same Steward. The Navigator read us the Riot Act and the Merchant Shipping Act but we stood firm and the Steward was replaced with an Australian Steward.

While we were in Sydney we were taken out and about by the Seaman's Union Members and it was a good three weeks for everybody, we took on board as much food as it was possible to stow. Every locker and cupboard was filled with tins or bags of food. On 7th September 1947 we prepared the tow for the trip connecting to his port anchor cable, 20 fathoms wire to 140 fathoms 18ins manila and that night we had a party on board the *Canberra* with the run crew and shipping officials, the run crew consisted of twenty-eight deck and engine room hands and there would be steam for steering and lighting as far as Singapore. The ship's main shaft was disconnected from the engine to allow free momentum to propeller and eliminate as much drag as possible.

Rumania

We left the berth at 09.00 on 8th September assisted by two tugs and crowds of people in yachts following us down the harbour, there was a banner hanging over Sydney Bridge saying 'Farewell Canberra'. We cleared Sydney heads and dropped the Pilot and tugs at midday, there was a terrific swell running, we streamed the tow and set away full speed 14.00 hours. I remember coming off watch at midnight and looking astern could still see the lights of Sydney, I thought in my own mind we are not going to do it on our own, it was then blowing a full gale and we increased to maximum full speed and were making four knots at midday with the weather moderating we had run 68 miles. The Engineer notified the Skipper it would be impossible to maintain those revs (92 rpm) so we reduced to (78 rpm) which became the norm for the whole tow and proved to be satisfactory, all round giving an average towing speed of 6½ knots and 10 tons of fuel.

We re-entered the Great Barrier Reef and the Master of the Canberra gave us courses and positions via radio, as it was his home ground, we had about sixteen days of idyllic towing conditions, we stopped abreast two little islands while Canberra sent boats away with gear for lighthouses.

We cleared the Barrier Reef and arrived at a position off Cape York twenty days from Sydney, we shortened the gear and lashed up alongside, the general drift was seawards but we kept engines slow ahead and remained tight alongside in fine very hot weather, we rigged bunkering gear and drums were lifted from the ships hold three at a time on to the main deck then rolled to the trough and tipped. Everything went fine until midday when the sun became so overpowering the Aussie's who had been well paid for this, refused to carry on without a four hour break; Griffo ordered us aboard, while he manned the winch. We carried on until the sun went down and the ship's crew carried on. We were doing everything as planned until early hours of the second day we had the main steam joint start to blow and there was no way to repair that without a complete shutdown, so it was decided to make for anchorage at Thursday Island (a Leper Colony then). It was like Dante's Inferno below while towing into Thursday Island, we found a good anchorage, carried out repairs and bunkering and took fresh water from Canberra, we had been three days in all, and were ready for sea at 20.00 hours, Griffo decided to make it daylight. We all went aboard Canberra and the run crew Firemen presented our Firemen with twenty-four pints of beer each, which at that time and place was worth more than gold with temperatures 100 degrees Fahrenheit plus; when the crew found out we were paid a month what they got weekly they couldn't understand our enthusiasm.

We left Thursday Island at daylight and towed up through the islands arriving at Singapore forty-seven days from Sydney. At Singapore the Greek owners took over and put seven men on board, the Aussies flew home. We were advised that from Singapore there would be no more steam for steering or winches and lighting would be paraffin. It took twenty-eight days from Singapore to Colombo in good weather but the ship was sheering always to port on this leg of the tow.

The crew had three days in Colombo, on leaving Colombo and streaming tow the P.O. Canton almost came between the Tug and the tow; we had fine weather all the way to Aden, twenty-one days, on arrival the Port Authority would not allow the tow into port without steam so we had to engage a Danish tug to hold tow outside while we bunkered and stored which took twenty-four hours. From Aden to Suez we had continuous gales all the way up the Red Sea with the tow broad off to port most of the time, we took eighteen days to tow 1,300 miles, arriving at Suez on 23rd December 1947.

On Christmas Eve, we went through the canal and spent three days at Port Said, and I must say that Watkin's had cabled our Agents to supply us with extra Christmas Fayre and a few bottles. While we were in Port Said we had a Naval Officer come on board and told us we had been chartered for the British Government to tow craft down to Mombasa, and anywhere in East Africa in conjunction with the 'Ground Nut Scheme', after completing this tow to Italy. He gave us £25.00 each, this never went down very well with married men but we were on two-year articles. We took twelve days to Genoa and delivered the tow to the owner's four months from Sydney.

The Empire John was in Genoa waiting to start the same contract as us, we had been away almost a year. It was good to meet up with your mates, a good time was had by all for over a week while we carried out repairs and prepared for another long spell in the tropics. It was while we were in Genoa the Chief Engineer, Master Navigator and Second Mate, paid off sick and returned to England. The usual tug procedure was used, everybody moved up one and lower hands were picked up from shore.

The Empire John and Rumania left Genoa together for Port Said, after running through the Straits of Messina, we ran into bad weather. On arrival at Port Said we had to tow a Naval pontoon to Haifa, while Empire John went to Suez. We eventually arrived at Suez and found that we had eight converted L.C.T.'s and two tugs to tow to East African Ports. The Empire John had four large barges and had left with two. We connected two L.C.T.'s and one tug in tandem; the L.C.T. had three men on board, our destination was Dar-es-Salaam 3,500 miles, we took fourteen days to Aden in very good weather, we left Aden without taking a full supply of fuel and water stores owing to rioting and strikes by workers, so we had water and food rationed on board for twenty-one days until arriving at Dar-es-Salaam.

While we were towing down the East African coast it was noticed that the small tug we were towing was sinking, we lowered a boat and inspected but it was too late to save her, all entrances were welded and water was pouring in via the tail end so we slipped gear abreast of Zanzibar, we spoke to Empire John and told him about conditions at Aden, he advised he was going to run right to Suez providing we didn't require anything from him; I believe he achieved this.

On arrival at Dar-es-Salaam we were told by the Union Castle Agent that we could go aboard Dunnottar Castle for meal and drinks which we much appreciated. I think Dar-es-Salaam is the hottest place we had been to and couldn't get away quick enough, we ran light to Aden in about ten days, where things were back to normal.

On the run up to Suez we passed *Empire John* and he informed us this was his last trip and he was returning to the UK. I think everybody aboard *Rumania* was a bit browned off by now and that news didn't help. We took two more L.C.T.'s and one tug bound for Mombasa, on approaching Aden the *Empire John* was coming out bound home. I think that was the only time in my life afloat I really felt homesick.

We secured the tows to buoys in Aden and were bunkering when Sparks received two Maydays, one from up in the Red Sea and one from a loaded T2 Tanker at the mouth of the Persian Gulf a 500 mile run; we knew that *Empire John* was heading up the Red Sea and tugs were running from Suez, so we made for the Persian Gulf and steamed flat out with four hands down below all the time, but *Rumania* had been too long away from dry-docking, the best we could make was 11 knots but the nearest tug was 1,000 miles away and steaming to position at 14 knots. We arrived after about fifty hours and found the Tanker *Gladys Moller* ashore after having complete engine failure, we ran gear away in the lifeboat and commenced towing at midnight, by 04.00 we had the ship clear and began towing towards Aden at four knots which was our average, taking about six days to complete. The award was eventually £15,000 and was the last salvage award paid out tax free, my share being £100 or four months wages, the Chief's was £380.00, the Skipper £850. We then picked up our tows and carried on to Mombasa it was on this run that everybody seemed to go down with something. Heat rash, crabs, exhaustion, dysentery, and ringworm we had the lot on board. Griffo said it was the pets we had, nine caged birds, four monkeys, two parrots, two cats, one mongoose, one dog, and two doves. On arrival at Mombasa we had a boiler clean and fumigation, which we carried out ourselves taking about a week.

We had to escort a coaster down towards Durban but after three days he released us and we ran back to Aden. On arrival we were told to wait there as our salvage job was having problems with repairs and may require towing to England; after staying alongside the ship for a few days he told us he was going out on trials and carry on to Suez if everything was OK, so we stayed with him for thirty-six hours then when he was gone over the horizon. On this run up the Red Sea we ran into a dust storm and had to batten down, it was terrible you had a job to breathe. The sea temperature went up to 68 degrees Fahrenheit and stokehold 132 degrees Fahrenheit On arrival at Suez we were told this would be our last trip as the *Zealandia* was on its way from the Thames with two barges and would take the last two L.C.T.'s.

We left Suez in record time for Mombasa, I believe we were in and out of Aden in eight hours and Mombasa in four. On the run back we took on as much fuel as possible at Aden so all we had to stop for at Suez was water and to pay off the two Greek Firemen; we did this and then went through the canal, not stopping at Port Said, on the way out of the harbour we passed *Zealandia* coming in. We only had four hands below so we worked four-four to Grimsby, an eighteen day run. The sea growth was so bad on the hull that our average speed was eight knots, we arrived at Grimsby on 18th July 1948, nineteen months after signing on and the distance run was 47,000 miles. England to England of which 38,000 was towing. British Ropes took away 120 fathoms of 16 ins manila, which had

been in use on all tows for their Exhibition Room.

I re-joined the *Rumania* after a refit on 19th August 1948, we ran light to Gravesend and signed two-year articles at Tilbury.

We ran light to Portsmouth, which took one day and picked up a new built oil survey and research vessel for the Persian Gulf (Bahrain).

Portsmouth to Port Said took twnety-eight days.

Port Said to Suez (overnight in Ismailia), two days.

Suez to Aden took eleven days

Aden to Bahrain anchored for two days with boiler trouble nine days.

Bahrain to Sultan of Muscat anchored in bay awaiting orders sixteen days very hot and uncomfortable on board, no shore leave.

The tug ran light to Karachi (India), four days.

Karachi to Bombay towing B.I. Ship, nine days.

We ran light to Suez, thirteen days

Through canal to Port Said awaiting orders, went to assistance of Greek ship sinking off Sicily in a Gale, towed ship to Naples (Salvage) lost our starboard lifeboat and foredeck vents due to heavy weather, seven days.

Ran light from Naples to Samos Island in the Greek Adriatic towed Norwegian ship to Spain (Carthegena), twenty-one days

Ran light to Malta whilst steaming past Pantelleria Island went to the assistance of *Fort Patreux* ashore on the island, no assistance required, five days. On arrival at Malta chartered by Port Admiral as a rescue tug, as Naval tugs were on manoeuvres with the fleet, towed L.S.T. to Famagusta (Cyprus), returned to Malta, six weeks on Naval charter.

Left Malta with lifting craft for Genoa very heavy weather tow parted twice, ten days.

Ran light to Port Said, six days.

Through Suez to Aden, light, eight days.

Anchored at Aden awaiting Naval tug towing L.S.T. from Ceylon, took tow over at Aden and towed to Suez, fourteen days. Whilst on passage O.S. Haydon was taken ill with peritonitis and transferred in the Red Sea to SS *Clan Cumings*.

Port Said to Algiers, sixteen days

Drifting for two days with engine trouble whilst doing repairs, bad weather all the way.

Algiers to Milford Haven, twenty-one days. Dense fog from Cape St. Vincent to Lundy Island on arrival at Milford Haven received news of my father's death a month before.

Milford Haven to Grimsby, three days. Paid off.

Re-joined *Rumania* at Grimsby, and ran light to Gravesend sixteen hours.

Towed three-masted Bargue *Viking* to Antwerp, and then ran to Amsterdam to tow two hoppers to Piraeus, a total of nineteen days.

Ran light to Port Said and had serious boiler trouble on the way. On arrival at Port Said a Lloyds' Surveyor came on board, we ran through Suez Canal to Port Tewfik awaiting sixty boiler tubes to arrive from the UK. It was nine weeks before we were ready to get under way. The tug ran down the Red Sea and assisted three Naval tugs with a dry dock to Malta, fourteen days.

Left Malta light for England and received orders to call at Gibraltar and laid in Gibraltar ten days awaiting orders.

Ran light to Malta and towed L.S.T. to Milford Haven, Malta to Algiers took nine days, Algiers to Milford Haven, twenty-one days. We had extremely bad weather Hove to Abreast of Oporto taking four days.

Milford Haven to Gravesend, three days after which we towed *Lady Enchantres* from Gravesend to Dartmouth, we sheltered in St. Helens Roads as the tow was making water, a total of six days.

Ran light to Falmouth awaiting orders.

On salvage Station, twelve days.

Ran to sea on two Mayday calls but outclassed by *Turmoil* and *Zwarte Zee*.

Ran light to Gravesend, two days.

Ran light in company with *Empire John* to Arromanches to tow dismantled Mulberry Harbour sections to Iceland, eight tows in all both tugs. Arromanches to Skagerstrond twenty-eight days. Very bad tow, making water and covered in sea growth, *Empire John* had to return to Arromanches with his tow. Owing to being unable to keep up schedule, the contract went to the Dutchman, our part of the contract was to tow sections to Amsterdam where they were made ready for towing to Iceland, we had delivered seven safely, taking four or five days on each tow, on the eighth we ran into very bad weather abreast of Cape Grenez we had to cut tow adrift and a Destroyer came and depth charged the half submerged concrete Mulberry.

We ran light to Dover and the Skipper told us this was our Salvage station when not on towing jobs.

We had many Mayday calls whilst on this station but outstanding jobs were *Francine Clore* a loaded tanker, which had complete engine failure abreast of Beachy Head, towed to Purfleet assisted from North Foreland by river tugs. After discharge we towed a ship the *Rotterdam* with *Cervia*, £14,000.

SS Generton ashore on Redsands towed clear with *Kenia, Challenge* and *Napia* £16,000. *M.V. Goldenia* ashore on North Goodwins, towed clear £5,000.

Picked up a French dredger, which had broken adrift from her tug in heavy weather towed into Calais, £1,800.

Ran down channel to a position South West of Brest and took in tow Norwegian ship *Bonga*, towed to Antwerp contract tow which took six days.

Ran to Ghent and towed a tug to Liverpool, a total of four days.

Ran to Milford Haven towed two Corvettes to Hamburg, eight days.

Ran to Antwerp, towed a ship to Hamburg, we ran into bad weather and thick ice off the Elbe, we picked up eight survivors from a German Coaster, a Salvage Tug from Cuxhaven came and helped us into the Elbe, six days.

Ran light to Gravesend, two days.

Towed *Black Swan* from K.G. Dock to Newcastle, three days.

Ran to Hull, towed two trawlers to Grays for scrap then ran back to Dover on station.

Ran light to Milford Haven to tow four Corvettes to Hamburg, owing to the time of year we were only allowed to tow one at a time, each round trip taking about ten days, during these tows we ran into bad ice conditions in the Elbe and sheared rivets in No. 4 fuel tank and had to dry dock in Hamburg. Owing to the severity of the weather, the crew had to sleep ashore.

We ran light to Dover, and then ran light to Greenock accompanied by *Cervia*, where we towed British India Steam Navigation Company Ltd ship *Kenya* to Falmouth in very bad weather, five days.

Ran light to Lisbon and towed an Empire ship to Sunderland, fourteen days.

On the return to Lisbon we towed another ship to Sunderland, nine days.

Ran light to Antwerp, towed a ship to London and then returned to Dover on Station.

By this time it was September 1950 and I left *Rumania* to return to River Thames tugs.

Len Smith then returned to the river/coastal tugs at Gravesend and was Chief Engineer from 1965.